Still Hungry
After All These Years

Recent Titles in
Studies in Social Welfare Policies and Programs

STILL HUNGRY

AFTER ALL THESE YEARS

Food Assistance Policy from
Kennedy to Reagan

Ardith L. Maney

Studies in Social Welfare Policies and Programs,
Number 11

GREENWOOD PRESS

New York • Westport, Connecticut • London

Library of Congress Cataloging-in-Publication Data

Maney, Ardith.
  Still hungry after all these years : food assistance policy from
Kennedy to Reagan / Ardith L. Maney.
    p. cm. — (Studies in social welfare policies and programs,
ISSN 8755-5360 ; no. 11)
  Bibliography: p.
  Includes index.
    ISBN 0-313-26327-2 (lib. bdg. : alk. paper)
      1. Food relief—Government policy—United States. I. Title.
II. Series.
HV696.F6M35   1989
363.8′83′0973—dc19   88-7711

British Library Cataloguing in Publication Data is available.

Library of Congress Catalog Card Number: 88-7711
ISBN: 0-313-26327-2
ISSN: 8755-5360

First published in 1989

Greenwood Press, Inc.
88 Post Road West, Westport, Connecticut 06881

Printed in the United States of America

The paper used in this book complies with the
Permanent Paper Standard issued by the National
Information Standards Organization (Z39.48–1984).

10 9 8 7 6 5 4 3 2 1

Contents

Abbreviations

AFDC	Aid to Families with Dependent Children
AFL-CIO	American Federation of Labor–Congress of Industrial Organizations
AMS	Agricultural Marketing Service
ASCS	Agricultural Stabilization and Conservation Service
BAE	Bureau of Agricultural Economics
BOB	Bureau of the Budget
CCAP	Citizens Crusade Against Poverty
CDGM	Child Development Group of Mississippi
CEA	Council of Economic Advisers
CMS	Consumer and Marketing Service
CNI	Community Nutrition Institute
CORE	Congress of Racial Equality
FNS	Food and Nutrition Service
FRAC	Food Research and Action Center
FSA	Farm Security Administration
FSRC	Federal Surplus Relief Corporation
HEW	U.S. Department of Health, Education, and Welfare
NAACP	National Association for the Advancement of Colored People
NSA	National Student Association
OBRA	Omnibus Budget and Reconciliation Act
OEO	Office of Economic Opportunity
OMB	Office of Management and Budget

SCLC	Southern Christian Leadership Conference
SDDP	Surplus Dairy Distribution Program
SSI	Supplemental Security Income
TEFAP	Temporary Emergency Food Assistance Program
UNFAO	U.N. Food and Agriculture Organization
USDA	U.S. Department of Agriculture
WHCP	White House Central Files
WIC	Special Supplemental Food Program for Women, Infants, and Children

Preface

For over half a century, the U.S. Department of Agriculture has been making surplus food available to low-income Americans and subsidizing what they purchase in the regular channels of trade. At first, because of low benefit levels, cumbersome administrative requirements, and a focus on the policies' farm income goals, these programs were much more helpful to agricultural producers than to low-income people. Beginning in the mid-1960s, however, under sustained pressure from civil rights and poor peoples' groups, the nation's food aid efforts were revised and expanded in order to serve better the needs of low-income individuals and families. These changes were so great that this group of in-kind social welfare programs is one of the most important legacies of the Great Society period.

This book began as an attempt to satisfy my curiosity about why food aid programs, such as food stamps and school food assistance, that arose in rural America emerged as highly visible elements in the federal government's response to the problems of poverty in urban areas. It has evolved into a study of the contemporary American policy process as well. Several subjects that have concerned observers of American national government over the past two decades—the roles that citizen groups and bureaucrats play in the development of domestic policy initiatives, the uncertain costs and benefits of social programs generally, and the effects of political stalemate and divided government that have overtaken the nation since 1970—are in evidence.

The principal source of research support for this book came from Iowa State University. I am grateful to the Graduate College, the College of Science and Humanities, and the Political Science Department for funding various aspects of data collection and writing. Two colleagues whose expertise on agricultural politics and policy are widely recognized, Ross Talbot and Don Hadwiger, provided important intellectual stimulation and encouragement. Staffers at the USDA's Agricultural History Branch and the National Archives also deserve thanks, as do their counterparts at the Kennedy, Johnson, and Ford presidential libraries, the Minnesota State Library, and the Archives of Urban and Labor History at Wayne State University. Finally, I would like to acknowledge numerous debts that I owe to Annmarie Walsh and Lee Ann Osbun. Both have been extremely able critics and advisers. I am sure that I will call on their help again in the future.

Still Hungry

After All These Years

1

Introduction: The Importance of Food Assistance Policy

During the recession of the early 1980s, a record number of Americans, almost 23 million people, received aid from the federal government in the form of food stamps (Senate Committee on Agriculture, Nutrition, and Forestry 1985:172). At the same time millions of people qualified for food aid in other forms. Children received free, or partially subsidized breakfasts and lunches in school or while attending day-care programs. Other Americans ate free meals in soup kitchens or stood in line to take food home for themselves and their families. Despite the operation of these and other in-kind income-transfer programs designed to supplement the food purchasing power of low-income individuals and families, newspaper editorials, television news reports, and testimony before congressional committees all pointed to the continued existence of hunger and malnutrition in America after twenty years of concern about food assistance as a form of governmental aid to low-income people and as a significant public policy issue. Hadn't this problem already been solved? Why were all these people standing in line to get surplus food?

The objective of this book is twofold: (1) to analyze the policy process that resulted in the series of domestic food aid programs administered by the U.S. Department of Agriculture (USDA); and (2) to examine the politics of food assistance policy, showing how various interests gained and lost from decisions (and nondecisions) made during the last quarter century.

Food aid policy is important for several reasons, including its sheer size and expense. During the 1980s, it was second only to Medicaid and Social Security in its claims on the federal treasury, far outdistancing the federal government's contributions to such better known income support programs as Aid to Families with Dependent Children

(AFDC) and Supplemental Security Income (SSI). Decision making on food aid policy illustrates many of the conflicts and strains that have characterized the policy process in the United States during the post-war period. The social programs that have survived as the chief legacies from the Great Society period are those that provide in-kind rather than cash assistance to low-income people (Browning 1986; Schwarz 1983; Weaver 1985). Because food aid policy has been a focal point for arguments about governmental activism on behalf of low-income people by both supporters and opponents, it contributes to an understanding of how policy designed to assist low-income Americans is formulated and implemented.

The remainder of this chapter is in four parts. First, federal food aid decision making is examined in light of scholarly literature about the policy process generally. Then, the plan of the succeeding chapters is outlined with particular reference to four cycles of food aid policy making and implementation. This is followed by a brief discussion of policy and program design, that is, how the programs' architects expected these in-kind social welfare programs to operate. Then, the chapter ends with a discussion of the first cycle of food aid policy making during the 1930s.

THE DYNAMICS OF THE POLICY PROCESS

The policy process consists of several stages: (1) agenda building, a process of group competition designed to bring problems to the attention of governmental officials; (2) formulation of specific policy options and debate about alternative solutions; (3) adoption and legitimation of a preferred solution as the new policy; (4) its implementation in program form by a bureau or agency of the federal government; and (5) ongoing formal and informal evaluation of the results designed to guide further policy making. The policy process is continuous, not linear. No policy's content is ever final and no program can be said to be fully implemented because the decision-making process is always open to change (Ripley and Franklin 1980; 1986).

The process begins when officials within government, interest group activists, and others advance specific problems for governmental attention. Some problems languish for years (even decades) until key publics perceive the dangers they represent for themselves or for society as a whole. Others may go unacknowledged because they challenge entrenched interests or the *mobilization of bias* present in the political system (Bachrach and Baratz 1962; Schattschneider 1960). Calling problems to official attention and formulating plans to deal with them present nongovernmental groups and individual activists with significant costs that they pay for with money, access, votes, or other political resources available to them. Influencing the political agenda is an example of *who gets what, when, and how* from government (Cobb and Elder 1972; Lasswell 1936; Page 1983).

Complications arise because political actors (e.g., citizen activists, interest group leaders, bureaucrats, members of Congress, etc.) advance competing problems for public attention and disagree about how their objectives can best be achieved. Food aid policy presents a case in point. Food stamps, the child nutrition programs, disposal of surplus food to low-income families, and other domestic food aid programs administered by the USDA were designed to support farm income. However, program supporters have disagreed over what method would best achieve that end. Most supporters of the agricultural economy favored schemes whereby USDA officials made highly targeted purchases for disposal of specific foods to the needy whenever those foods were in oversupply. Part of the appeal of this approach was that it disaggregated benefits to interest group sectors (e.g., peanut butter, milk, and potato producers) influential in Congress, with the president, and within the USDA.

A competing perspective favored by departmental economists, some politicians concerned about the agricultural economy, and others favored a demand-side approach. If consumers' purchases could be subsidized, the government could get out of the business of buying surplus food and low-income consumers could shop for food in the supermarket like everyone else. During the 1960s, these long-standing debates over method grew sharper and the consensus over program objectives weakened. Concern about hunger and how to improve the diet of low-income consumers gained equal status in law with the earlier objective of helping the farm economy. Finally, by the 1970s, this second objective overtook the first. Once the food stamp and child nutrition programs were expected to assist low-income consumers as their primary objective, food aid's new supporters began to push to improve their design and operation.

Food aid policy also casts new light on discussions about policy adoption as a stage in the policy process. The typical view is that adoption by Congress of a new policy direction occurs after one particular alternative has survived a complicated legislative obstacle course in Congress, a process that may take several years. However, as food aid policy making shows, authoritative policy also may derive from judicial action (e.g., from rulings by the Supreme Court and other federal judges), and decisions, such as executive orders or regulations, issued by executive branch officials serving at the pleasure of the president.[1] There have been frequent additions and changes in the base of food assistance policy during the period under study here. This book is concerned with how and why these policy changes occurred and with the struggle over what happens when new policies are administered by federal executive departments and agencies such as the USDA.[2]

Implementation is the term commonly used to encompass the wide range of activities that take place "after laws are passed authorizing a program, a policy, a benefit, or some kind of tangible output" (Ripley and Franklin 1980:6). It involves such activities as marshaling financial and other resources, planning and designing program operations, preparing regulations and other written directives, organizing bureaucratic activities, and actually extending program benefits or enforcing rules and regulations (Rabinowitz, Pressman, and Rein 1976). Because these are complicated and often technical undertakings, bureaucrats are considered the most important political actors during this phase of the policy process.[3]

Officials charged with administering federal programs and policy mandates operate within a political environment that can come under pressure from several influential political actors. Program managers hear from a core set of *significant others*, which includes budget and domestic policy advisers to the president, the members of Congress who authorize and fund their programs, and interest groups with strong stakes in what they do.[4] Officials charged with overseeing implementation also face intense but less frequent scrutiny from the media, the courts, and other federal agencies. Finally, elected state and local government officials seek to influence implementation when, as is often the case, their agencies are the ones that actually administer national government programs and policies (Maney 1987b).

This study suggests that the more political scientists study implementation, the more activities it must account for in order to remain a meaningful tool of analysis. Implementation proceeds more smoothly during periods when executive branch officials dominate policy formulation and adoption. When the president and Congress are at odds politically, as has often been the case with the USDA's food aid programs, implementation becomes a key political battleground. Legislative policymakers seek to ensure that implementation activities reflect the intentions embodied in policy formulation. Meanwhile, presidential budget and policy advisers are tempted to try to reverse losses suffered at earlier stages of the policy process. Readers should not be surprised to see periodic surges in congressional interest in food program administration and attempts to reshape existing policies and programs, especially during periods of divided party control of the executive and legislative branches of government (e.g., the Eisenhower, Nixon, Ford, and Reagan administrations).

FOOD ASSISTANCE POLICY CYCLES

Because such a wide variety of political actors can become involved, implementation is not always so well demarcated as a separate stage of the policy process in practice as it is in theory. At the end of the 1980s, after fifty years of activist government, national government policies and programs exist in relation to almost every important domestic policy issue.[5] How should we treat changes in policy enacted by Congress or enunciated by executive branch officials after a program has gone into effect? These changes are made because policymakers now see a problem differently or wish to correct difficulties that have arisen during implementation.

This study addresses these issues by further developing the concept of *policy cycles* (May and Wildavsky 1978:12–13). Because food aid policies have changed so much since the 1930s, it is useful to think of distinct cycles of policy making and implementation. When such policy shifts occur, they affect bureaucratic routines in Washington and the arrangements and results of implementation carried out in the local policy environment (Maney 1987b; Van Horn 1979, 1985). Four major shifts in food assistance authority, scope of program activities, and resources will be examined in the chapters that follow. During the first food aid policy cycle from 1933 to 1946, executive branch officials dominated all food aid decision making. Working under a broad grant of power from President Franklin D. Roosevelt, Agriculture Secretary Henry A. Wallace and his aides fashioned a series of initiatives to cope with the economic emergency facing the nation. The chief beneficiaries of these policies were agricultural producer interests.

Other groups associated with the political coalition that supported New Deal policies for national recovery (e.g., mayors, county commissioners, and other local government officials whose jurisdictions were strapped for funds to underwrite relief and recovery programs in their areas) also benefited. Later, as World War II came to an end and Harry Truman succeeded Franklin Roosevelt as president, party lines tightened and Congress began to reclaim prerogatives that legislators had ceded to executive branch officials during the period of most acute economic emergency. This second cycle, from 1946 to 1966, which can be characterized as one of shared governance between the executive and legislative branches, is taken up in chapters 2 to 4. During most of this period, little formal change occurred in the food aid programs that remained from the Depression years. The few policy changes made came about because executive branch decisionmakers acquiesced to specific surplus disposal initiatives put forward by agricultural producer groups influential in Congress.

Chapter 2 analyzes the new debate over the purpose of food aid policy that began during the 1950s. Was it still a useful adjunct to general agricultural policy? Or could it also be a way to marshal resources from the agricultural sector to deal with problems of the wider national economy? Eisenhower administration officials vociferously disagreed with the latter view, but tolerated a small surplus disposal effort since they did not have the political resources in Congress to eliminate it altogether. Kennedy administration officials, on the other hand, took important steps to expand food aid initiatives immediately after coming to office in 1961.

Chapter 3 examines how powerful agricultural interests exercised influence over the New Frontier's initiatives once they began to be implemented. Then Chapter 4 shows the reactions of all of the affected interests when Johnson administration officials sought congressional support for two purposes: (1) to make the Kennedy food stamp program permanent; and (2) to strengthen the school lunch program's ties to the Great Society's war on poverty. After Congress approved those changes in the mid–1960s, a new stalemate on food assistance policy set in. White House and congressional liberals had demonstrated that they could enact new food aid program efforts designed to help low-income Americans. However, these policy statements turned out to be little more than an exercise in *symbolic politics* (Edelman 1964) since congressional conservatives retained control over major implementation decisions through the congressional appropriations process. This tension over program objectives, which reached a boiling point toward the end of the Johnson years, led a new group of program supporters to push for a third cycle of policy formulation. From 1967 to 1977, a vast number of important policy changes took place. Taken together, they represent the significant deepening of food aid policy's ties to welfare policy suggested earlier. Chapter 5 shows how this redefinition of the objectives of food aid policy (away from supporting farm income and toward the problems of hunger and severe malnutrition) got started.

During the time period covered in chapter 6, antipoverty and civil rights activists turned their attention to food aid policy making and implementation. First, they took direct aim at how the food stamp and commodity distribution programs were being administered in the rural South, pressuring federal officials through the national media to make changes designed to broaden program coverage. Chapter 7 shows White House advisers responding to this charged political environment in 1968. That year, presidential advisers almost suceeded in getting President Lyndon Johnson to make hunger and malnutrition a top domestic priority. Although these efforts failed, enough political pressure remained that the Nixon administration presided over an unprecedented expansion of the federal government's role in subsidizing food consumption by low-income Americans.

Executive–legislative branch conflict, not shared influence over food aid policy, was the norm during most of this third period. Whenever this conflict erupted, Congress won out. Mostly what Congress wanted was food aid program expansion and greater program spending. Chapter 9 shows the beginning of a final policy cycle, which started in 1978 and continues into the Bush administration. Its roots go back to attempts by executive branch officials during the Ford administration to challenge congressional dominance of food aid policy making. These efforts contributed to growing political conflict in the *Washington community* (Young 1966) over the costs of domestic spending. In this last cycle, policymakers view food aid as a key part of both welfare and budgetary policy. As such, it was subject to the pervasive political stalemate that overtook policy during the 1980s.

Except for brief periods, such as 1977–1979 and 1981–1983, when Congress and the president have been united, this period has been marked by strong conflict over food aid policy, a prospect for which there appears to be no easy resolution in the near future. Through it all, both liberals and conservatives on Capitol Hill, those still pushing for food program expansion and those more concerned about fiscal and administrative accountability, have been sharply divided. They have, however, agreed on two issues—placing the various food aid delivery systems under greater congressional scrutiny and pushing for greater centralization in program operations. Neither side, it appears, trusts federal program managers at the Department of Agriculture or state and local implementors.

UNDERSTANDING FOOD AID AS SOCIAL POLICY

Before examining food aid policy making during the Great Depression, it is important to sketch out briefly how these complex programs work. Implicitly or explicitly, policymakers make assumptions about how a new program or policy ought to operate. These assumptions usually come down to four concerns: (1) how the policy will work; (2) who it is supposed to serve; (3) how much assistance should be provided; and (4) what service delivery mechanisms will be used. By applying these judgments to food aid policy, it is possible to place it in the context of domestic and social policy generally.

How Is the Policy Supposed to Work?

All government programs and policies contain assumptions about how means and ends fit together. In the case of a policy designed to help a certain category of agricultural producers, economists and other program designers in the USDA ought to be able to say what effects a program or policy will have. This is what Paul Berman has called a program's *technical validity* (Berman 1978), that is, how good a policy initiative is at what it is supposed to do. Policymakers know that many factors influence what occurs during the complex chain of events be-

tween enactment of legislation framing a new program's operations
and the actual flow of benefits to recipients. They want to know if the
means they choose will lead to the proximate or final goals embodied
in the architecture of the program.

For an agricultural support program, policymakers try to calculate
the collective results of individual decisions producers make about
what crops to grow and what inputs to use. For a social welfare policy,
it would include expectations about how a particular federal government program would ameliorate the situation in which low-income
people find themselves. Questions of technical validity associated with
farm income support objectives proved to have been exceptionally complex in the case of food aid policy. Furthermore, the results have always
been subject to debate, even within the agricultural policy community.
The case for using these programs to help low-income people, however,
seemed self-evident, especially to food aid advocates. They approached
the issue as follows.

If the federal government is going to respond to political pressure
from agricultural producers by buying up surplus foodstuffs, why not
use some of it to increase the food available to low-income people? The
issue of technical validity was understood the same way intuitively by
all concerned; if people get more to eat, their health and well-being
will automatically improve. If the food they consume is subsidized
directly (i.e., without recipients having to make any out-of-pocket purchases), the results are still better, so the reasoning went, because
recipients can dispose of more of their meager income according to
their own priorities. Once they became familiar with the USDA's food
assistance programs in the mid–1960s, antipoverty advocates found
these programs irresistible. Food aid was a simpler proposition than
were other forms of welfare or income support policy. The latter can
get caught up in complicated arguments about policy effects on family
life, dependency and self-sufficiency, and other issues. At least, they
reasoned, the national government can get food to people for whom,
by getting more food to eat, some concrete problems of poverty such
as hunger and malnutrition could be more easily assuaged.

What Populations Is It Supposed to Help?

The way policymakers and program managers have answered this
question has varied over the half century since food aid programs have
been in existence. The first food aid programs were executive branch
initiatives begun under emergency conditions. Guidelines for policy
implementation often were sketchy, but the intent was nevertheless
clear—agricultural producers were to be the principal beneficiaries.
The side benefit of helping low-income people was welcome but sec-

ondary in the eyes of administration officials. During the nadir of the Great Depression, no one worked out how many poor people might benefit or at what level. Administration planners simply took for granted that a large part of the total U.S. population could stand to improve their diets.

Federal officials allowed local relief administrators to decide who would receive surplus food and who would be eligible for participation in a pilot food stamp program according to local judgments about eligibility and administrative arrangements developed for other federal relief programs. Until the early 1970s, the issue of how many needy people could be served by food aid at any given time did not depend on the objective needs of client groups. Instead, program size rested on the interplay of three other factors: (1) the total amount of resources available at any given time, (which, in turn, depended on the current political needs of the administration's farm program); (2) decisions by state and local government officials about whether, and how intensively, to implement these federal programs; and (3) local welfare agency eligibility and certification practices. Local officials acted as gatekeepers to program participation and their decisions depended on local political and economic conditions.

In short, since implementation was so thoroughly entrusted to local officials, the answer to the question of who got what food aid benefits was extremely contingent. *Some* food was available to *some* people *some* of the time, as long as recipients behaved themselves according to norms of political behavior set and enforced locally. The changes that Congress made in the 1960s and 1970s were designed to ensure that food aid reached a larger proportion of those living in poverty according to standards set nationally, without additional conditions imposed by local implementors. Since then, Congress has further refined the list of categories of who would be served, and income levels, eligibility requirements, grievance procedures, and other issues have been changed over and over again through legislation, administrative regulations, court decisions, and other authoritative policy statements.

Like other U.S. welfare programs, the federal food programs still do not enroll all of those who qualify. But as redesigned, they have proven to be fairly responsive to demand from low-income people, especially during periods of economic recession. Experience with food aid policy strongly suggests that the issue of who is actually being served by a given social program cannot be accurately estimated just by examining statutes, appropriations bills, administrative regulations, court decisions, state plans, and other authoritative policy statements. It is also necessary to examine how people hear about and sign up for particular programs and how benefits are delivered. Unless eligibility requirements and benefit levels are set in concrete, the experience of the 1980s has shown that policymakers will squeeze back on programs serving low-income people in order to meet budget targets whenever domestic spending cutbacks become politically attractive.

What Level of Assistance Will Be Provided?

Policymakers need expert information about how much assistance people need and what that will cost in order to decide how much government can afford to pay. Someone has to decide who gets benefits and how costs are assessed. For the food stamp program to work as policymakers intend, USDA officials have to make two complicated sets of calculations: how much food poor people need to maintain a nutritionally adequate diet and how much that kind of diet actually will cost at the supermarket checkout counter. Nutritional research and information about food buying patterns must be brought together, refined, and reduced to standard tables before they can be used in welfare offices all over the country. This complexity has ensured a big role for experts in program design.

How costs to government are fixed in the food aid programs is also important to understand. Food aid policy owes its origin to the availability of slack resources set aside to help the agricultural economy recover from the Depression. Later, after food aid efforts began to draw on regularly budgeted funds, total expenditures depended on a mixture of (1) presidential priorities and congressional interest; (2) general economic conditions (e.g., the need to increase federal spending to poor people during economic downturns, pressures to rationalize or reduce domestic spending at other times); and (3) the strength of whatever poor people's lobby existed at each moment. When food advocacy groups have been active, the cost for these programs has grown; when their voices have been muted, food aid has had to compete along with other domestic programs for scarce funds.

Federal assumption of most food stamp and child nutrition program costs distinguishes food aid from welfare programs like AFDC. Attempts by Republicans and conservative Democrats to shift some of the financial burden of federal food aid policy to state and local governments have all failed. Instead, congressional policymakers have preferred the present hodgepodge of separate, partially overlapping programs with different delivery mechanisms and have refused to enact reform proposals designed to further intergovernmentalize food aid costs and service delivery.

What Service Delivery Mechanisms Will Be Used?

Two characteristics of food aid administration are key: the intergovernmental character of program administration and use of multiple service delivery mechanisms. Each program depends on a different mix of involvement by state and local government agencies and some also use nongovernmental organizations (e.g., nonprofit community groups and the regular retail channels of trade) to get food to needy people. Each set of programs pumps funds through a specially designated state agency charged with coordinating program services. That means health departments in the case of the Special Supplementary Food Program for Women, Infants, and Children (WIC), the state education agency for most of the child nutrition programs, and the state welfare or human services agency in the case of the food stamp program.

Local service delivery mechanisms are even more complex. In each case, policymakers grafted food aid programs onto established missions of existing organizations. Not surprisingly, this has yielded great variety too. The distribution of surplus agricultural commodities, which can take place through a wide variety of local organizations (e.g., food banks, churches, soup kitchens, etc.), represents the most eclectic approach. The food stamp program, which usually operates through county welfare offices, is the most rigidly organized. The others fall somewhere in between. For example, a wide variety of health agencies (e.g., clinics, hospitals, community action programs, and other local organizations) can be WIC agencies. Schools, private day-care centers and homes, nursery schools, summer camps, and recreation programs offer one or more child nutrition program.

What happens at the local level where program benefits are actually disbursed is extremely important to program critics and supporters. Each of these service delivery mechanisms reflects the results of past battles, some won by self-styled antihunger or food advocacy groups seeking increased food aid spending and greater national government control over implementation activities, some by conservatives concerned about program costs or allegations of fraud and abuse. In the late 1960s, advocates of increased food aid benefits criticized the degree of discretion that welfare officials and local elites exercised. Interest group supporters of food aid policy sought additional reforms, including eligibility and benefit liberalization, expanded outreach activities, and stronger due process protections. Their chief concern has been that everyone involved in program implementation—executive branch officials, USDA and state program managers, and local implementors—have as little discretion as possible.

Ironically, when their turn came, conservatives followed the same strategy. Conservatives were concerned that county welfare officials and other local implementors would be too lenient in encouraging people to apply, certifying their eligibility, and calculating their benefit levels! So, they pushed for tighter eligibility standards and sought benefit cutbacks and administrative reforms designed to ensure greater financial accountability. In short, neither group trusts local officials, but for exactly opposite reasons.

THE NEW DEAL FOOD PROGRAMS AND THEIR TIES TO AGRICULTURE

Much has changed for American farmers and for the urban and rural poor in this country since food aid initiatives began during the 1930s but one common thread that has remained is the linkage that these programs have to macroeconomic policy concerns. When the Roosevelt administration took office in 1933, prolonged turmoil in agriculture was contributing to depression in the national economy. Moreover, widespread rural poverty was overburdening relief efforts and contributing to wider social dislocations as families were uprooted from their place in the agricultural economy. To meet these problems and staunch further declines in farm income, administration officials quickly obtained authority from Congress in 1933 to begin payments to agricultural producers in return for promises to take part of their land out of use. Thereafter, payments, production controls, and the vicissitudes of weather all had important effects on the income that farmers received during the period up to the entry of the United States into World War II (Benedict 1966; Cochrane 1979; Leuchtenburg 1963; Rasmussen and Baker 1972; Schlichter 1959). As a side effect of these new agricultural programs, the federal government began accumulating vast amounts of surplus agricultural commodities. Accordingly, the nation's first food aid initiatives were developed under the authority of the Federal Surplus Relief Corporation (FSRC) in 1933 as part of the implementation of broad national farm and relief policies (Benedict 1955).

Disposal of surplus agricultural products to the rural and urban poor was politically attractive to New Deal policymakers for several reasons. They hoped it would help rebuild normal demand for agricultural products, distract attention from the embarrassing prospect of ever-increasing government-owned stockpiles, and assist needy individuals and families. Accordingly, the FSRC had two objectives—to help the government deal with the growing burden of surpluses and to provide supplemental in-kind relief to the needy and unemployed—that is, to subsidize the producer interest directly but help out consumer interests in the process. Administration officials were mindful of other possible political benefits. For example, relief efforts put some unemployed people to work handling food distribution around the country.

In 1935, Secretary of Agriculture Wallace acquired new budgetary authority from Congress under Section 32 of the Agricultural Adjustment Act. Soon thereafter the FSRC was reorganized and Agriculture assumed the preeminent role in federal government surplus food efforts.[6] The legislative language in *Section 32* (as it came to be known) of this act reserved 30 percent of U.S. custom funds in each year to the Department of Agriculture. The secretary could use these funds for a number of purposes, including one designed to "encourage the domestic consumption of [agricultural] commodities by diverting them, by the payment of benefits and indemnities or by other means, from the normal channels of trade and commerce" (U.S. Statutes at Large, Vol. 49, Ch. 641, 774). Roosevelt administration officials read that language to mean that they could go ahead with surplus disposal plans without applying to Congress for additional legislative authority or specific appropriation.

Two points about the department's program authority need to be emphasized. First, the department's Section 32 authority continues today. Nearly all of the food aid programs discussed in this book began under Section 32 authority. Through this automatic source of unbudgeted funds, the agricultural sector of the national economy received permission to draw on the federal treasury. In turn, executive branch officials used some of this money to move foodstuffs to needy people around the country. Second, all the New Deal surplus disposal efforts were structured and brokered by the Secretary of Agriculture according to that official's judgment about how best to help food producers. That officials at the secretary, undersecretary, and assistant secretary level play key roles in packaging and managing policy initiatives has long been understood, especially with relation to constituency-oriented departments such as Agriculture, Commerce, and Labor (Heclo 1977). What is striking in the case of the New Deal's food aid policy initiatives, however, is how little legislative activity and oversight were involved.

From the perspective of Secretary Wallace and other USDA officials, the major decisions at any given time were which commodities to purchase and groups of agricultural producers to help. Wallace and those advising him believed that food aid could be used for three purposes simultaneously. The most important use was to support farm income; but officials were also interested in increasing the consumption of food products by low-income people and restructuring the agricultural economy for a healthier future. However, producer groups and their allies in Congress believed that Section 32 had been designed expressly to serve the needs of agriculture as defined by producer organizations. As a result, they wanted Wallace to concentrate solely on the first objective and to distribute only those foods in surplus at any particular time.

Since these complaints came mostly from the Roosevelt administration's political opponents in the Farm Belt, they meant little during the New Deal years because the president was popular generally and the amounts of money involved were quite small. Another reason was that since there were no hearings or floor debates on food aid bills, there was no congressional forum handy to criticize the programs. However, this opposition did reinforce the administration's predilection to cut back on surplus disposal efforts once most people went back to work in the wartime economy.[7] During the Roosevelt administration, White House officials paid only sporadic attention to the Department of Agriculture's initiatives. They saw the food aid programs as temporary measures to get the country out of the immediate crisis caused by the Depression. No one expected the surplus problem to linger after the war.

Administration political strategists, including Secretary Wallace, also hoped the food aid programs would help them forge an urban-rural alliance that would be available to assist the department in other political battles. Most of those outside the USDA who supported increased welfare spending during the Depression years—mayors, urban liberals, local relief administrators, and social welfare professionals— overlooked the food programs because they operated out of an unusual venue, the Department of Agriculture. When they did notice the programs, these supporters tended to be critical, either out of distaste for all relief-in-kind efforts or because of their murky ties to agriculture policy. Why should relief recipients receive large quantities of peanut butter or lard just because Agriculture had those particular foods on hand during a given month?

THE DESIGN AND OPERATION OF THE NEW DEAL PROGRAMS

The food aid programs that operate today owe much of their design to the administrative arrangements begun in the New Deal period. Roosevelt administration officials started out using Section 32 funds for two types of programs: (1) distribution of food in bulk to families and individuals using the same state and local relief agencies that the FSRC had relied on; and (2) donations to institutions such as schools and hospitals (Benedict 1955:382–84). USDA administrators later claimed that these programs were successful and widely liked, but in fact they operated with extremely low political profiles and were exceptionally complex; as a result, their putative success is hard to evaluate. Few people outside the USDA understood how the programs actually worked.

Secretary Wallace and his aides made decisions about what foodstuffs to buy and then worked out arrangements with state and local officials to distribute the products to schools, hospitals, relief agencies, and other institutions. They based their decisions on an eclectic mix of factors: their technical expertise about particular market conditions; judgments about how to benefit the agricultural economy generally; and specific political pressures from farm groups. Sometimes USDA officials heard pleas for help from producer groups directly; on other occasions they received pressure indirectly via Congress and the White House.

Most of the programs that distributed surplus foodstuffs to individuals, families, and institutions during the Roosevelt years operated without any consumer charge; when federal officials bought surplus commodities and gave them away, they were diverting food from commercial outlets where prices were too low for farmers to make a living. Soon after these programs had gotten under way in 1933, departmental officials began hearing objections from grocery trade officials and local merchants that this new competition from government was hurting them in their dealings with consumers. Whenever the government made surplus milk or peanut butter available, smaller amounts of these same products were sold in stores. Consequently, departmental economists began to develop plans to use the established national network of grocery stores, supermarkets, and other retail outlets in the department's surplus disposal efforts.

Merchants feared that poor people might be able to satisfy all their needs from food made available at government warehouses and spend the income that usually went for food outside the agricultural economy altogether—on shelter, for example. As a partial remedy to this problem, departmental economists proposed a subsidized cash purchase or food stamp program that would expand, rather than displace, domestic demand for agricultural products.[8] Recipients would be required to buy a set of orange stamps in an amount roughly equivalent to their customary out-of-pocket expenditures for food. Purchasing these orange stamps made relief recipients eligible for a free category of blue stamp foods that would represent a net increase in their dietary consumption. The second set of food items would be the ones that were in surplus at any given time.

By using this complicated two-tier system, administration policymakers hoped that recipients would no longer be able to substitute free foods for their usual diets and that both food processors and retailers would benefit. Money would circulate in the local economy as retail food stores redeemed cash for the stamps through their banks. The banks, in turn, would draw on special Treasury Department accounts paid for by Agriculture with Section 32 funds. Agriculture officials decided to leave eligibility and certification issues to local relief officials. After all, they reasoned, local government agencies already distributed the relief payment that people would use to pay the original purchase price for the orange stamps. Another implementation feature was equally important. Although departmental economists stressed the role that the purchase price would play in the farm income-related objectives of the food stamp program, they were later surprised at how little cash actually changed hands during program operations.

Relief recipients often paid for their food stamps with script which they received from local welfare officials, rather than with cash. Because so many poor people lived totally outside of a cash economy during the depth of the Depression, federal officials' desire for uniformity in relief administration gave way to the practicalities of intergovernmental administration and the strong pull of local autonomy that characterized the federal system in the United States at that time. Benefits were administered by city and county relief agencies that received funds from Washington, but responded to local political elites and conditions for guidance on most substantive issues. This bow to the strong forces of a decentralized political system helped local Democratic party institutions allied with the Roosevelt electoral coalition (e.g., labor and political party organizations in the North and the traditional white power structure in the South) play important roles in policy implementation and program administration.

In their reports on program administration, USDA managers minimized problems with food stamp policy implementation posed by the "no-cash" problem and played up evidence showing that the department had broadened its mandate by reaching to poor people outside rural America.[9] For example, the authors of an influential USDA report published in 1940 noted that the department had gone far beyond its traditional constituencies and was serving the interests of farmers, low-income consumers, and food dealers alike (Gold, Hoffman, and Waugh 1940:2). Not coincidentally, this triumvirate closely resembled the political coalition at the heart of the New Deal. It is also one that has remained dear to Democratic party officeholders as they have tried to keep the same voting block together, or reassemble it, ever since.

The USDA's pilot food stamp program began in 1939 as a supplement to the surplus disposal initiatives already in place and continued until 1942. Only about 60 percent of all recipients were able to buy stamps in the manner that planners had intended because so many local relief agencies gave aid in the form of grocery vouchers, not cash. About 20 percent of local relief programs, including many in the South, made cash payments that were so low recipients could not afford to buy the orange stamps and program planners had to give them blue ones without requiring any purchase price at all, a major, although little publicized, adjustment in the program's design.[10] It is also important to note that the pilot food stamp program never reached anywhere near all needy Americans during the Roosevelt administration. At its height, the program reached a severely "restricted clientele" (Ripley and Franklin 1980:80–83) of about 6 million people out of a much larger total population that could have benefited from participation in the program.

Part of the reason for such low enrollment was the program's administrative complexity. In order for a local government to participate, USDA officials first had to go through a time-consuming process of arranging for the cooperation of local banks and grocery trade associations. The program's decentralized implementation procedures allowed localities to opt not to participate at all or to severely limit eligibility. For example, some counties only admitted families already on the relief rolls, although a much larger number of needy people could have benefited from a food-buying subsidy. The USDA's program managers were aware of these limitations but felt that they could do little about them. They estimated that a nationwide food stamp program encompassing all relief recipients would have cost $400 million a year to operate, far more than the administration was prepared to fund out of Section 32 authority (Gold, Hoffman, and Waugh 1940:27).

A program designed to include all low-income families (i.e., relief recipients and those members of the working poor with incomes below $1,000 per year) would have been still larger. Extended to all cities with populations over 2,500 people and open to all low-income residents, food stamp program eligibility would have increased to about 23 million people, about the same number actually served during the worst of the recession of the early 1980s. If rural areas were included on the same basis, the number of eligibles could have risen to a grand total of 35–40 million. The yearly price tag for a complete program along these lines would have been about $1 billion, far too high a price for the administration to pay. After all, food aid was not principally a welfare policy, but a temporary adjunct to farm policy with secondary, but welcome, social policy benefits.[11]

2

The Kennedy Administration's Food Aid Initiatives

During the Truman and Eisenhower years, more food was available in more variety than ever before and at prices that most Americans could afford. But many low-income consumers still could not fully participate in the nation's cash economy. Public policy failed to solve their problems of unemployment and underemployment in the postwar period, and the nation's agricultural economy suffered because of low demand for what it was able to produce. Many battles were fought over farm policy in Washington during this period (Christenson 1959; Matusow 1967) but decisive changes in agricultural price support legislation, which might have changed the mixture of incentives offered to agricultural producers, were stymied because of weak and divided party control of Congress. The Eisenhower administration's principal solution was to dispose of surpluses abroad so as to disturb the domestic market as little as possible—to sell on the world market if possible, to give food away as an adjunct to American foreign policy if necessary.

The bulk of the surplus diverted from the market was stored at home, with most of the remainder going abroad under the auspices of the Agricultural Trade and Development Act of 1954 (Peterson 1977). PL 480, as this came to be known, drew broad bipartisan support and became one of the major legislative accomplishments of the Eisenhower administration's program for agriculture. At the same time, powerful producer groups used political leverage to push for the development of new surplus disposal schemes at home. For example, school lunch legislation based on the New Deal approach, that was enacted with broad bipartisan support in 1946, benefited a broad range of agricultural producers. Having a clear legislative base freed agricultural producers from total reliance on the administration's willingness to use Section 32 funds for surplus disposal.

Individual commodity groups also succeeded in legislating the disposal of specific foods in this period. In 1954, for example, milk producer groups and their congressional allies won approval for a program expanding the sites where children could receive reduced-price milk (e.g., in schools where the school lunch program was not available and in other institutions like summer camps). Whenever, as in this case, Eisenhower administration officials faced united Democratic party and interest group support for expanded agricultural programs, they tempered their philosophical objections to greater governmental involvement in the marketplace with political realism and grudgingly accepted the new responsibilities. The stalemate that existed over farm policy during the Truman and Eisenhower years also extended to domestic food assistance policy. Food aid was not a major priority at USDA during the Truman administration, although officials did not strongly oppose it either. Eisenhower administration officials, however, were much more critical. They grudgingly administered the scaled-back distribution programs funded under Section 32 that they inherited on coming to office, but opposed most legislative initiatives proposed in Congress during these years.

Nevertheless, some changes did take place at the margins of this stalemate. Besides outlining how they came about, this chapter also addresses two related issues: (1) how proposals for a revived food stamp program advanced to a prominent position on Congress' agenda by the time a new administration assumed office in 1961; and (2) why expanding food aid efforts was an attractive political option for Kennedy administration officials. It was, after all, the first domestic policy initiative that they undertook after taking office in January of that year. In the process, there is a fascinating glimpse into the role that bureaucratic policy specialists can play in the formulation and adoption of important public policy initiatives.

REVIVED INTEREST IN FOOD AID POLICY

George Aiken, Republican of Vermont, one of the most important and atypical farm policy leaders in the 1950s, served as the chairman or ranking member of the Senate Agriculture and Forestry Committee during most of the postwar period. Starting in 1943, when he collaborated with fellow dairy state senator Robert LaFollette (R-Wis), Aiken worked doggedly for congressional enactment of what he called a food allotment plan. A speech that Senator Aiken delivered to the National Farm Institute on February 15, 1957, in Des Moines, Iowa, is typical of his views on the disposal of surplus agricultural commodities. On that occasion he argued the case for a domestic food assistance program combining the farmer's concern for price with some response to the problems of America's needy.

According to Aiken, the major problems facing American agriculture were underconsumption and low farm income, that is, "underfed people and underpaid farmers in a nation which is presently enjoying unprecedented prosperity" (Kennedy Presidential Library, Pre-Presidential Papers). In Aiken's view, farmers were not overproducing; food buyers were underconsuming. His measure would allow agricultural producers to soothe their consciences and help themselves economically at the same time. Aiken's food allotment scheme was also preferable, he argued, to the skeleton surplus commodity distribution program then in effect. Two-thirds of the budget for agriculture in 1956 went to control or store surplus agricultural products, he reminded this knowledgeable farm audience. A food allotment plan would cut back on government activity and competition with the private sector, since it would operate through banks, grocery stores, and supermarkets.[1]

Besides Senator Aiken, the most prominent advocate for expanded food assistance for the poor along the lines of the New Deal food stamp plan during the 1950s was another congressional maverick, Representative Leonore Sullivan (D-Mo.). Almost immediately upon being elected to Congress in 1954 as the representative of an urban district that included parts of the city of St. Louis, Sullivan began to introduce food stamp legislation.[2] Her leadership on this issue belies simple explanations of committee and subcommittee influence in Congress or the hegemony of the White House in creating agendas of public policy. It is especially surprising in light of her extremely junior status in the House. At that time more than now, the House invariably used seniority to guard the two chief routes to congressional power—gaining influence in important subject matter committees or in party leadership positions.

She was not a member of the House Committee on Agriculture or of the informal congressional agricultural policy subsystem that included the subject matter committees and the agricultural appropriations subcommittees in both houses. Instead she shared the northern liberal and urban orientation of those members of Congress who headed the presidential wing of the Democratic party at that time. After introducing her own food stamp legislation in 1955, only to see it buried unceremoniously in the House Agriculture Committee, Sullivan pushed to have the idea incorporated in the Democratic party platform at its nominating convention in 1956 and reintroduced her bill in 1957. This time she proposed it in the form of an amendment during debate on the floor of the House on extension of the popular Agricultural Trade and Development Act of 1954 authorizing PL 480 surplus disposal programs abroad. This attempt failed as well, but it prompted Chairman Harold Cooley (D-N.C.) to promise that the House Agriculture committee would hold hearings on all of the food stamp proposals then current.

Besides Sullivan, those who testified in favor of some kind of a food stamp or food allotment plan at the subsequent hearings included welfare officials, food industry representatives, some urban elected officials, social work professionals, a few rural and urban liberals in Congress (e.g., Democratic Representatives George S. McGovern, S. Dak., Lee Metcalf, Mont., and John Dingell, Mich.) and representatives of several farm groups (the National Farmers Union, the National Milk Producers Federation, and the National Grange). These hearings show that urban supporters viewed food stamps as a welfare program and preferred administration by the newly created Department of Health, Education and Welfare (HEW), while farm organizations like the Farmers Union and the Grange favored expansion of surplus food programs within the jurisdiction of the USDA (House Agriculture Committee, 1958).

With the Democrats in disarray—many northern Democrats would have supported either of the plans presented while most southern Democrats seemed as ready to oppose all of them—agricultural interest groups divided on this issue, and executive branch officials prepared to veto any legislation that the president and USDA officials did not approve, the chance for a successful legislative initiative was extremely low. Except for Aiken and a few farm state liberal Democrats who saw food assistance policy as beneficial both to rural and urban people, most proponents simply wanted more food to go to the unemployed and needy. They talked about a food stamp or allotment program as a means to this end because one had existed before, but they really saw food assistance as a surrogate for increases in welfare spending generally and were ready to use a variety of means—school lunches, bulk commodities, and food stamps—toward that end.

With each initiative Sullivan got a little closer to her elusive goal. Her partial success in 1958 reinforced a point she often made in congressional debate: urban interests were becoming more interested in the costs and purposes of farm programs (House Agriculture Committee 1958:40). In 1959, by again tying her food stamp bill to consideration of the USDA's popular PL 480 program, she finally won passage of food stamp legislation. This amendment allowed (but did not require) the Department of Agriculture to initiate a small food stamp effort modeled on the New Deal program. Predictably, the Eisenhower administration chose to ignore this permissive legislation. Still, Sullivan had succeeded, almost singlehandedly, in keeping the issue before the House of Representatives for several years by perfecting a legislative strategy of linking food stamp legislation to whatever agriculture bill was handy. She had also begun to receive help from prominent Democrats in Congress. In 1959 Senators Hubert H. Humphrey (D-Minn.) and John Kennedy (D-Mass.) introduced rival bills, which were supported by liberal farm groups and labor unions, calling for expansion and improvement of Agriculture's existing surplus distribution programs. These were also proposals designed to appeal to broader segments of the electorate than just farm state voters.

JOHN KENNEDY'S POLITICAL EDUCATION ON FOOD ASSISTANCE POLICY ISSUES

Kennedy became interested in farm policy when he ran for reelection to the Senate in 1958. Before that, he had had only infrequent contact with or interest in agricultural policy issues.[3] In 1958 Kennedy hired Myer "Mike" Feldman, a lawyer with previous Senate staff experience, as a second legislative assistant to work with his chief aide, Theodore Sorenson. Feldman immediately began collecting information about farm issues from interest group and labor newsletters, setting up meetings with liberal and Democratic party farm policy activists, and establishing informal contacts with academics knowledgeable about farm policy. The second phase of Kennedy's attempt to be a credible Democratic party spokesperson in rural America got under way at the same time.

Armed with a comfortable lead at home, the senator ventured away from his Massachusetts base to appear before midwestern farm audiences on behalf of fellow Democratic candidates during the 1958 election campaign. For example, drawing on ideas that Feldman received from corresponding with former Truman Secretary of Agriculture Charles Brannan, Kennedy addressed the National Farmers Union Corn Picking contest in Iowa in October 1958. In this first attempt, Kennedy portrayed his general position on agricultural issues as similar to that of such midwestern farm state legislative activists as Hubert Humphrey and William Proxmire (D-Wis.) (Kennedy Presidential Library, Pre-Presidential Papers). Kennedy's work with Feldman allowed him to deflect Humphrey's claims to be the party's true champion of rural interests and join with Farm Belt Democrats in denouncing Eisenhower's Secretary of Agriculture Ezra T. Benson.[4]

His staff also drafted some farm-related bills for Kennedy to introduce in the Senate in 1959. With help from interest group activists like John Baker of the National Farmers Union and Clay Cochran of the American Federation of Labor–Congress of Industrial Organizations' (AFL-CIO) Industrial Union Division, Feldman's first attempt was a bill calling for a modest increase in food aid spending. The bill, titled the Food Assistance Act of 1959, proposed to increase federal food aid to state and local governments, establish uniform federal standards of eligibility, and transfer program administration for part of the commodity distribution program from Agriculture to HEW. In June 1959, hearings were held on this and related bills, including the latest version of Senator George Aiken's food allotment plan and a Humphrey-Symington food stamp bill (Senate Committee on Agriculture and Forestry, 1959).

Even though none of these bills achieved final passage before the election-year congressional session wound down in 1960, Kennedy had accomplished his major objective. His food aid proposals placed him squarely in the middle of the pack of Democratic challengers on an important agricultural policy issue. Work on the bill also helped Feldman assemble the nucleus of a farm issues staff to advise the candidate during the 1960 presidential campaign. Baker and Cochran's participation did not commit their organizations to support Kennedy's bills or his candidacy. Rather, it reflected an interest common to many in the Washington interest group community to be on good working terms with influential senators, especially those with presidential aspirations.

The election campaign itself influenced the Kennedy administration's food assistance policies in two crucial ways. First, while campaigning in key states like Wisconsin and West Virginia, Kennedy promised to take particular food aid initiatives if elected. Then, during the general election campaign, Kennedy talked about how the food assistance programs he advocated would fit into the context of general farm policy. Kennedy's farm advisers saw food distribution schemes as providing a range of benefits similar to those that had guided Roosevelt administration officials. Expanded food aid would stimulate greater food consumption and bolster farm income. Social welfare and other humanitarian considerations came second. Privately, Kennedy and his political aides would probably have acknowledged a third set of benefits—that food distribution schemes were good politics in a presidential election campaign.

In researching issues to be included in the candidate's speeches, Feldman helped Kennedy strike a balance between increased food aid as a desperately needed short-term measure to help economically depressed areas like Appalachia and the need for more fundamental reforms. In his speech on "Aid to Depressed Areas," given at Huntington on April 20, for example, Kennedy linked the two issues (Kennedy Presidential Library, Pre-Presidential Papers) and in the process gave an indication of the direction that his administration would take in response to the need for economic development and recovery. He also promised at several campaign stops to increase the kinds and quantities of food that would be available for distribution by the USDA in his administration and to try out some form of food stamp program. Along the way, it became increasingly likely that West Virginia would be one of the test sites for such initiatives should a Kennedy administration actually assume office.

THE KENNEDY ADMINISTRATION'S FIRST FOOD AID INITIATIVES

By 1961, when he was sworn in as president, John Kennedy had successfully used food aid policy as a technique to deepen his involvement in and understanding of farm policy issues. Because the USDA already had authority to distribute surplus food on a greater scale if the president desired, Kennedy's campaign promises on the subject suited the theme enunciated in his inaugural address when he promised to adopt a more activist stance toward the nation's domestic problems. Besides fitting his natural inclination to mix an activist style with caution about legislative substance, this approach was even more congenial when the new president found out he had been elected president with only a slight congressional majority. That fact made new legislative initiatives less likely during his first two years in office in any event.

To run a more activist Department of Agriculture, Kennedy turned to an urban figure from an agricultural state, the outgoing governor of Minnesota, Orville L. Freeman.[5] Kennedy wanted to spend more Section 32 money on the surplus commodity or food donation program immediately after taking office and institute some kind of food stamp plan as soon as possible thereafter. As his first official act on his first day in office, the new president implemented one of his goals by signing an executive order that significantly enlarged the USDA's surplus distribution programs. Feldman remembers preparing it in about one half hour, taking it in to the president to sign, and giving it to Press Secretary Pierre Salinger to release to the media before any of them knew the established procedures (Kennedy Presidential Library, Feldman Oral History, 335–36).

At his press conference on February 21, 1961, the president's announcement of the sites of the first food stamp projects was the second public indication of new directions. Members of the Kennedy farm issues staff from the campaign—a group that included John Baker, Clay Cochran, and agricultural economists Willard Cochrane and John Schnittker—had been working with USDA economists on a broader food stamp program than the proposal that had been put forward by Sullivan and other food aid supporters in Congress during the last years of the Eisenhower administration, one that would apply to most food sold in modern supermarkets. Even before settling into his new

Washington office as the USDA's new chief economist, Cochrane had drawn together a committee on food distribution policy in the department's Bureau of Agricultural Economics. Chairing this working group was Frederick V. Waugh, the USDA official who had been the strongest advocate within the department for two decades of subsidizing consumer demand for the food produced by American farmers.

Because administration officials implemented the plans for the new food stamp program so quickly, they relied on Waugh and other career staffers for assessments of the program's likely costs and benefits. The committee's plan contained several assumptions, the implications of which no one questioned at the time. These same assumptions were later incorporated, again without being independently examined, in the legislation that the White House and USDA officials drafted in 1963 when the administration asked Congress to make the food stamp program permanent. This is not to say that Congress would have opposed (or would have changed) any particular elements of the committee's plans. It is simply an illustration of the weight that bureaucratic policy experts and technicians can wield in the contemporary policy process when time is a crucial constraint.

THE REVISED NEW DEAL FOOD STAMP PROGRAM

Waugh and some of his colleagues were part of a small group of officials who had worked on food stamp policy issues at the USDA off and on since the 1930s. For example, in 1955 under pressure from Senator Aiken and Representative Sullivan, Acting Secretary of Agriculture Earl Butz had set up a Food Stamp Plan Committee in the department so that administration officials could respond to congressional inquiries. Its membership had included USDA officials who worked with the commodity distribution, school lunch, and special milk programs on a daily basis. It also included Frederick Waugh, one of the agricultural economists who had helped design the original food stamp plan for Secretary Wallace in the 1930s. In good bureaucratic fashion the committee had summarized the New Deal food stamp program for Butz without expressing preference for any particular option.

Subsequently, when Butz testified before the House Agriculture Committee, he stressed the problems rather than the successes associated with the New Deal food stamp program that the Food Stamp Committee had mentioned in its report. But in various research reports, journal articles, and presentations to professional meetings over the years, Waugh had made his own position clear. Food assistance efforts, and especially a revived food stamp program, would have to be a continuing feature of American farm income policy for the foreseeable future (Waugh 1961, 1962). This and later reports by the committee provide a fascinating glimpse into the role that bureaucrats can play in the development of new public policy initiatives. As the department's resident expert on food stamp issues, Waugh was part of a kind of a government-in-exile that had existed within the USDA during the 1940s and 1950s. Thus, when the Kennedy administration took office in 1961, Waugh and his colleagues were able to provide Secretary Freeman with a detailed plan in just a few weeks.

Most of the features of the food stamp program unveiled by the Kennedy administration in the spring of 1961 had been worked out in the reports the Food Stamp Study Committee had made to Eisenhower administration officials in 1956. In a report, "An Analysis of Food Stamp Plans," the committee had noted that the original food stamp program had been effective in obtaining a net increase in food consumption among participating families. That meant that low-income consumers had not been able to substitute free foods for what they usually consumed. Second, according to data that the committee had reviewed, most of the administrative problems cited by program critics could be charged to the complicated two-tier design of the original program. The committee's report in 1956 offered less guidance about another set of administrative problems that they traced to the earlier program's overdependence on local government agencies for certification and administration and even for choosing whether to participate at all (Agricultural History Branch Files, Food Stamp Plan folder, 1).

This working group also had compared distribution of surplus foods in bulk (which they called the commodity distribution program) and the cash subsidy (or food stamp) approach as mechanisms for helping families and individuals. Top department officials would have to choose one or the other if expanded assistance schemes were to be seriously considered. The working group's members decided that the food aid programs aimed at local institutions (surplus foods directed to schools, hospitals, etc.) could be expanded without major administrative changes. Congress liked these programs because individual senators and representatives could claim credit from their farm-sector constituents for helping local producers. When particular market problems arose, senators and representatives urged the Secretary of Agriculture to purchase peaches, potatoes, or whatever was in temporary or chronic surplus at that given time.

If the question was phrased differently—which program option best reduced agricultural surpluses—the bulk commodity program looked good because the government had more flexibility to make particular foods available. However, a food stamp plan did a better job of upgrading diet and nutrition while at the same time maintaining normal food expenditures. Thus, even during the Eisenhower administration when the political leadership at the Department of Agriculture and the White House steadfastly opposed any expansion in food assistance programs, departmental bureaucrats had already developed a decided preference for the food stamp approach over the distribution of surplus foods to needy people. By accepting the thrust of the second Waugh group's recommendation for a broad food stamp program in 1961, Secretary Freeman understood that the USDA would not be able to target specific foods that were in surplus at any given time.

Instead, Willard Cochrane later recalled, the program would operate to increase demand for food overall, but probably to the greatest extent among what department officials considered "high ticket" items, that is, meat, cheese, produce, and some other milk products (Kennedy Presidential Library, Cochrane Oral History, 23). Over the long run, departmental policymakers also realized that such a food subsidy program would help producers of these foods more than it would those (except for dairy) whose products had been going into the bulk commodity or school distribution programs. This is an important point to understand since Freeman, Cochrane, and other USDA policymakers knew which regional agricultural economies and producer constituencies grew each kind of food.

Members of Congress and producer groups might prefer dealing with particular surplus foods, but Freeman and his advisers were hoping that the food stamp program would have positive effects on the agricultural economy. In response, some farmers would shift away from producing crops perennially in surplus in favor of livestock and feed grain production. They also hoped that a successful food stamp program would eventually supplant the other family food program run by the department, the distribution of surplus agricultural commodities to needy people. The food stamp program also was attractive to them for the same reason New Deal planners had liked it, because it did not compete with the private market. A food stamp program would still be able to operate if and when the administration's proposed new legislative programs for the agricultural economy began to take effect and dry up the accumulating surpluses. In the meantime, according to a March 1, 1961, memo from Willard Cochrane to the secretary discussing plans for the food stamp program, the school and other smaller institutional feeding programs would operate on an expanded basis as tools to target disposal of particular surplus items (National Archives, Farm Program 6–1).

WORKING OUT THE DETAILS ABOUT FOOD STAMP PROGRAM OPERATION

Departmental economists were the only ones who paid much attention to these details at the time, however. Secretary Freeman understood the outlines of these arguments, but was more concerned with the legislative and appropriations battles starting up in Congress over the department's mainstream farm income programs. These economic assumptions are important, however, because they severely limited the options that decisionmakers had when the program came under close public and congressional scrutiny later on. For example, the informal understanding shared by USDA economists and program managers that a food stamp program ought to supplant the commodity distribution program grew to mean that both programs ought not to operate in the same locality under any circumstances. There is no evidence that Feldman or Freeman, let alone the president, ever considered that issue and reached a decision about it in 1961 when the program began.

Instead, a series of tentative conclusions made jointly by staff and line experts soon hardened to become the lore of the USDA operating agency, the Agricultural Marketing Service (AMS). An important part of the reason for leaving the details to officials at the USDA was that the program did not have to be submitted to Congress in 1961 and administration officials did not have to go on record about its operating assumptions at that time. Instead, White House officials got it running with Section 32 money. Another set of assumptions was more technical, but equally important over time. The Waugh group reported to Cochrane and Freeman that the department should test certain aspects of the program after it started by analyzing results from the pilot projects.

Yet because the program's planners assumed from the start that a food stamp program was superior to commodity distribution—an assumption that was never examined by policy generalists in the office of the Secretary of Agriculture, by presidential aides, or in overhead agencies like the Bureau of the Budget (BOB)—no serious attempt was made to operationally compare the two approaches from the standpoint of such program goals as efficient disposal of surplus foods or nutritional supplementation; but when the subsequent evaluation studies were completed, they only measured selected aspects of how individual food stamp pilot projects performed.

Another aspect of program design also had wide ramifications. The Waugh group did not commission research studies on typical food expenditures by needy families in order to measure both what amount people actually spent on food and what they needed to satisfy their nutritional needs. Instead, members of the Waugh committee designed a purchase schedule for the stamps based on their own estimates of the amount of money poor people spent on food. These estimates did not take into account regional, ethnic, or religious dietary preferences. Such oversights are particularly surprising in light of the expertise available within the Department of Agriculture at that time. After all,

home economists and other consumer specialists in Washington, researchers in the land grant universities, and staffers in USDA field
offices around the country could have applied a body of research that
was already in existence to these questions.

Instead, the food expenditure estimates that went into the design of
the food stamp program were based on fragmentary studies done several years before. Estimates of dietary requirements were only slightly
better substantiated. The main reason for these oversights was that
the program's designers were used to responding to the problems of
farmers, not those of low-income consumers. This point was taken up
in a memo Willard Cochrane sent to Freeman at the beginning of
March. In it the program's designers admitted that the *economy* food
budget used to calculate the amount of food stamps to which each family
would be entitled was somewhat arbitrary.[6] The department's experience with the pilot projects would allow it to pursue studies later
about the shopping patterns of low-income consumers and the actual
amount of cash they spent on food.

Any changes or modifications could be made before the program was
expanded and made permanent. This promise was lost sight of later,
however, as control shifted from its designers in the Bureau of Agricultural Economics (BAE) to program managers in AMS, who were
more concerned about program continuity, expansion, and other daily
administrative concerns. The final Waugh report in 1961 also built on
the premise that needy families would contribute some of their own
money to the purchase of the stamps, a restatement of the concept of
normal food expenditures that had been a feature of all of the schemes
developed by food stamp program supporters at the USDA since the
1930s.

Kennedy administration planners assumed, although they did not
substantiate this independently, that more low-income Americans
were participating in the national cash economy in 1961 than had been
during the Depression. Equally important, the food stamp program's
designers also assumed a family with no money at all (and thus a
household that made no cash outlays for food) could receive enough
food from participation in the food stamp program to constitute an
economy diet absolutely free of charge.[7] However, USDA officials soon
lost sight of this key point and the issue of what to do about people
who had no normal food expenditures became blurred after the first
pilot projects began to issue food stamps. Finally, no one considered
any changes in local administration from the system that had prevailed
during the Depression. By leaving the determination of eligibility to
local welfare officials, the program's designers guaranteed that the
food stamp program would be built on the existing federal–state welfare system with its wide disparities in amounts, conditions of assis-

tance, and responsiveness to local elites and values at the expense of national standards and uniformity in local program operations.

After being ratified by Secretary Freeman and White House officials, the pilot food stamp program followed the outlines of the Waugh committee proposals exactly. It was an exceptionally complicated and technical undertaking that uneasily juggled several different emphases. Until 1968, when food program critics had mastered its intricacies, USDA economists were almost the only ones to fully understand its economic and philosophical underpinnings. At the same time, AMS staffers became the custodians of the technicalities of program operations and the chief source of information for the state and local officials who signed people up and actually distributed the food stamp coupons (Berry 1984).

CHOOSING THE FIRST FOOD PROGRAM SITES

While they relied on Waugh and his colleagues for the program's design and operating philosophy, Secretary Freeman and White House decisionmakers were more interested in the next step in the policy-making process, picking the pilot food stamp sites. Staff recommendations set the overall parameters for site selection based on two factors: (1) a locality's previous experience with USDA food relief efforts; and (2) partisan political considerations. Departmental officials understood the political necessity of using government programs to reward the president's friends and allies and incorporated that principle into their original recommendations. Because a far larger number of cities and counties could justify federal aid of this type than could be accommodated in such an experimental program, it was fairly easy to find six or eight sites that could be justified both programmatically and politically.

That AMS officials set the tone for the site selection process can be seen from recommendations entitled, "The Expansion of Food Donations to Needy Families," included as an attachment to a February 9, 1961, memo from Cochrane to Freeman. AMS officials suggested that Freeman consider a cross section of economically depressed areas where the department already had experience working with local welfare officials and where they thought the food stamp program would do well. Almost 80 percent of the food given away by the department during the last month of the Eisenhower administration had gone to urban and rural locations in just eleven states and Puerto Rico. The mining industry had been hard hit in Pennsylvania, West Virginia, Kentucky, Tennessee, and parts of Michigan. Detroit and other midwestern cities had been hurt by cutbacks in sales of major consumer goods. And besides these urban and rural industrial employees, Agriculture Department officials noted that many farm workers were also receiving large amounts of the existing federal food aid, especially in parts of the South such as Alabama, Arkansas, Louisiana, Mississippi, Oklahoma, and Texas because of the trends toward greater mechanization in cotton production and consolidation of farm holdings there (National Archives, Farm Program 6–1).

White House officials allowed Freeman to start with eight sites. Six were concentrated in economically depressed mining regions. Fayette County, Pa.; Floyd County, Ky.; McDowell County, W. Va.; and Franklin County, Ill., were all in AMS' original report. Parts of St. Louis and Itasca counties on the Minnesota Iron Range in Freeman's home state and Silver Bow County in Montana copper country represented in the Senate by Mike Mansfield (D-Mo.), the new majority leader, were added. Finally, the city of Detroit and San Miguel County, N. Mex., rounded out the experiment with urban and rural components respectively. While plans were being finalized, Freeman kept key Democrats in Congress and around the country informed about the status of program planning.[8]

Several other tasks also needed to be done before the program could begin. A memo from the AMS' O. V. Wells to Freeman on April 10 shows that the secretary prodded lawyers in the department's legal branch to justify the program's legality under his Section 32 authority rather than Representative Sullivan's legislation (National Archives, Farm Program 6–1–1). AMS officials prepared background materials for Freeman to use when he briefed members of Congress, communicated with state and local officials, and talked with representatives of retail food organizations about how the program would operate. They also worked closely with officials of the American Bankers Association, the Federal Reserve System, and the U.S. Treasury Department in arranging for the design and redemption of the coupons. Once the first sites had been agreed on, congressional supporters rewarded, and the public announcements made, the chief interest that President Kennedy's White House advisers had in food aid administration was to monitor program costs.[9]

From the beginning, the principal limitation holding down food aid program activity was budgetary. Freeman discussed finances for all of the food aid programs with Sorenson, Feldman, and the president at regular times in the budgetary cycle. And top officials at the BOB and the Council of Economic Advisers (CEA) closely watched Agriculture's use of Section 32 funds as part of a broader concern about the high cost of the department's farm income programs. Secretary Freeman asked to make the program permanent just a few months after the first program sites began operations in June 1961. White House aides turned down this request, but did approve a small expansion in spring

1962, after the secretary assured them that he could manage all of the old and new sites with the $50 million in Section 32 funds allocated for that fiscal year.[10]

EVALUATING NEW FRONTIER FOOD POLICY

The proposals adopted by the Kennedy administration were unusual instruments of public policy in several important respects. First, members of Congress were only minimally involved. Following New Deal practice, they arose within the executive branch and, after being approved in brief outline form by White House officials, went into effect without being enacted by Congress. Second, conventional interest group lobbying was little in evidence. The president and his appointees at Agriculture adopted proposals based on ideas developed by career officials within government, not those proposed by interest groups or congressional supporters of the administration. Officials at Agriculture shared a concern for the health of the farm economy, but disagreed about specific policy approaches and responded differently to interest group pressures. A small cadre of policy specialists in the career bureaucracy had been able to continue to research alternative policy options even when they had been out of favor with policymakers. After years when the idea of subsidizing demand for food by low-income consumers had attracted little interest, when administration priorities changed, proposals quickly flowed out of the hothouse atmosphere of bureaucratic politics.

Finally, compared to the work done by presidential domestic policy staffs during later administrations, White House involvement with the food stamp program in 1961 seems especially ad hoc. During the presidential campaign, the candidate had repeatedly promised expanded food aid, but it was only after White House officials assumed office that they considered specific programmatic responses, including a particular USDA version of a food stamp program. Because White House officials adopted such a low profile during this round of food assistance policy making, Orville Freeman emerges as an especially key figure. The Secretary of Agriculture had two main goals: (1) he was concerned with how the food distribution programs fit into the framework of general agriculture policy; and (2) he wanted to use them to achieve political benefits for the administration's farm program in his dealings with friends and allies in Congress. In the process he adopted a role that Cabinet officers often play, that of advocate for their own departmental programs and missions in administration councils.

3

Implementing Food Assistance Policy

Launching the New Frontier's food assistance programs and administering them on a daily basis meant that Secretary Freeman and other USDA officials had to respond to different kinds of political pressures. President Kennedy's appointees at Agriculture made the decisions outlined in the last chapter in an environment remarkably free of the constituency and interest group pressures that usually surround executive branch decision making. Instead two other influences predominated: (1) macropolitical concerns that White House officials inherited from the 1960 presidential campaign; and (2) preoccupations with program philosophy and design on the part of bureaucrats at the USDA. Once the new programs actually began to operate, however, members of the president's team at Agriculture had to manage them within a broader context, which included interest group and congressional scrutiny, administrators' best judgments about the role of the food programs within the department's missions generally, expectations among middle-level managers and other career USDA employees about how the department's programs ought to operate, and periodic White House interest in the specifics of program operation.

How Secretary Freeman and his aides responded to these often contradictory pressures on food aid administration is the subject of this chapter. It begins with a discussion of how the new Kennedy appointees became accustomed to the political stakes that agricultural interests had in the day-to-day operation of the department's surplus disposal programs. Interest by producer groups and their congressional allies is easily understandable; the prospect of gluts and other changes in market conditions prompt producer groups to ask USDA officials for help. These contacts take place through visits or communications from commodity groups and trade associations, backed up by political pressure from sympathetic members of Congress. To further complicate matters, Freeman and his aides sometimes found themselves faced with contradictory and competing producer demands for action, all of which could not be accommodated. At the same time, White House officials also had important political stakes in the mechanics of food program operation.

Usually, presidential interest in implementation decisions showed up in connection with other battles the administration was fighting in Congress. Decisions that Secretary Freeman made on specific surplus disposal issues could be used to convince influential senators and representatives to support other parts of the administration's legislative program. Kennedy administration officials saw food program issues as part of several larger domestic policy concerns; this chapter examines three of the most important: (1) civil rights enforcement; (2) governmentwide antipoverty efforts; and (3) macroeconomic policy, especially budget concerns. Thus, even at the beginning of the 1960s, before the spotlight of public scrutiny focused on them directly, the USDA food programs were being pulled in several directions. In debates about food aid program administration, Secretary Freeman tried to stake out a position between the two main sources of pressure—more inclusive than the concerns of individual commodity sectors within the agricultural community, but less all-encompassing than those of White House officials who had to balance Agriculture's claims with those of the other parts of the administration.

SPENDING SECTION 32 MONEY: A CLOSER LOOK AT PRODUCER INTERESTS IN FOOD PROGRAM ADMINISTRATION

With the exception of the new food stamp program, which operated through regular commercial food-buying channels, all of the other food assistance efforts depended on decisions made by department officials about which foodstuffs to buy under existing program authority, such as that included in Section 32, designed to bolster farm income.[1] Everyone concerned—members of Congress, White House officials, USDA staffers, Freeman and his aides, producers, wholesalers, retailers, and consumer groups—knew that departmental purchases influenced the price and availability of specific commodities in regional and national markets. Also because of the wide variety of growing conditions across the country, the surplus food decision-making process knew few seasonal boundaries. Pressure on departmental decisionmakers to help out producer interests was unceasing.

Once a problem came up, decision making had to be quick and flexible because of the vagaries of weather and other problems that occurred with little advance notice and needed prompt attention. Two such issues that USDA officials faced during the Kennedy years—commodity decisions involving orange juice and peanut butter—illustrate some of the complexities involved. In late 1962, Secretary Freeman had to decide whether or not to purchase citrus products for distribution to schools and other institutions. Consideration of this issue by officials on the secretary's staff began after AMS staffers reported that producers were worried about a glut of oranges at the end of the current growing season. In response to these concerns, AMS officials recommended that the department purchase more than 383,000 cases of concentrated orange juice.

Memos from AMS official S. R. Smith to Assistant Secretary John P. Duncan on January 5 and 11 and February 2, 1962, provide a good overview of how USDA officials saw the agency's responsibilities to producer groups (National Archives, Farm Program 8-Domestic). Smith argued that this action would be justified under the secretary's Section 32 authority because a surplus of the magnitude expected with the next crop of fruit would otherwise severely depress producer prices. This case illustrates how complicated Section 32 decision making could become. Shortly after senior department officials gave permission to make the purchase, a harsh December freeze reversed earlier estimates of a citrus glut. In response, USDA officials dropped their plans for that contract and a similar one for grapefruit. That change in plans, however, drew complaints from local school officials, who often faced last minute changes in the surplus foods they received.[2] That USDA officials usually put producer interests first made menu planning and their own food buying—school officials received only a fraction of the total foodstuffs that they needed from the federal government—confusing at best and sometimes chaotic.

Besides direct pressure from producer groups (such as happened in the citrus case), USDA's officials also heard from important members of Congress on behalf of producer groups. USDA records show that not all commodities—or all legislators—were treated equally. Senator Spessard Holland (D-Fla.) and Representative Jamie Whitten (D-Miss.), who chaired the congressional subcommittees that guarded the purse strings of the Sections 32 and 416 programs used to fund the surplus food distribution programs, were especially influential.[3] In the orange juice case, producer groups like those represented in Holland's home state prevailed over the objections of school officials and other weaker constituencies of USDA activities. But what happened when agricultural interests made competing claims for USDA's assistance, when, for example, California citrus producers complained about help given to Florida growers? Or when producers raising rival products—sugar cane versus sugar beets—both jockeyed for favorable action by departmental officials?

A case involving peanut growers and peanut butter processors shows how difficult it could be for department officials to satisfy all of their agriculture-related constituencies. In a January 20, 1963, letter to Undersecretary Charles Murphy, James E. Mack, general counsel of the Peanut Butter Manufacturers Association, expressed concern about the effects on his members of an adverse USDA action (National Archives, Farm Program 8). Mack complained about recent government purchases of surplus peanuts designed to help peanut producers. By making peanuts available to needy families through the food distribution system, USDA actions made peanuts scarcer in commercial channels. That, in turn, threatened to raise prices to peanut processors and depress market demand for the finished product. Mack invoked his organization's close ties with members of the House Agricultural Appropriations Subcommittee by pointing out that that body had inserted language into a recent report favorable to the industry's position.

While using formally deferential language in his letter, Mack conveyed a definite threat to USDA officials—that they could expect a hostile congressional reaction if they stood by their peanut decision. From Freeman's perspective, every interest always wanted something, but his job was made more difficult by the fact that many people wanted contradictory things simultaneously. Sometimes that meant that the secretary had to give in, but in other instances USDA officials had room to maneuver. When he was under pressure from rival producer interests, Freeman could make decisions based on his own view of what was best for the agricultural economy as a whole, not just what commodity interests, agricultural policy specialists in Congress, or officials in individual USDA agencies wanted at a given point in time. Freeman rarely felt any pressure on commodity decisions from consumers or anyone outside of agriculture's close friends in Washington in the early 1960s.

Concern for the health of major producer groups was deeply institutionalized within the department. Many USDA officials at the bureau and agency levels had learned not just to wait for producer groups to make appeals, but to anticipate their problems. The reality for Freeman (and Undersecretary Murphy to whom the secretary delegated responsibility for major commodity purchases) was that almost every producer group and other agriculture-related interest had sympathetic allies somewhere within the department, and on one or more of the congressional committees responsible for departmental legislative authority and program funds. The secretary could only hope that the benefits balanced out among the department's various claimants over the long run.

In order to deal with the reality of producer interests, Freeman adopted a strategy of exchanging favors with influential legislators for help on other departmental business.[4] Before each meeting with some-one like Whitten, Holland, Chairman Allen Ellender (D-La.) of the Senate Committee on Agriculture and Forestry, or Representative Cooley, head of the House Agriculture Committee, Freeman had his staff prepare a list of issues upon which the member wanted depart-mental officials to act. Such concerns commonly included agricultural products with which that member wanted surplus disposal help from the USDA and requests to locate major departmental facilities in his or her district.

Freeman's responses to these requests for help were an executive branch variant of *distributive* politics, a term usually applied to defense installations, dams, and other public projects that members of Congress want for their districts (Lowi 1964, 1972). In this version, Agriculture officials made the formal decisions that resulted in individual legis-lators winning benefits for their districts. What the secretary gained in return was aid in moving a departmental or presidential program out of committee, support on an appropriations committee matter, or help in an important floor vote in the House or Senate.

What the secretary gave away was the public political credit for a surplus food decision that he probably would have made anyway. Keep-ing this network of relationships with key members of Congress in good repair during the early 1960s took up a great deal of the time that the Secretary of Agriculture spent on congressional matters in-volving the food aid programs. Freeman's staff also used similar "box scores" as backup material for presidential meetings with key members of Congress and as ammunition when arm-twisting on floor votes in-volving the president's legislative program. All the players understood what was going on. After all, Freeman's most important job as Sec-retary of Agriculture was to sell the farm community and its allies in Congress on the administration's farm program, not to adapt it to the social welfare concerns that were less central to the objectives of the USDA's food aid efforts.

Freeman's task was complicated by the stranglehold that conserv-ative (mostly southern) Democrats held on important positions in the congressional agricultural policy subsystem, people like Whitten, Hol-land, and the leaders of the House and Senate Agriculture committees. Most opposed administration policies on a wide range of nonfarm do-mestic policy issues. USDA decisionmakers also were trying to achieve broader administration economic policies by creating incentives that would lead producers away from crops in chronic surplus. A June 7, 1963, memo shows how difficult this balancing act sometimes became (National Archives, Farm Program 6). In this memo and an accompanying report, Willard Cochrane, Freeman's chief economic adviser, reported to the Commodity Credit Corporation directors about the effects of the department's surplus disposal objectives.[5]

Sometimes, as was the case with potatoes, turkeys, and eggs, Cochrane noted, government action tended to replace commercial demand and encourage overproduction, both of which department officials hoped to avoid. Cochrane also raised another thorny issue associated with the school lunch program. While USDA contributed a combination of cash and commodities, state and local school officials still had to purchase additional foodstuffs themselves. Department officials wanted to encourage producer groups to make the most of this local purchasing power and Cochrane was concerned that the federal government often wound up competing with local school officials in their food buying. Thus, the department was constantly being tugged in different directions by its long-term goals for agriculture, its new responsibilities for improving the health and nutrition of low-income people, and the short-term demands of producer groups described earlier.

As time went on, policymakers like Cochrane, Murphy, and Freeman grew increasingly frustrated by their inability to convince producer groups that more flexibility for USDA officials would be beneficial to them because it would contribute to the development of a large and stable future market for the foodstuffs they grew. A good sense of the expanded demand argument is conveyed in letters that Assistant Secretary John Duncan wrote to William H. Stephens, Jr., on August 25, 1961, and Senator Olin Johnston (D-S.C.) on March 7, 1963 (National Archives, Farm Program 7—School Lunch Program). To most producer groups, that argument sounded similar to the one that the Kennedy administration had used in order to justify the design of the new food stamp program. Departmental officials were holding out uncertain hope for producers in the future, rather than taking specific commodities off their hands when they were in temporary surplus. Instead of sermons and vague promises of future benefits, commodity groups and their Washington representatives preferred to have emergency help available at the time when they most needed it.

They did not want federal officials telling them to change to another crop. They wanted assistance immediately each and every time an emergency occurred. Furthermore, they considered Section 32 funds to be the principal mechanism for that objective and disliked having the administration using this authority for the kind of generalized increase in consumer demand that the food stamp and school lunch programs promised to achieve. As they negotiated this political mine-field, USDA decisionmakers had to keep another objective in mind, that White House officials wanted Section 32 funds used as a mechanism for increasing administrative flexibility just as the law said. Section 32 should be used at the discretion of the secretary to benefit the overall agricultural economy, based on the best expert advice he could get from his staff and from the various USDA agencies involved. In summary, during the early 1960s, Agriculture Department officials acceded to more producer demands than they would have liked, but they also kept trying to change the behavior of agricultural producers and other subsystem members.

WHITE HOUSE FOCUS ON FOOD AID ADMINISTRATION

Compared to the unrelenting nature of subsystem pressure, attention from White House officials on food aid policy was sporadic. When it did come, however, Freeman had to give it very close attention. On several occasions, White House officials pressed Secretary Freeman to include food aid program implementation within the context of domestic policy priorities. Examples of such attention—civil rights violations associated with food program administration in the deep South, short- and long-term antipoverty planning, and concern about farm program costs—will be briefly discussed in this section. Most of the time however, once food stamp siting was completed and specific commodity decisions made, USDA officials left decisions about day-to-day program administration to state and local officials.

Over the years, county welfare officials and local school district authorities who operated the surplus disposal programs had become accustomed to having very little supervision from USDA officials stationed in Washington or the regional offices that dotted the country. In parts of the South, local control over program administration was even stronger. State and local officials there, who had grown up with and shared the same values as the federal officials who had the legal authority to oversee program operations, were used to running USDA programs as they thought best. Early in the Kennedy administration, a situation arose that cast doubt on the wisdom and equity of operating such a decentralized implementation structure (Maney 1988).

In the spring of 1961, complaints about discrimination in the USDA's surplus disposal activities began to reach White House and Justice Department officials from civil rights workers in rural areas of Mississippi and Tennessee. Among other allegations was the charge that local government officials were attempting to use food program benefits to enforce traditional norms of social behavior on the part of black sharecroppers and farm tenants. Specifically, civil rights groups charged that in some parts of the Mississippi Delta area county welfare officials were refusing to certify blacks for participation in the food distribution program if they had registered to vote.

After investigating these charges, Secretary Freeman instructed AMS officials to bypass the usual implementation process and take more of an active role in food program administration in order to prevent such discrimination from taking place in the future.[6] The results of the new federal–state cooperative arrangements that were soon put into place in Haywood and Fayette Counties in Tennessee and in nearby Le Flore County, Mississippi, stood as a warning for what might happen elsewhere in the cotton South if civil rights activism continued to grow. It is also important to note the objections that AMS officials raised to bypassing the established intergovernmental structure in food program operations. The Section 32 authority that the secretary had was, they admitted, flexible enough to justify this approach.

AMS officials were accustomed to having the department's programs adjust to local political conditions, especially in the cotton South, where they had become a fixture of the local political economy.[7] The officials worried that any changes in program administration would prompt local governments in these areas to withdraw from participation in the federal programs altogether. At the end of that process, they argued, the Department of Agriculture would emerge with a new set of financial and administrative obligations. These arguments were rejected, however, and after the new arrangements had gone into effect in Tennessee and Mississippi, participation in the food distribution program increased dramatically. Still, AMS officials remained critical of the increased federal role in funding and administration that these civil rights initiatives represented.

White House officials also influenced the implementation of food assistance policy when they included it within the administration's larger antirecession and antipoverty efforts. During most of the 1950s, both urban and rural poverty had been largely invisible to middle-class white America, as Michael Harrington reminded the country when he published *The Other America* in 1963. The Kennedy administration's response to the conditions of poverty in America consisted of two parts. First, there were attempts to alleviate emergency conditions (e.g., in West Virginia, Kentucky, etc.) while officials worked on broader schemes to bring economic recovery to depressed rural areas. Then, after the administration's main economic recovery program was in place, attention shifted to dealing with structural poverty of the kind Harrington had publicized, an admission that the economic recovery that the administration had planned was not likely to reach all segments of the society.

It was this second category of activity that came to be explicitly titled an antipoverty program, but both sets of initiatives focused on conditions caused by poverty and both included USDA programs in their arsenal of weapons. When particular problems of poverty came to light during the Kennedy years, the administration's reasoning was similar to that which guided the disposition of the civil rights cases just described. Each time a new problem was brought to White House attention, the president and his aides requested that Freeman increase the distribution of surplus food in the area concerned. In the Tennessee and Mississippi cases, federal officials secured the cooperation of state welfare officials by making clear that they were prepared to go ahead unilaterally if necessary. Administration legal strategists concluded that the USDA had the authority to take unilateral action in crisis situations if state and local government officials would not cooperate in joint efforts at alleviating local economic conditions. But even when state and local officials were sympathetic, problems could arise if the affected jurisdictions did not have any money to put into expanded food aid efforts.

The administration's efforts in eastern Kentucky illustrate this dilemma. During the fall of 1962, White House officials became concerned about newspaper predictions of a looming crisis in depressed parts of eastern Kentucky. Ted Sorenson, the president's chief aide, organized a working group to prepare an administration response. The problem was the stagnant regional economy, which affected the entire Appalachian area (Caudill 1963; Harrington 1963). Unlike the Tennessee and Mississippi cases where race was an issue, state and local elected officials in Kentucky wanted to alleviate the conditions that poor people faced. But their ability to increase relief and welfare payments was severely strained because tax collections were down, and the local economy was under severe stress. In response, Kennedy administration officials decided to deploy a package of federal social and economic development programs, including expanded food aid.

This time because state and local governments were more cooperative than their counterparts had been in the civil rights cases discussed earlier, AMS officials successfully argued against the federal government setting up its own direct distribution programs in counties where neither a surplus commodity program nor a food stamp project was already in existence. Although White House officials chafed at the variety and variability of benefit levels that existed across local government jurisdictions in the area, they did not consider overhauling the various welfare and economic development programs that already existed. Overlapping programs, differing benefit levels, and local discretion in implementation were characteristics of the dramatically decentralized intergovernmental delivery system with which AMS officials were accustomed to work. The eastern Kentucky case is important in the development of federal food aid policy because it tied these programs more closely with the administration's economic recovery priorities. It also was the first time that Kennedy administration officials experimented with a multiprogram approach to poverty as a focus for federal government action.

THE USDA'S EXPERIENCES FIGHTING RURAL POVERTY

The Tennessee, Mississippi, and Kentucky initiatives illustrate the extent and variability of the problem of rural poverty that the nation faced thirty years after the Great Depression. To what degree should the USDA be responsible for alleviating these conditions? Rural poverty had caused problems for USDA officials during the Roosevelt and Truman administrations (Baldwin 1968; Kirkendall 1982; Tugwell 1959) as influential critics charged that large landholders were the biggest beneficiaries of the New Deal's policies for agriculture in the South.[8] Several studies focused on the plight of black farmers, tenants, and sharecroppers (Baldwin 1968; Conrad 1965; The People Left Behind 1967). Critics also cited evidence that departmental policymakers had intervened at key points to discipline USDA officials who questioned these policies. More often, however, departmental staffers at all levels had responded to the pressures of agency socialization and the structure of incentives for career development within the department by censoring their own actions and avoiding the problems of rural poverty in favor of those on the agenda of mainstream commercial agriculture.

When Orville Freeman took office, it was already possible to see the outlines of the critique of USDA programs and policies that civil rights and antipoverty activists would soon put forward against the department. These liberal critics believed that the department had contributed to, rather than alleviated, rural poverty. First, the Department of Agriculture's policies had not been evenhanded. Landholders had benefited more than tenants, and whites far more than blacks. USDA farm income programs had contributed to the shakeout in agriculture, which was forcing millions of people off the land and into the cities. Its major programs benefited the larger and more prosperous and politically powerful farmers and agribusinesses. Second, USDA policies too unquestioningly embraced "progress" via science and technology, which have been the major engines driving the trends toward more concentration and corporate penetration of the agricultural economy (Fite 1980, 1984; Hadwiger 1982).

Other side effects, according to this indictment, have included negative impacts on the nation's environment through overuse of agricultural chemicals, depletion of the soil, and the introduction of chemicals and additives into the food supply (Carson 1962). The USDA especially ignored the impacts of these trends on those least able to deal with them: agricultural laborers generally and black southern farm workers in particular. Finally, critics would allege that implementation of the department's mission of fostering the mainstream agricultural economy caused spillovers into other areas of legitimate public concern. For example, the farm support programs that were popular with agricultural interest groups and their spokespersons in Congress were contributing to migration from rural to urban areas. This put additional stress on employment training programs and governmental social welfare efforts generally.

Agriculture had been becoming more capital- and less labor-intensive ever since the first two decades of this century. As a result, the workforce needed for American agriculture was already much reduced in size. Willard Cochrane, who came to Washington in 1961 to be the Kennedy administration's chief agricultural economist, has shown that farm employment began to slow as early as 1870 and then to decline after 1920 (Cochrane 1979). The 1960s was to be a key period of social and economic change, yet few people in Washington seemed aware of its likely magnitude. Agricultural policymakers in successive presidential administrations had underestimated the role that science and technology would play after World War II in increasing the nation's food supply (Matusow 1967). Agricultural economists working for the department, or like Cochrane at the land grant universities, could see that the continued application of scientific advances to agricultural production would continue to have massive effects on the farm workforce. However, few talked publicly about the likely magnitude or the political implications of the directions of postwar agriculture (Fite 1984).

It is also important to note that the problems and successes of American agriculture in the postwar period differed from region to region in the country. Economic concentration had proceeded rapidly in the newer growing regions of California and the southwest, where large factory farms had started specializing in single crops like cotton or fresh produce. Parts of Freeman's midwest were specializing in feed grain and livestock production, but there the farms remained, by and large, family-sized units. However, it was in the deep South that the costs of economic change took the longest time to become visible and where planners, bureaucrats, and policymakers turned a particularly blind eye. Gilbert Fite has described the lag that occurred between the advent of a prototype of the mechanical cotton picker in the 1920s and 1930s and the beginning of its widespread use twenty years later (Fite 1980).

The political and social realities of life in the cotton South meant that when change finally came to that region special displacement costs would be borne by large numbers of black farmers and laborers who were especially ill-prepared for such a change in their way of life. According to Fite, by 1950 only 5 percent of American cotton was being picked by machine. By 1963, that figure had jumped to 72 percent. However, a large part of this total applied to the southwestern cotton areas, which had adopted the new technology faster than deep South producers had. This, in turn, suggested that much of the impact of mechanization remained to be felt in the South at the time when the Kennedy administration came to office. Contemporary USDA technical publications estimated that as much as 30 to 50 percent of the farm labor force would ultimately be thrown out of work in some states (Fite 1980:190–207).

The effects of postwar farm policy on rural poverty and unemployment extend further than just to the department's price support programs and agricultural research missions. Sidney Baldwin (1968) has argued that the continued existence of chronic rural, or agricultural, poverty has been hidden by general adherence to an American "agrarian myth." This set of beliefs and values romanticized the reality of farming and exaggerated the role of the agriculturalist as the nation's true Jeffersonian democrat. Many of the policymakers who came to the USDA in 1961 joined program managers, technicians, and researchers there who shared this creed. This belief reinforced the department's disposition to concentrate on the problems of commercial agriculture and helped structure the views of USDA officials about agriculture's role in the larger national economy.

Agricultural scientists and technicians tended, by training and inclination, to specialize in projects that would be useful to the major regional agricultural economies around the country (Hadwiger 1982; Kirkendall 1982). The extreme specialization of many of the department's scientific professionals, part cause and part result of this affinity for immediate practical applications, in turn contributed to a concentration on technical questions and a willingness to leave the policy implications of their work, or even the interrelationships among the various regional agricultural economies, to be drawn by others. Finally, Hadwiger (1982) has argued that these officials also shared a feeling of defensiveness caused by the older isolation of rural America from the currents of change in the larger society.

Even with expanded domestic food assistance programs on the New Deal model, no one could have reasonably expected the USDA, or any other federal department acting alone, to provide for all of the country's growing welfare needs in rural areas, or to tear down the system of racial segregation that constituted the foundation of much of southern agriculture. Freeman faced more problems than his Republican predecessor, however, because Kennedy administration officials did not share Secretary Benson's position that alleviating the effects of this revolution in agriculture was no part of the department's business.

AGRICULTURE'S ROLE IN PLANNING FOR THE WAR ON POVERTY

When pushed, the Kennedy administration chipped away at the edges of the problem, but it did not launch an all-out effort at alleviating rural poverty. Decision making on antipoverty issues in 1963, showed the effects of the administration's efforts a few months before in eastern Kentucky. The first memos and background papers on what became the War on Poverty were prepared at the Council of Economic Advisers in the spring of 1963 at the instigation of Walter Heller, chairman of the council. Kennedy administration officials began to turn their attention to poverty as a structural problem after the president's tax cut legislation had passed Congress and been signed into law. Since something had been done for both the middle class and for business, so the administration's logic went, it now was time to help out other parts of the traditional Democratic party constituency. Heller asked Robert Lampman, an economist on the council staff, to prepare a memo on the possible contents of a Kennedy antipoverty program.

Lampman's response on June 10, 1963 linked success in fighting poverty to broader issues of economic policy. First, he argued that full employment, a successful tax cut, and other administration efforts, if successful, would have the greatest long-term effects on reducing poverty; that is, they would help return the situation to that of the ten-year period from 1947 to 1957 when, Lampman argued, most segments of American society, including minorities, had participated in and benefited from economic growth. However, Lampman pointed to three populations—older people, the disabled, and female-headed households—who needed special attention because they were structurally linked to poverty. When pressed to suggest programs for the benefit of groups likely to be left out of general economic growth, Lampman produced an inventory of existing governmental programs, including activities of the USDA's Extension Service and the various AMS food assistance efforts.[9]

He was suggesting that a Kennedy administration antipoverty effort ought to build on the base of federal programs already in place and target the poor wherever they were located. Clearly, food assistance policy would be part of that effort. Lampman also acknowledged some of the political limitations of any antipoverty program, calculations that set administration planners apart from influential critics of the current system outside of government such as Michael Harrington, whose recommendations implied much higher political costs. "Probably," Lampman cautioned in his June 10, 1963, memo to Heller, "a politically acceptable program must avoid completely any use of the term 'inequality' or the term 'redistribution' of income or wealth" (Johnson Presidential Library, OEO Legislative Background, 4).

Lampman's original memo contained no recommendations for participation by the poor themselves in the local operation of federal government programs. Authorship of the ideas calling for community action programs with *maximum feasible participation* by the poor usually has been credited to a second group working out of the Department of Justice and headed by the Attorney General's aide, David Hackett. Much of the perspective of this second group came out of foundation-sponsored social work projects such as the Ford Foundation's Grey Areas program. A third interdepartmental group was charged with sorting out the federal programs that were already in existence. That third group included representation by the same USDA officials who had been involved in the Kennedy administration's project in eastern Kentucky just a few months before (Kennedy Presidential Library, Kennedy Library - Brandeis University 1973).

After Lyndon Johnson assumed the presidency in November of 1963, administration officials assembled a bill for presentation to Congress by merging the work of the three groups. One part of this legislative package designed to demonstrate the country's commitment to the ideals of the slain president—an important part from the perspective of the president's appointees at the Department of Agriculture—later had to be dropped because of congressional opposition. Originally, there was a rural affairs section of the Economic Opportunity Act proposal (Fite 1984; Johnson Presidential Library, OEO Administrative History). If the original proposal had remained intact, problems of rural poverty might have emerged sooner to trouble officials at the USDA (Fite 1984). Instead, traditionally powerful rural political elites succeeded one more time in 1964 in limiting the official policy agenda of the poor in rural America.[10]

ADMINISTRATION DOUBTS ABOUT FARM PROGRAM COSTS

White House officials also kept close track of the size of farm program costs during the Kennedy administration. In the 1950s and 1960s, White House officials of both parties had fervently hoped to cut the share of the national budget that was going to the acquisition and management of agricultural surpluses. When it came to the use of Section 32 funds, the technique used by the Republican administration had been to keep as tight a lid as possible on Agriculture's budget, construe the department's operating authority narrowly, and do only as much as the law and political reality required. After 1961, the Democrats adopted a different approach. Kennedy administration officials were more aggressive in using funds that had traditionally been earmarked for the Department of Agriculture's mainstream farm programs for relief and social welfare purposes. Freeman also used Section 32 spending to encourage the restructuring of agricultural production and reduce the further accumulation of surpluses. Both of these initiatives increased conflict among the party's traditional political constituencies and made the secretary's job more complicated.

Concern by officials in the Kennedy White House about the overall costs of farm policy led them to direct the BOB to closely monitor the cost of agricultural surplus and support programs. Budget officials worried that if the administration did not summon the political will to curtail farm support programs, too many people would find it artificially profitable and remain in farming. Some of the trends working against small operators—consolidation of land holdings, more intensive use of capital, continuing advances in agricultural mechanization—were, in the view of administration economists, probably inevitable and ultimately would prove positive for the economy as a whole. No one in the White House was directly proposing to force people off the land and into the cities. Still, these dispassionate analyses circulating within the administration echoed sentiments held by mainstream economic researchers about the state of agriculture within the national economy (Cochrane 1965, 1979; Committee for Economic Development 1962).

Freeman was aware of these ideas and their implications for USDA programs. His reaction to the analysis and recommendations contained in a report by the Committee for Economic Development can be seen in his July 18, 1962, *White House Weekly Report* (Freeman Papers). This memo shows that Freeman saw the state of the agricultural economy in terms of that part of it that he knew best, the rural midwest. As people left farming, he argued, small towns in rural America suffered a loss in their economic vitality, then later in the quality of life that they could offer their citizens. Freeman also was concerned about the short-term political consequences of these trends, especially prospects for Democratic party losses in rural districts in the 1962 congressional elections.

Although these undercurrents swirled around executive branch decision making during the first years of the Kennedy administration, they did not come to the surface and generate much public discussion. Analysis of their political implications was confined to annual consideration of the administration's legislative proposals for agriculture. Freeman feared that these trends meant that USDA officials would face increasingly hostile urban opposition to their efforts on behalf of the agricultural economy. They were particularly sensitive to news accounts that described farm program mismanagement, fraud, and abuse for national (i.e., nonrural) audiences. On several occasions, Freeman responded to unfavorable press reports alleging spendthrift federal programs for farmers.

The media's message seemed to be that federal money was going to the greedy, not the truly needy. After the appearance of an unfavorable article by syndicated columnist Drew Pearson, for example, the secretary urged his staff in a June 21, 1961, memo to go on the offensive and launch a major public relations campaign on behalf of the department's programs (Freeman Papers). The proper response, Freeman asserted, was to compare subsidies to agriculture with those that routinely went to business or to veterans. The latter were actually much larger, he said, but less noticeable.

Despite his general enthusiasm, the secretary sometimes found it difficult to defend the full panoply of governmental efforts directed at rural America. For example, Freeman devoted his *Weekly Report* for August 1, 1961, to responding to an inquiry by White House officials about a story of a farmer buying a Cadillac with his government support payment (Freeman Papers). Another time the media criticized a Farmers Home Administration program that made loans available for the construction of golf courses in rural communities. Besides having to respond to particular charges, Freeman and his aides knew that press reports of this kind inevitably prompted increased White House scrutiny of other USDA activities.

Other favorite media topics in this period included exposés about the overall costs of the farm income programs, apparently outsized payments to individual agricultural producers, questionable decisions by local USDA officials, and rising prices that consumers had to pay for food. In the style of the popular Sunday newspaper supplements, the public also read about farmers in fancy cars driving into town to pick up their government checks. Readers were encouraged to imagine that after this arduous task had been completed, the rest of their day was spent relaxing at the government-funded golf course.[11]

All of this free time was possible, so the popular conception went, because producers were being paid not to grow their crops. It was not that the *food aid* programs were unpopular or had gained a bad press, rather, it was mainline *farm income* programs that were more apt to put USDA officials on the defensive. Food aid costs were minuscule compared with those of the major farm income programs. When and if administration officials asked for a congressional blessing and regular appropriations for the food stamp program, however, that would attract much greater public scrutiny. Instead, the sour public mood toward the high cost of supporting the nation's agricultural economy in general prompted Secretary Freeman to be increasingly defensive in his role as chief advocate and cheerleader for agriculture within the administration and in the wider Washington community in the mid–1960s.

4

Enacting New Food Assistance Programs, 1962–1966

After food aid policy's administrative base has been eximined, it is time to turn to legislative action designed to change it. This chapter examines the passage of three acts of Congress. These actions attest to increasing interest on the part of White House officials to poverty as an important domestic policy problem, and each illustrates a different degree of presidential involvement in legislative policy making. Virtually all of the substantive legislative changes made in food aid policy during the 1960s were included in these three laws. First, in 1962, Congress added a new section to the National School Lunch Act to provide cash grants-in-aid to school lunch programs in low-income areas. Two years later, enactment of the Food Stamp Act of 1964 gave congressional approval to the USDA's pilot program, which had begun administratively in 1961. Finally, the Child Nutrition Act of 1966 added several new program emphases to the existing school food programs and strengthened the national government's commitment to the antipoverty and nutritional aspects—as opposed to the surplus disposal functions—of food aid.

After this period of legislative activism was completed, a broad range of food aid programs was in place; none of these, however, was large enough to meet the needs of its projected clientele; nor were prospects good for major increases in appropriations in the near future. Expanded food aid spending was not yet a priority for anyone on the Washington scene. Secretary Freeman was preoccupied with the prospect of declining congressional support for the department's mainstream farm income programs and was under little or no pressure to alleviate urban or rural poverty. The president and other White House officials rated the USDA food programs fairly low among the administration's domestic policy priorities, giving more attention to the need to secure funds for the antipoverty and Great Society programs. Unless public or interest group pressure countered this balance of forces, congressional conservatives would be able to keep domestic food aid efforts underfunded for the foreseeable future.

ADDING SECTION 11 TO THE NATIONAL SCHOOL LUNCH ACT

The National School Lunch Act of 1946 had owed its origin to a combination of good timing, support from producer groups who wanted to find expanded uses for the foods they grew, and the fact that it had a popular set of beneficiaries, the nation's school children. Congress had approved the first school lunch legislation before partisan debates about postwar agriculture policy heated up. Thereafter, except for establishing a companion program in 1954, which made surplus milk available to the same constituency, the legislative branch had paid little attention to school lunch program operations. From the beginning, the school lunch program enjoyed wide support from agricultural producer groups and education lobbies. In Congress it was popular among liberals and conservatives, as well as rural and urban representatives in both political parties.[1]

Responsibility for the school lunch program spilled over conventional committee responsibilities. The House Education and Labor Committee and the Committee on Agriculture shared jurisdiction because program operations were supported by farm income programs. Discussions on funding involved the agricultural appropriations subcommittee in each house. In order to run the program, Agriculture entered into contracts with state government, usually the state education agency. The USDA paid for a portion of the food costs that the state agency incurred, donated surplus foods, and, as shown in the last chapter, purchased other food specifically for use in the school lunch program. When the special milk program was enacted in 1954, a broader range of institutions (such as summer camps) became eligible, but USDA officials operated it in much the same way.

During the late 1950s some members of Congress representing urban constituencies began to push for expansion of these child feeding programs. They argued that the formulas used in the legislation discouraged rather than encouraged participation by schools in their districts. Attention centered on Section 6 of the act, which provided for federal cash purchases apportioned according to a formula included in the law. In 1960, the House Education and Labor Committee reported out a bill introduced by Representative James O'Hara (D-Mich.) and others. Although this bill did not pass Congress during the election year, reforms aimed at expansion of the program in urban areas remained a priority for liberals after the new administration had taken office. In 1962, O'Hara and Education Subcommittee Chairman Cleveland Bailey (D-W.Va.) brought Congress' attention to the issue again. Because the idea had White House backing this time, its prospects for success seemed much improved.[2]

The bill discussed on the House floor in 1962 called for the addition of a new *Section 11* to change the appropriation formula for school lunch funds and introduce a rough measure of need based on each state's per capita income. Through this device its sponsors hoped to make special money available to urban schools (especially those in economically disadvantaged areas) in addition to the clientele already served by the act. During hearings on the bill, opponents did not directly criticize the provisions calling for special aid for low-income children. Instead they attacked the proposals obliquely by charging that the legislation placed too much authority in the hands of officials at the Department of Agriculture. It would be, according to Representative Peter Freylinghuysen (R-Pa.), the ranking minority member on the committee, a potential "slush" fund for the secretary (*Congressional Record,* 87th Cong., 2d Sess., 1962:9713).

Despite the discretion issue, the bill passed both chambers handily with only clarifying amendments added. As a result, a mild antipoverty focus was added to a program that already had broad bipartisan support. But when the bill's legislative sponsors pushed for funding, administration support disappeared. In a June 21, 1965, memo to Ken Birkhead, Secretary Freeman's aide Rod Leonard summarized what had happened. The USDA bureaucracy and many state educational officials had little enthusiasm for extending the school lunch program into low-income schools (National Archives, Farm Program 8). Section 11 remained unfunded for three years, even after the Johnson administration made poverty its chief domestic policy priority, until Senator Philip Hart (D-Mich.) successfully attached an amendment to the agricultural appropriations bill on the Senate floor. This same gap between authorization and appropriations would become a major stumbling block to the implementation of all the food aid programs adopted during the 1960s.[3]

WHEELING AND DEALING: THE FOOD STAMP PROGRAM AND THE LEGISLATIVE PROCESS

Congress also finessed the cost of the food stamp program when it was enacted in 1964 by leaving key aspects of its implementation up to localities and making its growth dependent on the appropriations process. White House officials began the process by including a bill drafted at the USDA in the legislative program that they sent to Congress in 1963. Its fate depended on two factors: (1) appeals that Secretary Freeman and other administration officials made to farm program supporters; and (2) interest generated among Democratic liberals. The administration had been unable to persuade agricultural producers to accept its supply management approach to the farm problem, and so the short-term commodity legislation that the administration had secured in its first year was about to run out (Hadwiger and Talbot 1965). Consequently, battles over farm support legislation loomed over the 1964 legislative session and threatened to complicate the food stamp program's legislative odyssey.

Most farm or food legislation considered in the House, except for the special case of the school lunch program discussed earlier, had to clear two major hurdles. During the 88th Congress, the House Agriculture Committee seemed divided on most issues into three fairly equal groups—loyal administration supporters, Republicans, and a key swing group of conservative southern Democrats. Legislation that could keep enough southern conservatives voting with the Democratic majority in committee would then have to face a much different environment on the House floor since many of the administration's natural supporters in urban America were unaffected by, or even hostile to, the claims of agricultural programs.

Although most of the legislative maneuvering that linked the fate of the food stamp program and cotton and wheat commodity program legislation in 1964 has already been examined elsewhere, the full range of USDA involvement has not been evaluated. Some commentators, interested in examining the legislative process generally and in delineating the rising strength of urban interests in particular, have focused on the role that the food stamp program played in the complicated bargaining process that took place (Ripley 1964). Others have written about the case from the perspective of agricultural policy interests, showing how the bill that finally passed Congress set a new pattern of legislative bargaining that later became institutionalized on agriculture issues (Barton 1976). Passage of the food stamp program reflected a new balance of power reached between urban and rural interests in the House and the ability of Democrats there to develop and enforce mechanisms for intraparty coalition building.

Here the emphasis will be placed on a third, complementary aspect, the role that Secretary Freeman played in brokering the administration's and the department's interests in farm and food policy. In orchestrating the urban-rural tradeoffs that were necessary to secure passage of the 1964 farm program, Freeman was motivated by a concern to get as much as possible of the Department of Agriculture's legislative program passed. The frantic vote trading that took place on the House floor was only part of the story. The secretary had to pay attention to the entire congressional process, especially what happened in the House Agriculture Committee, where negative decisions about the food stamp program might have produced adverse political consequences for other departmental missions.

Freeman's first worry was that a coalition of Republicans and southern Democrats would succeed in bottling up the bill altogether as had often happened during the 1950s, or damage its chances on the House floor by adding crippling amendments. Another concern was that after the bill had been reported out of committee, it might fail to interest the liberal Democratic supporters on which the administration had been counting. To achieve their objective, Freeman and his aides sent out two different messages at the same time. Liberals were directed to look for a sympathetic welfare program under the unlikely aegis of the Department of Agriculture, while farm state legislators were reminded that although they might be indifferent or hostile to this program, they would receive benefits from the companion farm bill.

The food stamp bill got through the House largely unscathed because of two important vote trades, one at the committee stage and one after considerable acrimonious floor debate. Freeman had opened the committee's hearings by describing the pilot program's successes and outlining what he considered to be the bill's two major policy objectives: (1) the social purpose of helping needy people; and (2) the economic benefits that a permanent food stamp program could bring to agriculture. At the committee stage, however, he concentrated on the second one, because it was of more interest to the agricultural policy community represented among the committee's members.[4] He particularly stressed the increased consumption of animal products by poor people that had occurred during operation of the food stamp program in the pilot areas since 1961 (House Agriculture Committee 1964).

Republicans, hoping to enlist the support of the southern Democrats holding the balance of power on the committee, concentrated on several criticisms. First, they claimed that it was not really a farm program. Food stamps would do less to alleviate specific surpluses than the other family food program, distribution of surplus food products, a point which Freeman and other USDA officials privately acknowledged. Second, they played to the concerns of southern Democrats in two ways: (1) by proposing more state involvement in funding and administration; and (2) by raising the specter of increased civil rights enforcement in food program administration (i.e., they threatened to attach explicit antidiscriminatory provisions that would apply to the program's implementation everywhere in the nation).[5]

In another tactic, committee Republicans linked the food stamp plan with Kennedy farm policy initiatives that were unpopular with this congressional swing group. For example, stressing the amount of discretion that the program placed in the person of the Secretary of Agriculture was the same approach that had been tried during the debate over Section 11. The alternative was to allow Congress—which really meant members of the House Agriculture Committee—to decide policy issues on a case-by-case basis through informal input into food aid decisions, the topic of subsystem politics discussed in the last chapter. By seeking a permanent legislative basis for the food stamp program, administration officials were seeking to remove it from the realm of subsystem politics, legitimize oversight by Congress as a whole—not just the agricultural policy community—and recognize it as part of the president's program.

This Republican southern strategy delayed committee action on the bill and forced administration officials to come up with some modifications in their original legislative proposal (Ripley 1964). At the same time that he was publicly courting support from southern Democrats on the Agriculture committee, Freeman was also looking ahead and working quietly with Representative Leonore Sullivan. Their first success was a bargain for rural and conservative votes on food stamps in committee in exchange for the acquiescence by urban and liberal Democrats for a bill that agricultural interests wanted. What Sullivan and Freeman had to offer conservatives was a tobacco research bill that junior Democrats had succeeded in bottling up in the House Rules Committee.

In communications with urban supporters, Freeman stressed the food stamp program's welfare aspects and downplayed its help to the farm economy. But he had to turn around and stress the program's advantages to agriculture when the bill reached the House floor and he needed to win over members from rural districts interested in price supports on cotton and wheat. Ripley has conveyed a good sense of the subtlety that is necessary to win this kind of congressional bargaining. For example, neither Freeman nor any other administration official ever made a public announcement about the vote trading they hoped to carry off. Instead they encouraged a certain "favorable psychological climate" (Ripley 1964: 196–97) to develop, nurtured it with quiet lobbying by USDA officials and key members of Congress, and then worked to keep their coalition together during the last tumultuous moments before the final vote on the House floor.

Freeman's actions are a good corrective to the emphasis that political scientists usually put on the role of White House congressional liaison quarterbacks like the Kennedy administration's Larry O'Brien in rounding up support for key roll call votes. Knowledgeable cabinet officers have to put in hard work at each stage of the legislative process if they are to be effective advocates for their departments' legislative programs. After the food stamp bill passed the House, Freeman continued these efforts using his appearance before the Senate Committee on Agriculture and Forestry to win further improvements.[6]

In most respects, the food stamp legislation that President Johnson later signed into law confirmed the operating principles of the USDA's pilot program. Several aspects of the legislative history of the 1964 act influenced program implementation in ways that its authors and supporters had not foreseen at the time of its passage.[7] The first issue, making sure that food stamp recipients still made their normal food expenditures, went back to the New Deal food stamp program. USDA officials insisted on including the concept of a purchase requirement in the legislation, which Congress considered in 1964 in order to preserve the normal pattern of low-income families' previous food expenditures.

AMS officials later claimed that in the legislation enacted in 1964 this injunction was ironclad and permitted no exceptions. Program recipients would have to pay for a portion of the stamps they received even if they had no money at all for food. This was a decided change from the proposals developed by the Waugh committee in 1961 as well as administrative practice under the pilot program and was a practical demonstration that USDA officials considered the program's objective to be preeminently one of supporting agricultural income. It also was bound to be controversial if the issue of poverty assumed major proportions.

Another issue that could become controversial was a prohibition on operating both a food stamp and a direct distribution program in the same locality except under emergency situations. What kind of conditions could be classified as emergency remained unclear. Freeman and other departmental policymakers later had to answer charges that they had construed this legislative language too narrowly. The most important hidden dimension of the program, however, lay in the law's silence on the expansion issue. The 1964 act gave legislative approval to the concept of a food subsidy along the lines of the one already in operation, but left program expansion in the hands of legislators who guided the congressional appropriations process. In the short run, this was a congenial approach for Freeman and White House aides to take because they had grown accustomed to disaggregating decisions about expansion, making them one by one in response to whatever political pressures operated at the moment.

This feature also meant that the program's availability to the needy lay in the hands of the congressional agricultural policy subsystem whose members were largely hostile to the idea of subsidizing the income of poor people. Most of those who dominated the House and Senate agricultural appropriations subcommittees were conservative southern Democrats like Representative Whitten and Senator Holland.

To expand, the food stamp program faced a multistage legislative approval process even more complicated than that facing Section 11 of the school lunch program. In 1964, program supporters had passed the first test by authorizing the program. The second stage, successfully securing funds for each authorization target, would have to be done on a yearly basis. Reauthorization and expansion, the third stage, would be tied to the cycle of farm program legislation. So, while presidential leadership on food aid had increased, Congress had not vested control of program implementation with those responsible for its passage.

PUTTING THE SCHOOL FOOD PROGRAMS INTO AN ANTIPOVERTY PERSPECTIVE

In the situations discussed earlier in this chapter, enacting Section 11 and the food stamp program, White House officials played a supportive role (to legislative activists in the first case or to officials at the USDA in the second). Although White House officials committed scarce political resources to secure their passage, neither initiative was really a top presidential priority. In the first case, Kennedy aides endorsed positions already staked out by congressional activists. The food stamp case was more complex; Lyndon Johnson inherited this legislative initiative from his predecessor, but the new president never made a major effort on behalf of the legislation. Another set of food aid proposals developed during the summer of 1965 was more closely associated with the Johnson administration's policy objectives, however.

After Johnson was reelected to office in the landslide of 1964, the president's domestic policy advisers reexamined the school lunch and special milk programs in order to prepare for reauthorization deadlines set for the next year. Since these were popular programs in Congress, administration officials considered whether they could serve as vehicles for the administration's policy objectives. As with other parts of the Johnson administration's legislative program, the school lunch amendments introduced in 1966 were the products of presidential task forces that were intended to put the president's stamp on the legislative proposals forwarded to Congress by executive branch departments and agencies.

The origins of the administration's child nutrition proposals can be traced to reports prepared in 1965 by two White House task forces.[8] The first, the Task Force on Agriculture and Rural Life, was concerned with the quality of life in rural America, food and nutrition policy, commercial agriculture, agricultural trade, and other issues. The section that concerned the child feeding programs echoed the strongly voiced concerns of congressional liberals like Representative James O'Hara (D-Mich.) that large numbers of poor children still did not have access to the school lunch program. Consequently, the report recommended that both the school lunch and special milk programs be expanded. Task force members also pressed for the addition of two new efforts, school breakfast and summer lunch programs, as logical extensions of existing food assistance efforts.

Using the same figures that Department of Agriculture officials had cited in testimony to congressional committees on behalf of Section 11 in 1962, the report noted that more than 9 million children attended schools that had no lunch program at all. Another one and a half million would qualify for free or reduced price lunches if Section 11 of the National School Lunch Act were fully funded and almost the same number would qualify for special milk (Johnson Presidential Library, White House Central Files, EX FG 6001, Task Forces). The Agriculture and Rural Life report proposed restructuring the school lunch and special milk programs into a comprehensive child nutrition act that would include all federal feeding activities directed at school children. Also included in the legislation would be a pilot school breakfast program and authority for a lunch program for low-income children during the summer when school was not in session. The same theme of broader educational opportunities for children whose families lived in poverty showed up in the Task Force on Public Assistance.[9]

These two reports represent the outer limits of what the Johnson administration wanted to accomplish in 1966. White House domestic policy chief Joseph Califano's next task was to package the proposals so that they were politically attractive and financially realistic. Already an ambitious plan for a school breakfast program drawn up by the National Milk Producers Federation had been circulating around government offices in Washington. In the process, it came to the attention of White House aides. That they were jealous of the favorable interest it had stirred on Capitol Hill can be seen in a memo written by Harry McPherson to Perry Barber on September 23, 1965 (Johnson Presidential Library, White House Central Files, EX AG 7). When Freeman was asked about these proposals, he relayed his wholehearted approval and reminded White House officials that Agriculture had wanted to do more in connection with the president's new Head Start program. However, because of language in the school lunch act restricting nutrition assistance to schools, he told McPherson in a memo on June 24, 1965, the USDA had been limited in its response (Johnson Presidential Library, Files of McPherson).

The department had made milk and other commodities available to several thousand Head Start sites, but the existing school lunch legislation had not allowed for similar assistance to child care centers and other sites where the Office of Economic Opportunity had many of its projects. Presidential aides really had two objectives: (1) establishing legislative authority for a school breakfast program; and (2) reorganizing and rationalizing the existing government-supported child feeding programs by extending them beyond the school setting. In other words, they were interested in making more meals available for low-income children in school settings, meals for their younger brothers and sisters attending preschool programs, and meals for children of all ages who were enrolled in child care and recreational programs during the summer when school was not in session. This was an attempt at comprehensive policy development—let's figure out where kids are located during the day and put a program into place at each site.

After they began to consider the costs for such an effort, administration officials retreated from the expansive language of the child nutrition recommendations contained in the task force reports. White House Counsel Harry McPherson summed up the dilemma in which they found themselves in a September 1, 1965, memo he wrote to Philip Hughes of the BOB. "[W]e need a good thumping program next year but...[we] can't afford to spend a great deal on it" (Johnson Presidential Library, Files of McPherson). What emerged was a legislative package putting the Johnson administration imprimatur on the existing school feeding programs. Because of budgetary constraints, the administration's strategy was the same that it had been for the food stamp program. That is, executive branch supporters would push for new legislative authority immediately and leave the issue of spending increases for later. At the last moment, however, increases in the defense budget necessitated by the widening war in Vietnam threatened to postpone the child nutrition proposals from the president's 1966 legislative program altogether.

In response, White House officials changed their plans and decided to ask for the elimination of the special milk program and the reorientation of the school lunch program from the middle class to the poor in order to offset the costs of helping feed more poor people in the new programs. Instead of *distributive* politics with something for everyone—even the poor—this would be *redistributive* politics with a vengeance! The milk program had long been a special target of BOB officials who viewed it as a congressional boondoggle for the nation's milk producers and the middle class. As Budget's Charles Schultze described it in a memo to the president on January 15, 1966, why should the administration subsidize milk purchases for middle-class parents when the money could go to poor children whose diets were substandard (Johnson Presidential Library, White House Central Files, EX AG 7)? But that led to another question. How to get Congress to pay for a low income focus with money that had previously been spent on the middle class? Liberals, especially those with dairy farmers among their constituents, wanted the new programs added on to the existing ones. And a lot of other people in Congress wanted the existing programs left unchanged.

Protest hearings were quickly scheduled in each house of Congress after the administration's plans to eliminate the special milk program became public. Democrats and Republicans both wanted an opportunity to criticize the president's plan. Many endorsed a substitute bill drafted by Wisconsin Democrat William Proxmire that promised to protect both the school lunch and special milk programs. Maybe the president was playing an extremely subtle game—publicly seeking budget cuts in order to earn conservative support for other domestic and foreign policy initiatives, but secretly hoping to force Congress to take the blame for increasing his budget. That seems unlikely because administration officials appeared genuinely surprised at the speed and scope of the opposition that developed. For a while, they tried to rally liberals behind the antipoverty emphasis in the plan. The needy would be protected through increases in Section 11 appropriations, they promised, and by the reorientation of the milk program provided for in the administration's proposal.[10]

Away from the public spotlight a compromise was quietly worked out. Meanwhile, at a May 12, 1966, Senate hearing, a USDA official allowed himself to be prodded by questioners into admitting that the USDA had been lukewarm all along in its support for the administration's budget-cutting proposals. Secretary Freeman had asked for a slight increase in the special milk program for 1967, he noted, but that request had been denied by officials in the Budget Bureau (Senate Committee on Agriculture and Forestry 1966c). In response to further questioning from Senator Spessard Holland (D-Fla.), the Agriculture official, George Mehren, defended the school programs and cautiously reminded the senator of the budgetary facts of life as seen from an agency's perspective. But Mehren also had to avoid offending White House officials and respond to signals sent from farm state liberals that the administration and the USDA ought to be ready to pay for both the old and new programs.

Freeman testified in person on June 21 after the compromise had been reached. It largely embodied liberal sentiments but did not commit the administration to seek full funding. According to the new plan, the school lunch and special milk programs would continue to operate as they had before and a pilot school breakfast program would be added. The administration agreed to ask for a small authorization of money to be spent on nonfood assistance, that is, money for food service equipment and aid for state administrative expenses associated with the school food programs. Most of the money for equipment would go to older schools, many of them in low-income urban neighborhoods. Newer schools that had been built to accommodate population growth in the suburbs already had the facilities to prepare and serve lunches that met USDA program regulations.

Freeman was on his best behavior that day, clearly relieved that he did not have to defend the administration's original proposal. The administration's main goal, to double the number of children receiving a free or reduced-price lunch, he admitted to liberals on the committee, could have been accomplished through increased appropriations from Section 11 rather than the new legislative language that the administration was seeking (Senate Committee on Agriculture and Forestry 1966b). The administration also acquiesced to language added by the agriculture committees in both houses that was designed to ensure the continued operation of the original programs by the Department of Agriculture (Senate Committee on Agriculture and Forestry 1966c). Congressional intent, as spelled out in the report accompanying the legislation to the Senate floor, stressed that the school lunch program would remain the major federal effort in the child nutrition area and serve as a model for the new programs.[11]

White House officials had little to say publicly about their defeat. Privately, however, Budget staffers continued to oppose the milk program throughout the remainder of the Johnson years on the grounds that it was a double-barreled subsidy directed at middle-income families and the nation's dairy lobby and not deserving of being a nutrition program. After all the excitement had died down, Department of Agriculture officials found themselves armed with new administrative flexibility and program responsibilities for the school food programs, but with little additional money to spend. The lesson seemed to be that, absent much stronger direct involvement by high-level White House officials or pressure from nongovernmental groups on their elected representatives, it was extremely difficult to reorient a program that enjoyed wide popular support in Congress.

Later on that year, another White House task force, on Nutrition and Adequate Diets, surveyed the administration's accomplishments and again considered ways and means to reach needy children with food aid both inside and outside of school. This group proposed legislation for a summer lunch program and administration planners extended their interest to the nutritional needs of infants for the first time. A similar summer lunch proposal had failed to receive congressional approval in 1966, but Congress did enact small programs for infants (a forerunner of the present WIC program) and the elderly. Thus, most of the major legislative authority that the USDA needed to fight a war against hunger had been enacted by the end of 1966.

What was needed after that was for existing legislation to be better funded.

Prospects for victories on appropriations issues did not seem promising. The legislative changes in 1966 had occurred while the Democrats held an overwhelming majority in the 89th Congress, but the midterm elections later in 1966 thinned out the ranks of the administration's supporters and exposed the president to criticism from fellow Democrats in Congress about the operation of the Office of Economic Opportunity and its many programs. Also, by the end of 1966 the dilemma of balancing spending for defense and domestic affairs had become more acute. None of the political actors concerned with food assistance as an issue at that time seemed inclined to lead more than a token battle for larger appropriations. The White House was increasingly preoccupied with defending Great Society programs from a growing congressional backlash. The Department of Agriculture was busy implementing the new child nutrition legislation and continuing with its modest expansion of the food stamp program. And congressional liberals were discouraged; they had labored mightily just to get tiny Section 11 appropriations, not nearly the magnitude of the spending needed to alleviate the conditions of poverty or malnutrition that actually existed around the country.

SUMMING UP: FREEMAN AT MIDTERM

All three of these legislative battles added significant authority in the area of food assistance policy. Each also tied the food programs closer to the issues of poverty and social welfare policy that had become an increasingly important focus for congressional liberals and administration officials like White House domestic policy chief Joseph Califano and his aides. By themselves, however, these two groups had not been able to win substantial enough appropriations from Congress to test whether the USDA's food aid programs could be an important weapon in the president's war against poverty. The major Johnson administration push against poverty still lay with the office of Economic Opportunity, not the Department of Agriculture. The process by which these programs were put in place is a reminder that the contemporary legislative process has an additional check beyond those envisioned by the eighteenth century founders of the nation.

For the food aid programs, legislative action was a painful two-step process. Authorizations could be achieved; however, appropriations actions were much more difficult for program supporters to accomplish. The legislative maneuvering that resulted in the passage of the food stamp program also is important because it brought a public admission by an important segment of the farm economy led by Freeman—although not all producer groups and their friends in Congress agreed—that farm programs no longer could be sustained legislatively on their own. Beginning with the legislation that Congress enacted in 1964, farm bills have had to be seen to contain something for national, that is, nonrural constituencies.

In 1966 White House officials had sought to strengthen the antipoverty focus of child nutrition policy over objections from within the president's own party by stressing their interest in broadened and improved program coverage. In hindsight the tactic employed, reorienting a popular program away from a target population with considerable clout to another with much less, seems doomed to have failed, despite the existence of overwhelming Democratic party majorities in both houses of Congress. When administrative officials temporized, legislators chose to add new programs for disadvantaged children onto the base of the existing middle-class programs.

As one of the few Kennedy holdovers serving in the same position during the entire Johnson administration, Orville Freeman had had to adjust to differences between Kennedy's and Johnson's outlook and presidential style.[12] By 1965 Freeman also had a record of his own to defend as Secretary of Agriculture and a keener sense than before of the difficulties of getting farm legislation through Congress. He had been defeated in several battles and was more reluctant to wage losing fights. While he had fought hard for passage of the food stamp legislation, his primary concerns were the tough battles with Congress over authority and funding for the department's commodity programs. In memos prepared for departmental officials during this period, Freeman reiterated his fears that urban and liberal interests, once mobilized, might realize that their numbers in Congress would soon be enough to pass food stamp and food aid legislation on their own. If urban legislators did not have to bargain for rural support, this would leave the declining number of rural representatives in the House unable to enact farm policy legislation that was of principal concern to them.

Freeman feared risking his popularity with the department's agricultural policy constituencies by adopting too close an identification with urban and consumer groups.[13] The results of the 1960 census had documented the continuing migration of Americans from the farm to the city and had meant new reductions in the number of House districts in rural areas. Freeman feared that these trends would intensify in future decades. So there is a paradox in the overall political strategy Freeman pursued, the merits of which he could never convince members of the congressional agricultural subsystem to accept publicly. Freeman pursued the food stamp program in order help ease farm problems. In seeking congressional approval for food programs, he got urban support for other more traditional farm policies and thereby postponed the time when rural interests would have to go it alone on the House floor. But he was playing a dangerous game; congressional subsystem leaders feared, and Freeman privately shared this view, that once urban interests secured a place in the USDA and a share of its budget in the guise of expanded food aid programs, they might dominate it completely.

The secretary was still spending most of his time on Capitol Hill trying to secure votes for farm legislation and, privately, he was increasingly skeptical about the ability of any Secretary of Agriculture to influence all the operations of the far-flung department. Yet his public stance remained that of a feisty and combative defender of his bureaucratic turf. For their part, officials in the Johnson White House, like their counterparts around President Kennedy, were relieved to be able to leave the daily routine of running the department in Freeman's hands. Presidential aides sometimes complained that the department's actions were more responsive to Congress and to agricultural producer groups than to White House direction, but they usually exempted Freeman and his immediate staff from this critique. After all, constituency influences on the USDA were expected to be relentless.

By late 1966, Freeman seemed especially discouraged. In a memo to the president, on October 24, he declared the last legislative session to have been his "most frustrating" so far (Freeman Files). The administration had won two battles—on foreign aid and child nutrition—but had lost the third and most crucial one, over agricultural appropriations.[14] In the same memo, the secretary warned the president of "bitter struggles" to come over nontraditional rural programs such as food assistance. The unstated question was whether the USDA and the White House would agree to spend the political capital that was needed to counter conservative interests in Congress. That, in turn, would probably depend on whether these struggles took place in public view or within the narrower confines of congressional committee rooms. While White House officials and congressional liberals could outmaneuver influential subcommittee chairpersons like Holland and Whitten in individual battles when they marshaled all their resources, the chairmen's influence over the Department of Agriculture remained pervasive and well entrenched through the appropriations process.

5

The Gathering Storm

This chapter marks the first attempts by groups outside the agricultural policy community in Washington to mount a major effort to influence Secretary Freeman and other USDA officials on food aid issues. These activities were part of a larger series of attempts by civil rights and public interest groups to challenge established policy subsystems or subgovernments in the 1960s. Washington-based public interest groups were aided by a cadre of civil rights and antipoverty activists, based in the rural South, who were critical of the implementation of food assistance policy and what they considered to be an arbitrary and discriminatory intergovernmental delivery system. After 1964, grass roots civil rights and antipoverty groups developed important political stakes in food program operations that paralleled those they had in other federal agencies. By 1965 and 1966, the white political establishment in the rural South and its opponents were struggling for influence over the operations of a wide variety of federal government programs.[1]

The rural South and its political economy occupy a special place in the history of the civil rights movement in the U.S. (Belfrage 1965; Fligstein 1981; Holt 1965; Watters 1971; Watters and Cleghorn 1967). Cotton agriculture in the Mississippi Delta represented the archetype of the southern caste system and a special test of the movement's political skills (Maney 1988). Civil rights activities were dispersed over a wide geographical area in the small rural settlements that dotted both sides of the Mississippi River in Louisiana, Mississippi, Arkansas, and Tennessee. Because it was an economy based on agriculture, the main federal government presence—sometimes almost the only one— was that of the U.S. Department of Agriculture. It is not surprising, then, that influence over the department's farm income and food aid programs became a major objective of the civil rights movement.

This chapter also provides new information about the range of strategies used by movement organizations and the division of labor among the movement's various subunits. The movement's overall objective was to bring black people equality of treatment and of opportunity. Most scholarly attention has focused on campaigns aimed at implementing constitutional protections of due process and equal protection of the laws. In addition to enlarging and enforcing the body of federal law mandating equal treatment, civil rights activists wanted poor whites and blacks to share in the benefits of federal programs that helped support the local economies and political systems where they lived. Movement activists represented population groups at the bottom of the income ladder, so the benefits encompassed in education, health, antipoverty, food aid, and other federal programs were especially important.

Because so much food program implementation was carried out by state and local officials, that meant a protracted series of conflicts with well-established local political interests. Low-income and minority populations were also concerned about the federal government's actions as an employer, not just in Washington but wherever federal employees worked around the country. Issues concerning personnel policies and questions about whether federal programs fairly served minority constituencies were of great importance in states like Alabama and Mississippi, where established one-party dominance meant that local Democratic party officials held crucial jobs in the field structure of federal departments and agencies like the USDA.

CIVIL RIGHTS GROUPS AND THE USDA: AN INTRODUCTION

Interest by civil rights and antipoverty groups in the operation of USDA programs in the rural South came in several stages. Beginning with the Tennessee and Mississippi cases discussed earlier, Freeman and his aides received warnings that trends in agricultural production—especially mechanization in the production and harvesting of cotton, the delta's main crop—would precipitate a crisis at some time in the future affecting tens of thousands of poor, mostly black, agricultural laborers. In the summer of 1963, for example, after meeting with a delegation from the National Sharecroppers Fund, a liberal organization that monitored the economic and social conditions of agricultural workers in the South, Freeman reported to his staff on problems that poor and minority people faced in the rural South on a daily basis. The main problem blocking expansion of family food efforts, he noted in an August 3, 1963, memo to Tom Hughes and others, was the degree of control that local government officials had over policy implementation, especially in areas such as rural Mississippi.

I wish you'd give this matter a little brainstorming. I predict that some fall when the jobs run out that there will be both great need and great pressure. There must be an answer to this. It's inconceivable that people in this country really do go to bed hungry and I'm frankly not satisfied with the answer that it's up to the local government—particularly when we know the local government is not very humanitarian oriented and is overwhelmed many places with hatred, negativism and emotion at this point. (National Archives, Farm Program 8–1, Domestic)

This memo is amazingly prescient. It shows that Freeman was aware of the effects of the department's reliance on state and local government officials to implement the food stamp and surplus commodity programs. County officials certified eligibility and handled distribution for both these programs; local officials performed the same functions in segregated school systems for the school milk and lunch programs.

Civil rights groups and activists were making the same criticisms of the USDA food programs that had been raised during the controversies over food aid implementation in Haywood and Fayette Counties in Tennessee early in the Kennedy administration: (1) that the intergovernmental delivery system was at fault (i.e., local officials could choose whether to participate or not and as a result programs were unavailable in many of the areas where they were most needed; and (2) that USDA officials must realize that many programs were administered in a discriminatory manner. The secretary offered no defense against the Fund's charges. When public pressure later built up, Freeman acknowledged the justification of his critics' charges in similar confidential memos to members of his staff. The best that officials in the secretary's office could offer was to try to use their influence with local officials to correct particularly flagrant situations. USDA staffers investigated allegations of discrimination and tried to push local officials to administer the programs fairly, but they seldom followed up to see if complaints were resolved on a satisfactory basis and made no attempts to affirmatively empower minority groups in the local administration of the department's programs.

At the same time, Freeman and other USDA officials defended the existing system publicly and seldom passed along their misgivings about future problems to the president or his aides. Backed by strong congressional support, agricultural producers and other traditionally powerful local elites remained the principal beneficiaries of USDA food aid policies in the delta region during the Kennedy and Johnson years. Most key implementation decisions—whether or not to apply for a food program, which one (surplus commodity distribution or food stamps) to request, and who would be eligible to participate—remained firmly at the discretion of state and county officials. The main reason why many counties joined the surplus disposal program each fall was to make sure that agricultural workers subsisted during the winter months. Too little aid might stimulate outmigration and diminish the needed labor supply. Too much might make it hard to find people to work in the fields the following spring.[2]

Besides representations from organizations like the National Share-croppers Fund, Freeman and his aides began to hear from other antipoverty, civil rights, labor, and religious groups in support of the rural poor, both black and white. In 1964, for example, USDA officials became embroiled in a controversy with the National Council of Churches and the National Students Association (NSA), which continued for several years.[3] These departmental critics knew that USDA policymakers had the authority, based on their response to the earlier Tennessee and Mississippi cases, to displace local administration of the surplus commodity program if sufficient evidence of discriminatory activities existed. They wanted minorities and other poor people to share in the political stakes of food aid administration. Ensuring minority access to federal benefit programs was just as much a civil rights issue, they argued, as voter registration, desegregation of public facilities, Head Start aid for alternative schools, and other community organizing projects.

The NSA posed an added dilemma for USDA officials by offering to operate surplus food programs in areas where no food program existed and/or where state and county officials had been engaging in discriminatory behavior. Fearful of offending powerful southern state and congressional officials, departmental officials turned down these suggestions and looked for some viable middle ground in what was becoming an increasingly polarized political environment. The solution that the Freeman administration decided on was to express sympathy with the goals of the civil rights groups and then use the threat of action by these outside groups to convince state and local officials in the delta region to start up their own programs and administer them in a fair and nondiscriminatory manner.

Shortly after NSA officials renewed their offer, Freeman aide William Seabron reported to Tom Hughes in a November 29, 1965, memo about two new developments. First, he noted the good news that ten more counties were now operating food programs in Mississippi. Second, the department had developed an informal goal of seeking to have a food distribution program in place in all Mississippi counties by that winter (National Archives, Farm Program 8–1, Domestic). That their offers of assistance might lead to broader food program coverage did not reassure civil rights groups that the new programs would be fairly run. They believed that USDA's field offices accepted protestations of nondiscriminatory practices by local government officials at face value and did little to verify such claims without pressure from Freeman's office.

COMPLAINTS ABOUT STATE AND LOCAL ADMINISTRATION OF USDA PROGRAMS

An exchange of letters between a community activist in Louisiana and officials in Freeman's office during the fall of 1965 provides further insight into the critique that civil rights activists were making about the administration of USDA programs and it suggests that the problems the department faced were not limited to Mississippi alone. During 1965, John Zippert, a staffer for the Congress of Racial Equality (CORE) in St. Landry's Parish, Louisiana, began corresponding with USDA officials about problems he saw in a number of departmental programs there.[4] Many of Zippert's letters focused attention on the administration of the food stamp program in rural Louisiana. At that time the food stamp program had only recently been approved by Congress and few sites had been opened in the south. So this was vital information that USDA officials needed to know. Criticisms of the food stamp program, if true, boded ill for the future. After all, USDA planners expected that food stamps would eventually supplant the commodity program nationwide.

Zippert told USDA officials that the food stamp purchase requirement, the program feature that guaranteed expanded food consumption, would not work in the rural South. Tenant farmers would not want to switch from the commodity program because they had no money to pay the purchase requirement. They would have to borrow money and pay interest on it in the form of "furnish," the term for money advanced by the landlord or from the storekeeper, who took over the stamps as collateral. Either option meant that food stamp recipients would pay a premium for a government benefit to which they were entitled by law. Second, when food stamp recipients went to the store owner to make their purchases, they were often overcharged on food costs in what was, in many cases, a captive consumer market. As a consequence, they ended up paying considerably more than program planners had anticipated; or, as Zippert put the problem in an October 28, 1965, letter to the USDA's John Slusser, "the actual amount of food the family eats is reduced anyway and the profit goes to the store owner" (National Archives, Food Stamp Program).

All of these criticisms came together in his account of the plight of one particular family in St. Landry's Parish. According to Zippert,

Willie Manuel worked "half shares," an arrangement whereby his landlord paid half of Mr. Manuel's expenses and took half of the crop. His wife's earnings as a maid in a nearby town went to keep their children enrolled in the school lunch program. The only other income the Manuel family regularly received was a small disability check for one son and money brought in by a daughter, who also worked as a domestic. Their income had recently been reduced when the daughter had married and again when the year's cotton and corn crops had been seriously damaged by storms. Now Mr. Manuel was encountering difficulty with local welfare officials. He had tried in vain to invoke the food stamp program's hardship provisions so that he could enroll his family in the program after his income had fallen so drastically. Besides the question of whether he qualified at all, a second issue was whether he had enough cash to pay the food stamp purchase requirement.

Over the next two years, many of the South's Willie Manuels would be thrown out of work because of the combined effects of the economic trends facing southern agriculture. Changes in the cotton allotment system, extension of federal minimum wage laws to agriculture, and advances in mechanization were allowing landowners to step up the pace with which they could replace farm workers with machines dramatically. Within that context, it is not difficult to see why rural counties wanted to phase out the family distribution program. Switching over to food stamps would transfer the burden of paying for a food assistance program from the county (which had to absorb transportation and distribution costs under the commodity program) to the individual and the federal government. If discarded tenant farmers could not afford the new federal food program and began to leave the rural areas altogether in large numbers, few tears would be shed by local officials. Soon, Agriculture officials might be overrun with thousands of individual complaint cases like those raised by Zippert.

News that officials in Freeman's office received from informants in Mississippi in 1965 confirmed much of what Zippert had outlined. They suggested that local officials might be switching over to the food stamp program not for legitimate programmatic reasons but in order to discourage participation by black sharecroppers and their families. USDA officials had been counting on expansion of the surplus food program into new areas of Mississippi; instead they were getting a large number of requests from county governments to start food stamp programs. What kind of evidence would USDA officials need to substantiate such charges? What kind of remedial action ought to be pursued? If this trend consistently occurred in areas with large minority populations, civil rights groups would see this as evidence of discrimination on a major scale by the local white power structure.

Department officials often cited two requirements to justify which areas they chose for new food stamp sites: (1) priorities expressed by state welfare officials; and (2) federal officials' sense of economic need. In practice, though, if there was strong support for a new food stamp program site from elected officials in Congress, USDA officials usually decided not on economic considerations, but political calculations that they hoped would help the administration's friends (or those members of Congress whose votes White House officials needed at the moment).[5] State officials usually proposed counties that they felt had the greatest need for federal food aid and that had no existing food distribution program. They left it up to the county government involved to decide on the form that food aid administration would take. Federal officials were caught in the middle. Food stamp startup (including switchovers from the commodity distribution) required the expenditure of considerable effort by federal officials. Taken together, these developments made it harder for Agriculture officials to show the dramatic gains in participation for Mississippi that they had hoped would happen during 1965.

When officials in Freeman's office questioned staffers for the Consumer and Marketing Service (CMS),—the new name for AMS—about how sharecroppers could come up with cash for the food stamp program's monthly purchase requirement, the response was usually more optimistic than Zippert's view had been. Landlords would provide the needed funds in the form of store credit or furnish, they said. No one noted that this might involve an additional charge on the consumer. These assurances may not have completely satisfied the secretary and his aides, but the press of other business prevented speculation on possible future ramifications. The department's plans for expansion of the food stamp program had no incentives or enforcement tools to ensure that the absolute number of food aid recipients increased compared with the people who used the food distribution program. After all, CMS officials were accustomed to seeing declines in participation as localities switched from surplus agricultural commodities to food stamps.

Food aid administration was in a critical period of transition by late 1965, so it was unlikely that any alarm bells would have rung at the department's Washington offices if outsiders like Zippert had not brought specific incidents to their attention. Another bad piece of news came when Freeman's staff received criticism from political allies in the South with more political clout than civil rights activists like Zippert. Their concern was prompted by the possibility of problems that sharecroppers faced who needed government food aid to get through the winter. In a September 22, 1965, memo to S. R. Smith, whose office was overseeing program expansion, Tom Hughes in the secretary's office raised this new issue. He passed along a warning that he had received from Aaron Henry, a prominent National Association for the Advancement of Colored People (NAACP) official in Mississippi, who was a long-time supporter of the administration (National Archives, Food Stamp Program). Henry was one of a group of moderate Mississippi blacks who had supported Lyndon Johnson and the national Democratic party during the struggle with more militant Mississippi civil rights activists over which delegation from that state would be seated at the 1964 national convention. That support had, in turn, earned him an important place as an administration adviser on civil rights issues.

Henry's warning came as a consequence of his membership on the USDA's Advisory Committee on Civil Rights to which he had been appointed by Freeman. Henry reiterated Zippert's point that the food stamp program could not work in what was, in effect, a "no money" economy. Because the other major food assistance program for families, the commodity distribution program, was being phased out in places where the food stamp program was being introduced, a large number of farm laborers and other members of the rural poor might wind up with no food program at all despite the administration's best intentions. CMS officials might be able to show on paper that the food stamp program was more convenient, more nutritious, and considerably less demeaning than the commodity program, Henry acknowledged, but that was not much solace for people who could not afford it.

THE CONNECTION BETWEEN POVERTY AND FOOD AID POLICY IS STRENGTHENED

During 1965 and 1966, USDA officials were hit from both sides as the traditional political economy of the rural South was slipping into crisis. As a consequence of the developments just outlined, department officials were increasingly being put on the defensive by civil rights activists and their liberal allies. At the same time, local officials and their representatives in Congress were putting equal and opposing pressure on department officials for designation of new food stamp program sites to help manage the costs of this economic and social change. With occasional exceptions for rumination and self-analysis, USDA policymakers avoided thinking about the extent to which the department's food and farm income programs had adapted themselves to established patterns of racism and discrimination in the rural South. As a result, they attracted the ire of liberal and grass roots critics, who charged that important USDA activities like the price support, loan, and food programs had systematically hurt, rather than helped, the rural poor.

The critical resource that Freeman and his aides most lacked was timely intelligence from CMS, the agency most involved, about the political landmines that lay ahead. No one in that agency was prepared to generalize from the few proven cases that had been brought to official attention to the existence of any larger structural problems. Here is a typical example of relations between Freeman's office and the USDA agency that administered food assistance policy. In July of 1965, Bill Seabron, a special assistant in Freeman's office with responsibility for civil rights problems, had reviewed the food aid situation in Panola County, Mississippi. CMS officials were reporting that Panola, in the Mississippi Delta, finally had signed a contract to begin a commodity distribution program. As part of their strategy of increasing food program coverage through quiet diplomacy, federal officials were willing to let county officials take credit publicly for starting it.

Everyone at the USDA, as Seabron's memos to Tom Hughes on July 13 and 29 show, hoped that county officials would keep their promises and begin operations before representatives of the National Council of Churches found out and claimed credit for it (National Archives, Farm Program 8–1, Domestic). An August 6, 1965, fact sheet, "Mississippi, a Crisis in Hunger," prepared by the NSA and the National Council of Churches, shows that food advocacy groups realized the role that Freeman's advisers had cast them for in this melodrama. Their leaders knew that southern counties preferred to run the programs themselves, rather than surrender control to federal agencies or to nongovernmental groups.[6] The department's grass roots critics wanted help for families who were being displaced by both temporary and permanent changes in the region's economy. Since departmental policy allowed local welfare agencies to decide who would be eligible for food aid, many southern counties did the minimum, enrolling only dependent children, the blind, the aged, and the disabled. Neither the unemployed nor the working poor, a majority of the population in most delta counties, got any help. The goal of USDA officials was increased program coverage, but their critics had a broader policy agenda.

When their organizing efforts in the delta region prompted a county to start a food program on a restricted basis, food assistance advocates did not count it as much of a victory. They continued to be concerned about the degree of local discretion USDA officials allowed (e.g., programs that operated seasonally and with a narrowly drawn range of beneficiaries) even if no overt racial discrimination was involved in their administration. Finally, they were still disappointed that USDA officials would not consider the option of allowing private groups to run food programs on their own along the lines that grass roots community groups were operating Head Start projects in Mississippi, under contract with the Office of Economic Opportunity (OEO) during this same time period.[7] In response to pressure from civil rights and antipoverty groups, USDA officials made another concession. They offered to pay startup costs for counties that could not afford the administrative costs necessary for the commodity distribution program.

All of these actions meant increased pressure on CMS' budget. As a consequence, in November of 1965 USDA policymakers decided to ask for financial help from their colleagues at OEO. Freeman formally approached Sargent Shriver on the subject in a letter dated November 18, 1965, after informal discussion had taken place among officials of both agencies (National Archives, Farm Program 8–1, Domestic). From USDA's perspective, this approach looked attractive. After all, OEO had been charged with responsibility for funding innovative approaches to the problems of poverty. Agricultural policy insiders in Congress might overlook this departure from established practice, that is, not requiring counties to pay the administrative costs associated with program operations, if neither regular appropriations nor unbudgeted Department of Agriculture funds had to be used.

The main stumbling block, not surprisingly, was Shriver's reluctance to give up a portion of his agency's budget to the Department of Agriculture and its programs at a time when his own agency faced deep cuts. Shriver also was dubious because OEO officials had heard about the USDA's dilemma from their own contacts in civil rights organizations. Many people at OEO considered Agriculture officials to have been overly accommodating to the very political system in the South that OEO was committed to change. Thus, the results of agency self-interest—the propensity for agencies to defend their budgets and their bureaucratic turf against raids from outside—and ideology coincided to make OEO policymakers cool to Freeman's overtures for help.

Freeman responded by going over Shriver's head. After White House officials mediated this dispute in Freeman's favor, OEO reluctantly agreed to put up money for a six-month experimental program in Mississippi. Freeman reported to the National Council of Churches' Henry McCanna that the OEO project was finally ready to get underway, in a letter on December 9, 1965 (National Archives, Farm Program 8–1, Domestic). This ploy allowed Department of Agriculture officials to bypass congressional conservatives like Holland and Whitten, who held the purse strings on food assistance funds. Freeman had bought additional time during which he hoped the number of Mississippi counties offering the commodity program could be substantially increased. Agriculture officials paid a price for this aid in the long run, however. By helping out, OEO officials acquired a legitimate stake in USDA food aid policy. At the same time, many OEO programs were also coming under attack from the white political establishment in Mississippi and elsewhere in the South for the role they were playing in empowering blacks and other segments of the rural poor.[8] It would be harder in the future for USDA spokespeople to claim that theirs were principally agricultural programs, that antipoverty considerations were less important.

By the beginning of 1966, the department's liberal critics had become much more knowledgeable about the operations of the family food programs, and through their work with the OEO's community action programs they had an alternative model at hand for how federal action could alleviate poverty, and give poor people a role in policy implementation.[9] To the discomfort of officials in Freeman's office, program critics were becoming increasingly adept at documenting embarrassing discrepancies between how the USDA was selling its programs in Washington and what effects they had at the local level. Civil rights and antipoverty activists in the South and their allies in Washington also had begun to direct critical attention to declines in food aid participation rates.

Consistent with the department's experience with that program elsewhere in the country, participation in individual southern counties dropped once people began paying for a portion of the food aid that they had been used to receiving free of charge. So, instead of increasing participation in the South as had happened in 1965, USDA policies were likely to lead to embarrassing declines in participation in certain counties during 1966. The fact of lower participation rates took on added importance because economic conditions in the delta area and other parts of the rural South were rapidly going from bad to worse in this period. A combination of weather-related problems, the legacy of systematic discrimination, and the effects of rapid technological advances in agriculture meant that a shocking amount of malnutrition existed in the South in 1966. Mississippi, the state where USDA officials were concentrating their efforts, was a special target for this indictment.

By 1966, Freeman and his advisers feared losing control of the implementation of food assistance policy to either or both of the forces most interested in local operations—civil rights groups and local welfare officials. There was only one bright spot on Freeman's political horizon. So far, critics had made their charges in private letters and memos supplemented only occasionally by grass roots protest action. The issue had neither been picked up by the national media nor received much publicity in Washington. The department's strategy still was to pursue expansion, funded largely through money provided by OEO, and hope for the best. The chief objective for the short-term was still to get some kind of program started as soon as possible in every county in Mississippi. USDA officials would worry later about how well run these new programs were.

FREEMAN AS PROPHET: TRENDS IN SOUTHERN AGRICULTURE

The predictions that Orville Freeman had made to his staff after meeting with representatives of the National Sharecroppers Fund in 1963 that were quoted at the beginning of this chapter were finally coming true three years later. Late in 1966, Fund officials released a new report on the plight of southern tenants and sharecroppers, citing disturbing statistics on the movement of rural blacks out of agriculture and away from the rural South. According to this information, the most acute problems centered on the plight of black tenant farmers in Mississippi. The Fund's statistics showed that the number of white farmers had dropped by 15 percent while the attrition rate for black farmers was more than twice as high or almost 33 percent. White tenants were leaving the land almost as rapidly as blacks, but because more blacks rented, the impact on minority farmers had been far greater and the likelihood was that they would continue to leave in greater numbers in the near future. It was estimated that 40 percent of the state's tenant farmers had left the agricultural economy in the period that the report covered.

According to a *New York Times* article that reported on the Fund's charges and publicized these dire figures, Mississippi still had more tenants than any other state, so that is where the biggest impact would continue to be. Freeman read this article and was stung by the political implications of the Fund's charges that farming was "gradually becoming an all-white occupation in the South." His immediate response was not to challenge the veracity of the report or the figures cited in the story, but to have his staff find out whether blame for these developments could be laid at Agriculture's door. "Would this be true," Freeman asked Ken Birkhead, his legislative liaison chief, "if our farm programs were reaching (black tenant) farmers as they should?"[10] The secretary received answers to this question from two high-ranking USDA officials within the next six weeks. Each corroborated different parts of the problem that the Department of Agriculture might encounter if newspaper accounts about the Fund's report prompted increased public scrutiny of the issues involved.

In a December 28, 1966, memo to Freeman, Birkhead corroborated the substance of the *Times* article, but absolved the USDA's farm support programs from major blame (National Archives, Food Stamp Program). The department's long-term job, he warned, was to help some of the tenants stay in farming through loans and the establishment of farm cooperatives; at the same time USDA programs should help others adjust to new jobs off the farm. He was not specific, however, about how the Department of Agriculture could accomplish either of these objectives. The most important short-term problem, though, was with food aid. The department would probably have to provide food on its own because state and local governments were not helping meet people's needs. This solution was politically difficult for the department to undertake. Birkhead was suggesting that the department's food aid budget be increased, which would mean directly confronting the southerners in Congress who held the purse strings on the department's Section 32 funds.

Freeman received an equally bleak assessment from Assistant Secretary John Baker in a January 18, 1967, memo (National Archives, Food Stamp Program). While not alone "responsible for direct displacement of tenant farmers, [the department's farm support] programs have accelerated the exodus," Baker acknowledged. The Department of Agriculture had not given enough attention to program effects on tenants and small farmers when it had created and administered farm income initiatives designed to increase agricultural capacity. With this disagreement with his colleague out of the way, Baker went on to agree with Birkhead about the need for expanded food aid, although he was more pessimistic that it would solve the problems of displaced sharecroppers. The food aid programs were underfunded already and might not really help those most in need. Thus, by the beginning of 1967 USDA officials were on notice that tenant farmers had not benefited from the department's producer-oriented programs and might, in fact, have been hurt by them. They were under few illusions that existing department efforts could change the migration trends already underway. They had a rough idea of the target population that would need expanded food assistance programs. Finally, they suspected that food aid issues would be even more politically sensitive during 1967.

After considering these bleak assessments during the winter of 1966–1967, Freeman confidentially instructed Rod Leonard, his new appointee to head up CMS, to develop policy alternatives to meet the dramatically enlarged food aid needs USDA officials would soon face. One possibility he wanted Leonard to explore was a reduction in the food stamp program's purchase price to a token amount such as fifty cents a month for families with extremely low incomes. Such a step would increase program costs and would be a clear admission to critics that the food stamp program, as it had operated to date, was not reaching the poorest of the poor.

This also was a tacit admission that food program critics were building political clout in Washington. USDA officials expected to spend much of their energy in 1967 dealing with the food program expansion issue in the South. Ironically, at about the same time, Mississippi finally met the department's earlier goal. By December 1966, all counties there were operating either a surplus food or a food stamp program.

Given the worsening economic circumstances in the state, however, the secretary could not expect that completion of that milestone would satisfy civil rights groups, antipoverty activists, or other program critics in the months to come.

6

When the Jobs Ran Out

In 1967, questions about the adequacy of the USDA's food aid programs in the South received nationwide media coverage. From all sides pressure built up on federal government policymakers to expand program coverage. Specifically, interest in the USDA programs by the Senate Subcommittee on Employment, Manpower, and Poverty (or Poverty Subcommittee) heightened the growing connection that they had with Johnson administration antipoverty and welfare programs. At two sets of congressional hearings that year, Secretary Freeman was called on to publicly explain the role of food aid in the battle against rural poverty and malnutrition. By helping organize these hearings and serving as a resource for media organizations interested in the issue, civil rights and antipoverty activists increased the level of public concern about food assistance policy still further, and the foundations were laid for institutionalizing pressure on department officials from congressional liberals concerned about attacking poverty and improving social welfare policy.

FOOD AID ADVOCATES MOUNT AN OFFENSIVE

During the winter and spring of 1967, several new initiatives got underway. First, civil rights and antipoverty activists became convinced that conditions in the rural South were reaching crisis proportions and that immediate ameliorative action by the federal government was imperative. At their winter meeting, members of the Mississippi Advisory Committee to the U.S. Civil Rights Commission took up the same issues that had preoccupied officials at the National Sharecroppers Fund and Secretary Freeman at the end of 1966. The general charge they made was that the USDA's food distribution and food stamp programs were not doing enough to alleviate conditions of unemployment and displacement in the cotton workforce. People giving testimony in their sessions alleged that local government officials were replacing the commodity distribution program with food stamps in order to spur black migration out of some rural areas. Advisory Committee members also were told about the drop in food program participation that had taken place at the time that several delta counties had switched over from commodities to food stamps during the winter of 1966–1967.[1]

As a consequence, fewer people in the Mississippi delta were receiving federal food aid of any kind at precisely the same time that more people were finding themselves out of work. Long-term trends in agricultural production (i.e., mechanization and diversification of production away from reliance on cotton as the main delta crop) were leading area producers to follow the example already set by their counterparts elsewhere in the country and seek to lower labor costs. The fact that these issues were being raised in late winter was also significant. It meant that the problems were likely to get worse in the short-term. USDA policymakers who heard about these new charges knew that they were under very specific time constraints. Traditionally, early spring was the time when farm tenants and their families returned to the fields. If the charges leveled by civil rights and anti-poverty activists were true, many of these people would not receive cash advances on the next year's crop, which they had come to rely on in order to purchase necessities.

The situation was made worse by the extreme degree of decentralized program operations that prevailed in other federal aid programs that might have provided assistance under these kinds of emergency conditions. In many deep South counties, needy people were not eligible for AFDC and other federal welfare programs. Now, by all accounts, the USDA's food aid programs seemed equally unavailable. Most of the delta counties that still distributed food aid in the form of commodities customarily suspended operations in the spring. Without work or cash advances, few families would have the money to pay for the new food stamp program where it was being introduced even if they qualified.

As a result of these developments, Freeman and his aides found themselves the targets of an unusual grass roots pressure campaign early in the spring. Mailbags full of letters and petitions, many of them laboriously handwritten, poured into the secretary's office from Coahama County, Mississippi, asking for increased federal food aid. Bad economic conditions, they wrote, made a food aid program vital in their community. The letters detailed the hardships of the many who could not afford to participate in the county's new food stamp program. Over a several week period, hundreds of people in that rural delta county described the same situation to USDA officials and similar reports about worsening conditions in Mississippi were reaching Washington-based staffers for two other key groups.

One group was the Citizens Crusade Against Poverty (CCAP), a labor union-supported antipoverty organization that had helped defend grass roots Head Start programs in Mississippi from attack by southerners in Congress. The other was the Poverty Subcommittee of the Senate Committee on Labor and Public Welfare.[2] CCAP officials responded by assigning the complaints about the situation in Mississippi to a working group devoted to problems of rural poverty. Meanwhile, members of the Poverty Subcommittee, led by Senator Joseph Clark (D-Pa.), tentatively decided to hold field hearings in Jackson, Mississippi, in order to investigate the operation of federal antipoverty programs there. Before long, staffers for the two organizations were exchanging information and exploring areas of mutual concern.

CCAP got started first. Reacting to the reports on rural/urban migration aired by the media since the previous November, CCAP officials decided to turn the organization's full attention away from OEO and Head Start to the subject of rural poverty. Accordingly, discussion at the first meeting of CCAP's new committee on rural affairs centered on possible Crusade protest targets nationwide. Examples included farm worker organizing efforts in the Southwest and West, initiatives to establish agricultural cooperatives in the South, and continuing problems with discrimination against minority farmers in the operation of mainline USDA agencies (e.g., the Agricultural Stabilization and Conservation Service (ASCS), the Soil Conservation Service, and the Cooperative Extension Service).

During the course of this meeting held on March 14, 1967, several participants urged that the committee focus all of its efforts on USDA food program operations in the South. One of the most articulate advocates for this position was Marian Wright, an attorney employed by the NAACP Legal Defense Fund in Jackson. Her views were seconded by several others in attendance including Clay Cochran, a member of the USDA's Advisory Commission on Civil Rights and long-time activist for liberal and labor causes. After Wright, Cochran was probably the person most familiar with the USDA's food aid programs as one of the original contributors to John Kennedy's legislative proposals on food assistance back in 1959. The Agriculture Department, Cochran declared at the first meeting, was afraid to act because of the power of congressional committee chairmen from the South like Whitten and Ellender (Draft Minutes, CCAP Files).

The position that the department had to be pushed by new constituencies to take remedial action was echoed by two other knowledgeable participants, Fay Bennett of the National Sharecroppers Fund and Howard McCanna of the United Church of Christ. CCAP's rural affairs committee had representation from all of the organizations— labor, civil rights, church, and other old-line liberal groups—that had monitored rural poverty in the South during the Kennedy–Johnson years. The minutes taken at that meeting show that before the participants adjourned, McCanna, Wright, Bennett, Cochran, Reverend James Vizzard of the National Catholic Rural Life Conference, and Arnold Mayer of the Amalgamated Meatcutters and Butcher Workmen's Union had been named to a subcommittee charged with developing an agenda for action. Soon thereafter, committee members agreed on a food aid policy agenda to push in Washington that year.

First, CCAP's food aid advocates believed that as a "matter of national policy" the poor should have access to a food program in all parts of the country "under conditions which do not permit infringement of individual liberties" (CCAP Fact Sheet, April 4, 1967, CCAP Files). This applied principally to the USDA's commodity distribution program. Second, these programs should operate continuously so that a loss of food aid could not be used to pressure people to return to work at one part of the year or another at less than the minimum wage. Another set of recommendations focused on shortcomings in the administration of the department's food aid programs, including problems that occurred whenever local governments decided to switch over from commodities to food stamps. People who had qualified for and participated in the food distribution program usually went without food aid while application and certification for the food stamp program took place.

CCAP's food aid advocates wanted certification for food aid to be continuous once family members qualified for the commodity distribution program. As a response to the minimum purchase problem, committee members urged that in areas "where income levels are so low as to preclude the purchase of stamps, an emergency should be declared, and both food stamps and commodity programs should be made available" (CCAP Fact Sheet, April 4, 1967, CCAP Files). They also wanted USDA officials to put in place and enforce a set of administrative safeguards, including a fairly administered appeals process in order to protect recipients from arbitrary and discriminatory practices by local officials. All of the recommendations outlined so far were designed to be implemented immediately, but the committee also discussed issues of longer range importance.[3] Before their recommendations could be taken seriously, however, CCAP members had to convince other influential publics of the severity of the problem.

THE INDICTMENT MADE PUBLIC

Program critics knew they had to engage congressional and White House officials on this issue in order to counteract pressure that Secretary Freeman regularly received from the conservative agricultural political establishment. Thus, they decided to use some of the same tactics that had proven successful in defending Head Start in 1966 and 1967. During the spring of 1967, CCAP officials further refined their policy agenda and discussed ways and means to achieve it. They believed that the secretary already had substantial discretion over how both family food programs operated and that he could make those changes on his own without further authority from Congress. The case for their charges about conditions in the rural South was advanced in two sets of hearings held by the Senate Subcommittee on Poverty during the spring of 1967. In both instances, media exposure and congressional attention combined to force Orville Freeman to take remedial action that went partway toward meeting CCAP's main objectives.[4] Food aid policy finally broke out of its traditional bounds within agricultural policy when members of the Senate Poverty Subcommittee and representatives of the national media unexpectedly traveled to Mississippi in April of 1967.

The Senate Poverty Subcommittee chaired by Senator Joseph S. Clark (D-Pa.) had already attracted national media attention during hearings about the administration's War on Poverty held in several locations around the country in 1966. The subcommittee's Democratic majority was supportive of the original intent of the Kennedy–Johnson antipoverty effort but increasingly critical of what was actually happening. CCAP's executive director Richard Boone had worked as an aide to Sergeant Shriver at OEO and had contacts with senators and staffers on the Poverty Subcommittee. Exchanges of information like those taking place in 1967 among civil rights activists, Washington-based lobbyists, and congressional staffers over food assistance policy are crucial elements in the early stages of policy development in the contemporary Washington political community.

Food aid advocates also had good working relationships with Adam Walinsky and Peter Edelman, the chief legislative assistants for subcommittee member Senator Robert F. Kennedy (D-N.Y.).[5] Subcommittee staffers expected to concentrate their attention in 1967 on OEO's programs and general employment conditions in Mississippi. However, the subject of the hearings shifted after CCAP officials briefed them on the emerging food aid crisis. Acting on this advice, Peter Edelman, who advanced the trip for the subcommittee's Democratic majority, agreed to contact the NAACP's Marian Wright as soon as he arrived in Jackson. After hearing her account of conditions in the state, Edelman asked her to testify at the opening session, rescheduled the subcommittee business originally planned for the second day, and added a guided tour by local antipoverty activists so that the visiting senators could observe conditions in the delta area for themselves.[6]

As a courtesy at the beginning of the Jackson hearings, subcommittee members first heard from Mississippi Senator John Stennis. Reports in the local press the next day concentrated on Stennis' testimony, which attacked civil rights and antipoverty activists, but the national media described a different story, graphic accounts by poor people and their spokespersons about poverty in rural parts of the state. This exposure to the scope and intensity of poverty in rural Mississippi on the first day of the subcommittee's hearings shocked the senators and the accompanying media. Democrats who had expected to criticize aspects of the local administration of the federal government's antipoverty programs suddenly found themselves on the defensive. Meanwhile, subcommittee Republicans jumped at the chance to blame OEO and the administration for Mississippi's problems.

Clark, Kennedy, and other northern Democrats in attendance were not prepared to attack Johnson and their fellow partisans in the executive branch wholeheartedly. Instead, their comments emphasized problems in program implementation; the policies were being administered by southern Democrats in different ways from what Congress had intended. They may also have been relieved to see that the Department of Agriculture, which was not theirs but another congressional committee's responsibility, was the principal focus of criticism. Finally, all of the subcommittee members who had come to Mississippi agreed before they left the state to sign a letter to the president calling the findings of their hearing to his attention for immediate remedial action. Then, after the hearing recessed around noon on the second day, all of the dignitaries except Clark and Kennedy returned to Washington.

As important as they had already proven to be, the subcommittee sessions in Jackson were only a prelude to the vivid media accounts about hunger in rural Mississippi, which were revealed on the second day. CCAP member Marian Wright led the remaining senators and the press to see conditions first hand in several delta counties. Peter Edelman, who was one of those accompanying Kennedy, Clark, and Wright on this half-day trip, later credited the television and press coverage of this swing through rural Mississippi for the true emergence of hunger as a national political issue. "It might have surfaced anyway, but this certainly gave it a good boost in surfacing" (Kennedy Presidential Library, Edelman Oral History, 8:13).

On two dramatic occasions—this Poverty Subcommittee trip through the Mississippi delta in April and the encampment in the nation's capital a year later by the Southern Christian Leadership Conference's Poor People's Campaign—those who constituted the base of support for the civil rights movement were as visible as they had been during the height of political action in the South in the early 1960s. At most other times, their demands for action were made indirectly by interest group and congressional allies, then packaged for public consumption by the print and electronic media. During previous economic and social crises in the rural South, blacks and other low-income people faced the extremes of rural poverty, but without the spotlight of media and congressional attention. This time two aspects were different. The civil rights movement had politicized people in minority communities throughout the Mississippi delta to push for changes locally. Second, activists and movement organizations were preparing to claim a share of the existing governmental programs that had been designed to ease these impoverished conditions.

AFTER MISSISSIPPI: THE PRESSURE CONTINUES

Almost as soon as highlights from the Mississippi trip were broadcast on network television, political shock waves were felt at the White House and the USDA. As he had agreed to do before leaving Jackson, Chairman Clark drafted a bipartisan letter to be sent to the president. He also tied a short fuse to the political dynamite implicit in the letter by scheduling follow-up hearings on the federal government's response in Washington at the end of two months. Democrats on the Poverty Subcommittee wanted to keep pressure on the Department of Agriculture and the White House without unnecessarily straining party and personal ties.[7]

Freeman used this two-month respite to work on his plan to lower the food stamp purchase requirement. Such a step might have been enough to head off criticism from congressional liberals if all other factors had remained constant. However, CCAP and other food aid advocates used this hiatus to increase the pressure on Freeman to expand the scope of conflict beyond Mississippi to the rural South in general. During the winter, Freeman and his aides had reached a consensus on the issue of lowering the food stamp purchase requirement to a nominal amount—fifty cents a month—for people whose normal cash expenditures for food were minimal. This was a clear admission that the program had not been reaching the poorest of the poor. Here is how Freeman aide Rod Leonard had put the issue in a February 22, 1967, memo to the secretary:

The Food Stamp program operated on a nervous compromise between those who insist it is not a welfare program and those who say it is. The program rests on the assumption that it will not—or cannot—replace the money a family normally spends for food. This works very well so long as there is a definable level of income. The program loses this prim and proper definition whenever it becomes difficult or impossible to determine the level—or even the extent— of family income (National Archives, Food Stamp Program).

The problem, Leonard noted in the same memo, is especially concentrated in the Southeast. CMS had "arbitrarily" set a figure of $2 as the minimum it assumed each family in that region spent on food each month (National Archives, Food Stamp Program). Leonard saw no evidence to support the view that all poor people had cash on a regular basis. He was admitting that no one at the USDA knew how much money rural black or white sharecroppers regularly spent for food or even if they participated in a cash economy. Like most of Freeman's immediate group of advisers at the USDA, Leonard was a product of the agriculturally prosperous midwest. Now he was having to come to terms with the realities of the southern rural economy.

Not surprisingly, CMS officials disagreed with the new direction that Freeman and Leonard were taking and strongly opposed any major change in the family food programs. In a February 15, 1967, memo, the agency's administrator insisted that each family had cash income from one or more sources: (1) money from monthly welfare payments for the unemployable; (2) wages from temporary, intermittent, or steady (albeit low-paying) jobs; or (3) government grants in the form of unemployment compensation (National Archives, Food Stamp Program). Furthermore, during emergencies when families were temporarily without income, they could apply to local government or private welfare agencies, which maintained emergency funds for this purpose. Even the poorest unemployed farm families had income of some kind, CMS officials confidently insisted.

They based this assessment on a survey conducted by local officials that showed the food stamp program operating in one locality without any major problems. They described the situation in the same memo.

In a recent survey in the delta counties of Arkansas, a number of unemployed farm families were interviewed. They had no regular wages because it was December. But they all had income—from a "day's work here and there"; money sent from a daughter in the city; advances from landlords; or borrowed money. (They were all buying food or purchasing food coupons.) (National Archives, Food Stamp Program)

There is no evidence that CMS officials made any independent study of their own there or in other parts of the South, or even that they systematically queried local welfare officials before reaching these conclusions. Instead this response amounts to a description of the best possible combination of assistance available and stands in stark contrast to the situation alleged by food program critics. In these memos, CMS officials also misstated Freeman's position; the secretary was not suggesting total abolition of the minimum requirement, something that he believed he did not have the power to do by himself.

He was asking for an informed judgment by officials at the USDA, who should know the local situation. What was at issue was a factual determination about the character of normal family expenditures for an important subset of the potential universe of food program recipients. Faced with pressure from Freeman for alternatives to the current minimum purchase structure, CMS officials reluctantly suggested "a scaling down of purchase requirements for the poorest families with the minimum purchase requirement reduced to fifty cents per person per month up to a monthly maximum of $3.00 per family" for the secretary's consideration (National Archives, Food Stamp Program). They were aware of the growing criticism that was being leveled at the minimum rates currently in place, but stood by their view that even modest changes would not be in the best interests of sound public policy. They recommended that the secretary not make any changes that, like the fifty cents proposal, would significantly shift the program away from its original orientation as support for farm income and toward a more general welfare program for the poor.

Freeman went ahead anyway. He accepted Rod Leonard's arguments for the fifty cents proposal and his ideas about a strategy to pursue in order to implement it. Freeman and his aide agreed that they would have to keep some kind of cash payment in order to placate congressional conservatives. Leonard recommended that the secretary adopt the fifty cents plan but delay its implementation until early summer so that legislative and budgetary action on the food programs could be completed before political retribution came from those in Congress who opposed it. As Leonard put the matter in a February 27 memo to Freeman, the minimum requirement should be "whatever token amount is low enough to ensure that no family is excluded from the program" (National Archives, Food Stamp Program). Since no one—neither USDA officials nor their critics—had yet quantified rural poverty by fixing exactly the amount of cash income received by the poorest of the poor, fifty cents seemed to be a reasonable compromise. By March of 1967, before the Mississippi hearings had begun, Freeman had privately accepted both Leonard's recommendations and his timetable.[8]

FREEMAN IN THE MIDDLE: KEEPING THE WHITE HOUSE INFORMED

The next step was to obtain permission from his White House superiors and acquiescence from important members of Congress for this change in administration policy. After the Clark subcommittee returned from Mississippi, Freeman briefed the president on his plans. In his *Weekly Report* of June 23, 1967, he told Johnson confidentially that he agreed with the senators' conception of the "very serious poverty conditions" that they had found (Freeman Papers, 6). He also warned White House officials that congressional liberals like Clark and Kennedy were using the emerging food aid issue to show that the administration's antipoverty efforts were not meeting national needs. The basic problem, the secretary wrote to Johnson, was "jobs, health care, and education. Failures in these in turn limit food and contribute to malnutrition. Because hunger is most easily dramatized the Committee has tended to concentrate on food inadequacies" (Freeman Papers, 6). If they had seen this memo, food aid advocates probably would have agreed with his assessment.

Freeman also briefed White House officials about the political problems involved. He told the president that he had held an unpublicized meeting with Senators Clark and Kennedy after their return from Mississippi at which he had outlined the fifty cents proposal and other changes that he hoped to make. They had promised to withhold additional public criticism in order to give the secretary a chance to get his reforms off the ground. The reaction of congressional conservatives was still worrisome, but would be less so after the food stamp extension bill, which was then pending before Congress, had cleared the House. In the meantime, he told Johnson, he looked forward to having positive initiatives to announce when the Clark subcommittee hearing reconvened.

Besides lowering the purchase price for those families and individuals at the low end of the income scale, Freeman also planned to step up efforts to launch a food distribution program as quickly as possible in all parts of the South where no family food program currently existed. Finally, Freeman warned the president and his advisers to expect more public criticism in the months to come. Food aid supporters would attack it as too little, while opponents would call the plan a giveaway and a perversion of existing food assistance policy. This report to Johnson is vintage Freeman material. He showed sensitivity to poverty's human toll at the same time that his political skills led him to appreciate the complexity of the problem before him. He portrayed his solution as a compromise and sketched in the political costs so that White House officials would be forewarned.

He also bared the combative side of his personality by venting the exasperation that he had been feeling at what he termed the "showboating" of the Democrats on the Clark subcommittee, and played to the president's ego by hinting at Robert Kennedy's political ambitions. This and other reports Freeman wrote to White House officials illustrate the complexity of the role of the contemporary cabinet officer. Presidential appointees like Freeman and Leonard constantly must make choices among alternative interpretations of congressional intent provided them from both inside and outside their own agencies. The case for change that Freeman presented to White House officials illustrates the confusing mix of short- and longer-term factors endemic in administrative policy making.

The secretary's instincts for political survival told him that this liberal interest in the Department of Agriculture's food programs would soon fade and he would be back to the situation where traditional agricultural policy constituencies dominated departmental activities. There is no awareness in Freeman's memos of this period that the issue of hunger and malnutrition was about to explode into the consciousness of the public at large, or that USDA officials saw it as an opportunity to operate outside of the political constraints that they had felt since coming to office in 1961. Instead, the Agriculture secretary wanted explicit White House backing because he feared a backlash from conservatives in Congress.[9]

Freeman knew he would face the ire of agricultural policy insiders whatever he proposed. So, having forewarned officials at the White House, the secretary informed Representative Jamie Whitten about what he intended. First he had his congressional liaison chief, Ken Birkhead, talk to Whitten in private, stressing that Freeman was considering some changes as part of an attempt to protect the department's food programs from undue influence by liberals and officials at the OEO. Then, on April 26, he sent off a carefully worded letter to the chairman advising him that he would be making a decision on the fifty cents issue in the near future (National Archives, Food Stamp Program). Freeman did not expect to receive Whitten's permission, but was following correct executive-legislative branch protocol and subtly letting the chairman know that enough outside pressure had built up for USDA officials to risk making such a change against Whitten's wishes.

Freeman's private relations with each significant group—White House officials, Whitten and other congressional conservatives, and Democrats on the Clark subcommittee—were well thought out, but most of the benefits of this masterful political maneuvering were soon canceled out by a lack of care in the secretary's public comments. He often allowed himself to be placed on the defensive during this period by belligerently defending aspects of food assistance policy and program operations in public that he was trying hard to modify. After all, lowering the purchase requirement was not one of the main objectives of food program critics; most of them wanted to improve operations in the commodity distribution program instead. Freeman passed up the chance to respond to other charges leveled by food program critics. One of these had been that the secretary had the power to declare an emergency in Mississippi and during its duration simultaneously operate both a food stamp and a food distribution program.

USDA officials usually had interpreted the legislative history of the Food Stamp Act to mean that commodity and food stamp programs could operate side by side during temporary natural disasters. Unlike the situation described earlier when bad weather had hurt farm income in Louisiana, the situation in Mississippi in 1967 was not seen as a natural disaster. USDA officials did not expect a reversal of the fortunes of agricultural laborers in the cotton South because of long-term trends in agricultural production. They judged the socioeconomic conditions of poverty in the Mississippi delta to be permanent, not temporary; under the law a permanent situation did not count as an emergency. Thus, they argued, there could be no change in policy.

Liberal critics of food aid policy, however, took another view. They believed the emergency concept should apply to the totality of traumatic effects that poor people were experiencing there. Should food aid supporters get the media to focus on details of poverty in Mississippi and bring increased political pressure to bear on the department's policies, it would be difficult for the secretary to continue to make such Solomonic judgments.[10] The stage was almost set for the second round of poverty hearings. CCAP strategists had monitored the media coverage that had been generated by the hearings in April and helped reporters follow up on stories of governmental inattention to poverty and malnutrition in Mississippi. By June, their offices were a mandatory stopping-off point for journalists who wanted to write stories about hunger in the South.

CCAP officials were also helping other interested groups gather and disseminate material about conditions in Mississippi. In late May, they arranged for a group of medical doctors, including specialists in pediatrics and childhood diseases, to make a trip to Mississippi under the joint auspices of the Field Foundation and a grass roots community action organization with close ties to civil rights groups. The purpose was to observe and document the effects of poverty and malnutrition on poor children there. CCAP officials also coordinated, publicized, and disseminated the findings of these and other groups. In June of 1967, CCAP officials distributed a report that included summaries of the doctors' findings and updated statistics on southern poverty. Prepared by the Southern Regional Council, it examined conditions in the poorest counties of the South and drew two main conclusions. Despite the extent of operation of the USDA programs in Mississippi, the state that had broader food aid coverage than any other, widespread poverty and hunger still existed there. Moreover, the department's food programs needed to be improved and expanded all over the South.[11]

CONGRESS AND THE MEDIA PUT MORE PRESSURE ON THE USDA

The next stage of the public drama about poverty and malnutrition got under way when Freeman, the Field Foundation doctors, and civil rights activists from Mississippi testified before the second round of Senate Poverty Subcommittee hearings in Washington in July. The resulting media images contained all of the trappings of the television age—persuasive testimony by program recipients, persistent and informed questioning from members of Congress, backpedaling by embarrassed and defensive government officials, and dramatic camera footage of conditions in impoverished parts of the rural South. These views were condensed and edited for full effect and presented with voice over reporting by each network's Capitol Hill correspondent on the evening news programs of the national television networks over several consecutive days.

Secretary Freeman escaped some criticism he would otherwise have faced by announcing that a package of administrative changes—basically the same ones that he had outlined to the president earlier in the spring—was already being put into effect in Mississippi. Nevertheless, at most points in the hearings the Agriculture secretary appeared defensive and insensitive. The most important new element that the hearings produced was vivid media testimony by the Field Foundation doctors about the effects of hunger and malnutrition on the long-term health of Mississippi's children. Freeman was caught off guard by this mixture of emotion and technical expertise on the subject of poverty and malnutrition. The doctors' testimony was particularly convincing in setting the tone of the proceedings and was crucial in swaying public opinion among those who heard and saw the graphic accounts over television at the dinner hour or read about them at the breakfast table the next morning.

Their accounts were in stark contrast to professions of ignorance about the extent of health problems in the South by federal and state public health officials who also testified. One of the doctors' presentations was particularly affecting. Speaking as both a physician and a white southerner, Dr. Raymond Wheeler told the committee (and via television the rest of the country) that he had been shaken by what he had witnessed. "Mississippi, it seems to me, is, for its poor and particularly for its Negro poor, a kind of prison in which live a great group of uneducated, semi-starving people from whom all but token public support has been withdrawn. They are completely isolated from the outside world" (Senate Subcommittee on Employment, Manpower, and Poverty 1967, 11). This kind of emotion was balanced by the dry recital of medical evidence in the accounts of the Field Foundation health professionals. For example, Dr. Robert Coles of Harvard University meticulously described the connections that existed between lack of food and the likelihood of serious disease, a process, he said, that begins in infancy.[12]

Freeman volunteered under questioning that an important policy objective that should be accomplished as soon as possible would be to extend program coverage to all of these localities. A more immediate effort, he suggested, would be to work for program coverage in all of the lowest one-third of the nation's counties as measured by per capita income. Accordingly, the secretary announced that the Department of Agriculture was prepared to pay the administrative costs associated with the start up of a food distribution program in the poorest counties whenever the local government could not afford to do so. This change in policy suggests the degree of pressure that had built up on USDA policymakers. The national news media immediately picked up on this promise because it could be used graphically to demonstrate the extent of hunger and malnutrition; hometown newspapers and television stations also developed stories, especially if their localities had been included in the national list of "hunger counties."

USDA officials hoped to show progress toward this objective by dramatically removing one county after another from the roll of dishonor but the substance of Freeman's responses got lost in the context of the new dimensions of poverty and malnutrition. The secretary's announcement of reforms in the food programs seemed anticlimactic, both too little and too late, as the emerging antihunger coalition—spokespeople for hungry people in the rural South, CCAP activists, sympathetic health professionals, and congressional liberals and their allies—tried to fix responsibility for poverty's effects somewhere. Both Freeman's defensiveness and the remedial actions that he announced helped set the agenda for changes in food aid policy over the next year.

Freeman's fifty cents proposal and his offer to pay administrative expenses in order to get the poorest counties to adopt some kind of food aid program are stark reminders of the leeway that departmental officials had in their administration of the family food programs. If Freeman could make these decisions on his own then why not earlier? If the secretary could pay administrative expenses for some counties, why not for all? Poor people were just as hungry if they lived in New York's Bronx County, where the secretary had forcefully reminded Senator Jacob Javits (R-N.Y.) that poverty also existed during the televised hearings. If Freeman could slash the minimum purchase price to fifty cents, why not, viewers wondered, to five cents or eliminate it alto-gether? The secretary hoped that these changes would satisfy program critics that USDA officials had moved to meet their charges. Instead, they reinforced the claims of food advocates that the USDA was still not doing enough.

LOOKING AHEAD: THE BROADENING HUNGER AGENDA

During the first half of 1967, USDA officials made major policy changes in food program operations under pressure from their critics. Because of statutory language basing the program on a family's normal food expenditures, Secretary Freeman was able to adjust the purchase requirement on his own authority just by changing his mind about how much cash poor people actually spent on food. Under outside pres-sure, USDA officials returned to a broad reading of the conditions under which they spent money for the commodity program. Each of these decisions would have greatly increased program coverage if considered separately. Taken together they had a much larger combined impact. Politically, however, both of these were complicated and risky ventures. In the circumstances of growing public awareness and continuing po-litical pressure, the Secretary of Agriculture got little credit for these decisions and USDA officials were in no mood to publicly acknowledge that pressure from antipoverty groups had freed them from some of the more burdensome constraints that had been imposed by conserv-ative subsystem insiders.

Within just a few months, food program operations had been sub-jected to unprecedented public attention. The logic that critics used can be summed up as follows: federal government farm programs have created a food supply of unprecedented proportions. Part of this bounty is regularly used to assuage hunger in other countries in order to support farm income and as an adjunct to American foreign policy. Yet, at the same time, millions of Americans are severely malnourished and regularly go to bed hungry. Federal government officials seem less concerned about these problems than they do about the plight of the poor abroad. Here was a situation where all of the misunderstandings and complexities about farm policy that had built up since the Depres-sion threatened to catch up with spokespersons for the agricultural sector of the nation's economy.

Technical experts and politicians might argue over the legal and philosophical issues involved, but stark and seemingly irrefutable med-ical evidence showed the deleterious effects of the current system; and all of this logic was conveyed through the persuasive medium of tel-evision. The new policy initiatives that Secretary Freeman promised

during the hunger hearings—the lower food stamp purchase requirement and increased federal spending on the commodity program—
would both cost money.[13] That guaranteed that the issue would be
brought to the attention of White House officials and subsystem insiders, who dominated the congressional appropriations process in the
months ahead.

7

The National Hunger Agenda Laid Out

The USDA remained the chief public target of food aid advocates for the last year and a half of the Johnson administration's term of office. During that period they won a slight rise in program spending, but were unsuccessful in getting Secretary Freeman to further liberalize food stamp or commodity program administration. Beneath the surface of this apparent stalemate, however, responsibility for food aid policy made two important shifts.

First, the White House got much more involved. During 1968, the most important governmental pressure for increased expenditures on food aid came from Johnson's domestic policy advisers. They presented the president with a broad range of options designed to meet the program commitments that Secretary Freeman had made to congressional critics in July 1967. This extended White House debate, which preoccupied Johnson's domestic policy chief, Joseph Califano, and his staff for several months in 1968, represents a dramatic centralization of responsibility for food assistance policy.

The second change continued the process begun in 1967 making food aid an important tool of social welfare policy in the eyes of congressional liberals. In 1968, members of the Senate expressed their dissatisfaction with the role that agricultural policy insiders had played in food aid policy by setting up their own watchdog unit, the Senate Select Committee on Nutrition and Human Needs, to monitor this emerging policy issue.

PROLOGUE TO 1968: MORE MEDIA CONCERN ABOUT HUNGER IN AMERICA

Neither Congress nor the president developed any new policy initiatives during the remainder of 1967. Congress' main hunger-related action that fall was the reauthorization of the Food Stamp Act of 1964. Because of the effects of media attention on poverty and malnutrition, few people in Washington were prepared to argue publicly that there was no need for a food subsidy program of this type. Congress passed a two-year extension that authorized program limits of $200 million for fiscal year 1968 and $225 million for fiscal year 1969. President Johnson's only public involvement with food aid policy during 1967 came when he signed the food stamp bill, PL 90–91, into law on September 27. Declaring that "no American should ever go hungry," Johnson responded rhetorically to the emerging hunger issue, but offered no commitments for further remedial action (*Congressional Quarterly Almanac* 1967:435).

White House aides had been content for Freeman to be the administration's chief expert on food and hunger issues in 1967. Presidential aides adopted this attitude for two reasons. Califano and his staff initially knew little about food and agricultural issues, so White House attention in 1967 had been desultory. The main concern of presidential staffers had been to hold down budget growth. They accepted continuation of the family food programs as part of the president's legislative program, but felt more emotional attachment to the child nutrition programs that administration officials had shepherded through the task force process. Second, since there was more criticism than praise for the Johnson administration in the broadening hunger debate, White House officials preferred to have Freeman shoulder the blame for the president.

Budget stringency was a strong motive at the end of 1967 when Califano and his aides put together the president's legislative program for 1968. Califano started the process off by asking up an interagency task force to prepare recommendations on food aid funding at two different dollar levels. The task force report endorsed the food stamp program as the best delivery system for Agriculture to reach low-income people with food aid. A memo from Califano late in the fall shows that the Johnson administration envisioned asking Congress to increase the food stamp authorization by $20 million for a total of $245 million in 1968 (Johnson Presidential Library, White House Central Files, Task Forces [1967] Interagency). Since that was more than the amount authorized in the food stamp legislation signed by the president earlier that fall, it guaranteed that the food stamp program would come before the Congress during 1968.

At the same time, food aid supporters were working to document the extent of hunger and malnutrition in the country as a whole. After the second set of poverty hearings in July, CCAP officials announced the formation of a national citizens board of inquiry made up of prominent private citizens. Its charge was to ascertain the extent of hunger in all of the United States, not just in Mississippi or the South. Food advocates were trying to raise the political stakes and widen the scope of conflict involved.[1] Simultaneously, a coalition of women's, business, civic, and church groups, the Committee on School Lunch Participation, began to study the objectives and accomplishments of that program. The increased media attention that followed stimulated demand for food aid program expansion at the grass roots level. That is, as CCAP and the women's groups held hearings around the country on aspects of food aid policy, more was written about the USDA programs, more people realized that they qualified for participation, and, consequently, local school officials began to receive pressure to increase the budgets they were preparing for the coming year. Their actions, in turn, put further pressure on USDA officials.

While all of this was going on during the summer and fall of 1967, articles on the hunger issue continued to appear in the national news media. Some were published in journals of national circulation, which reached private sector elite opinionmakers and important public officials in Washington. Examples of this type can be seen in stories published in the *New York Times* (Sherrill 1967) and the Dow Jones publication, the *National Observer*. An August 7 *Observer* article by Mark R. Arnold, "You Won't Find Many Are Dying of Hunger (But Malnutrition a Problem Even Here in Bounteous Iowa)," charged that people were going hungry in some of the country's most prosperous areas. With a flourishing farm economy, generally high per capita income, and almost complete statewide coverage by the USDA family food programs, Iowa still had people suffering the effects of restricted diets. "To discover hunger and malnutrition among Negroes in Mississippi, the nation's poorest state, is to suggest a problem of statewide or perhaps regional importance. To discover it in Iowa, among whites and Negroes alike, is to suggest a situation that may exist throughout the nation."

A second category of more specialized media coverage also influenced public opinion that year. It included a series of articles written for the midwest-based Cowles newspapers, which included the *Des Moines Register* and the *Minneapolis Tribune* by one of their Washington-based reporters. Nick Kotz's stories had an enormous influence because they were written for the audience at the center of Orville Freeman's political base in the upper midwest. Kotz used his access to internal USDA information and to the antihunger forces to skewer Representative Jamie Whitten, whom he referred to as the "unofficial secretary of Agriculture." Besides striking a raw nerve with Freeman, these articles also helped put Whitten on the defensive during the remainder of the Johnson administration.[2]

This kind of attention to food and hunger issues by the news media kept key elite audiences and the broader attentive public informed about unfolding events after the issue disappeared from the front pages of the daily newspapers and the prime time television news broadcasts. During these interludes in late 1967 and early 1968, USDA officials worked to implement the reforms that the secretary had promised during the second set of Senate hunger hearings. Freeman knew that the results of the new investigations undertaken by antihunger advocates would be released to the media early in 1968. The June 30, 1968, deadline that he had set to start a food program in all of the nation's poorest counties was a second factor to consider. Freeman and other cabinet officials were also concerned with putting their departments into the best possible political shape to help in President Johnson's campaign for reelection.

THE *NERVOUS COMPROMISE* BEGINS TO UNRAVEL: THE VIEW FROM THE OUTSIDE

At the beginning of 1968, when Freeman considered what else he could do to disarm critics of food aid policy and the administration, he could not stray too far from his role as chief spokesperson for the administration's farm policy and ambassador to its farm constituency. As Secretary of Agriculture, he had a responsibility to shore up the Democratic party's farm support in the upcoming election, especially in the midwest. As if this were not enough to worry about, the secretary also expected to have to work hard on short-term agricultural support legislation, an important bread-and-butter issue for the department and its most influential political constituencies. Consequently, during the first half of 1968, Secretary Freeman and the Department of Agriculture remained the principal lightning rods for public criticism of the administration's food assistance policies. Behind the scenes, however, a different battle was going on.

Freeman seemed determined not to let his rhetoric get out of hand when he adopted a low-key public response to CCAP's report, *Hunger USA*, on April 25. He welcomed the continued interest that CCAP and other groups had in his department's battle against the effects of hunger and malnutrition (Johnson Library, Files of DeVier Pierson). Soon thereafter, in a letter to the group's chairperson, Walter Reuther, on May 10, he said that he hoped the publicity would help the department in its battles with Congress.

Now that (publicity) must be translated into both legislation and appropriations, but mostly appropriations. With increased public support I can do a number of things that until recently Congress would not have permitted. But to make the real progress for which the stage may now be set, we will need to move skillfully and effectively in the Congress. It is time to be factual, skillful, and resourceful, rather than indignant and emotional. (Agricultural History Branch, Freeman Files)

He was cautioning the labor leader that he would not be bullied by overly strident criticism and that he, not outside groups, ought to control the pace and strategy for legislative reform.

White House officials also read the CCAP report with interest. Deputy Secretary John Schnittker reported to Freeman that Charles Murphy (whose place Schnittker had taken at Agriculture) agreed with its sense of urgency. USDA policymakers could count on Murphy, now a senior counselor to the president, as an important ally, Schnittker advised, if and when Freeman asked White House officials to approve more money for the food aid budget. In a memo to Rod Leonard on April 16, 1968, Freeman professed to be more impressed by the recommendations from the school lunch program study, *Their Daily Bread,* released the same month as the CCAP report. Prepared by the Committee on School Lunch Participation, this report castigated lax efforts by USDA officials to provide free lunches for low-income children (Agricultural History Branch, Freeman Files).

The report called for major increases in funding for poor children under the Child Nutrition Act. The report's recommendations also urged tougher scrutiny by the Department of Agriculture of state school lunch plans and program implementation, a criticism that echoed complaints made about implementation of the family food programs. This focus on the school food programs shows that once hunger and malnutrition became an important public issue, all of the department's food programs—commodity distribution, food stamps, school breakfast, and school lunch—began to be viewed as a single policy effort by the media and program critics. Antihunger activists wanted to increase the food available to low-income people no matter which program effort was involved.

By the time these two reports became public, most food program critics had developed a common position on what additional changes in policy ought to occur. This growing consensus was reflected in the recommendations contained in *Hunger USA*. In this view, Department of Agriculture officials ought to take several immediate steps. They should introduce and push for an open-ended authorization for the food stamp program along with reasonable appropriations so that the program could rise to meet the national demand that had been demonstrated to exist. Second, USDA officials should continue to enrich the commodity distribution program (that is, provide more nutritious foods where that program was still being offered), and further liberalize the rules concerning the department's power to supply commodities to the nation's neediest counties under emergency conditions via increased use of Section 32 funds. What's more, civil rights and church groups still wanted a management role for private organizations in the distribution of food aid to the poor.

Another set of recommendations addressed long-term problems in the operation of the food stamp program. Reforms would include offering free stamps to those with little or no income, overhauling the bonus schedule to assure minimally adequate diets, simplifying eligibility and application procedures, and other measures. Secretary Freeman already had ample authority to make all of these changes on his own, program critics argued. He could eliminate the purchase price altogether for the poorest of the poor and readjust it for others based on updated information about family income. At the same time, department nutritionists should evaluate just what was meant by adequate diets, that is, how much food ought to be made available. Critics did not disagree with the basic thrust of the food stamp program legislation; they worried about low participation rates and felt that it was not being administered as forcefully and creatively as it ought to have been.[3]

CCAP staff members were excited by the initial public and official reaction that their report had received and made plans to circulate it to as wide an audience as possible. Its tone of urgency was echoed in a CBS television documentary, "Hunger in America," which aired on national television in May 1968. Many of its recommendations were also reflected in the demands presented to federal officials in spring 1968 by the Poor People's Campaign. The campaign's organizers and their church and labor union allies wanted to focus on gaps between the promise of federal programs and their actual impacts on the lives of the nation's poor. Their main objectives were to question federal officials like Orville Freeman about their agencies' commitment to the needs of poor people and to keep public pressure on the Johnson administration and members of Congress through demonstrations, marches, and the sheer presence in the nation's capital of tens of thousands of poor people.

Given the attention that the USDA food programs had received from civil rights and other liberal critics for over a year, it is not surprising that the campaign's leaders planned to devote a large amount of their resources to the Department of Agriculture. The decision to make the USDA food programs a key element of the campaign's agenda came about because of the close working relationships that antihunger organizations developed with campaign leaders. The position papers developed by the Poor People's Campaign organizers asked for better treatment for minority farmers in the mainstream USDA farm programs, but the area of USDA activity that was most important to campaign officials was food assistance policy. Pressure on Freeman and the USDA took place at two levels. The Southern Christian Leadership Conference's (SCLC) Reverend Ralph David Abernathy led campaign supporters in two public meetings with USDA officials, which turned into raucous confrontations. Meanwhile, away from the spotlight of media attention, Marian Wright of the NAACP, by then one of the most knowledgeable people in the country about the intricacies of the USDA food aid programs, negotiated with USDA officials as a key member of the group's brains trust.[4]

THE HEART OF THE MATTER: MORE DELIBERATIONS ON FOOD POLICY AT THE USDA

What was Freeman doing while public pressure continued to build during the spring of 1968? Over the winter, the secretary considered, but finally decided against, taking any major new administrative actions, such as eliminating the food stamp purchase price altogether for the poorest of the poor.[5] Interestingly, the issue was not whether Freeman had the power to make such a change on his own for those who had no regular food expenditures, but whether the secretary ought to take such a step in view of the overall political environment of food assistance policy at that time. In a memo dated February 28, 1968, Freeman aide Rod Leonard suggested that the secretary wait until the new two-year extension of the food stamp program expired before asking Congress to make two changes: (1) free coupons for those at the lowest income level; and (2) an increase in the federal subsidy across the board to provide "a minimum diet to each household" (National Archives, Food Stamp Program). If recipients did not have to pay anything for the stamps they received, costs would increase even if the number of recipients remained unchanged. Case loads and costs both would rise significantly if the number of food stamp recipients increased as well, as seemed more likely.

USDA officials agreed with program critics that the number of people receiving aid usually dropped when food stamps replaced the commodity program in a given locality, and instituting a provision whereby the amount of food would more nearly approximate a minimally healthful diet would mean boosting the dollar value of the subsidy and lead to further increases in program costs. Changes of this magnitude really ought to be decided by Congress, Leonard seemed to be saying. But this recommendation not to ask for major policy changes did not solve the money issue. Leonard continued to be preoccupied with it that winter as he tried to ensure that the reforms that Freeman had promised half a year earlier would be implemented by the June 30 deadline.

The most important short-range problem that winter was securing enough money to pay for the changes the secretary was already committed to making. The combined effects of expansion into new areas and increases in participation that were coming with implementation of the fifty cents proposal were rapidly exhausting the department's existing food stamp appropriation. This problem had to be solved before July 1, 1968, when money earmarked for the new fiscal year would become available. Accordingly, Freeman instructed Rod Leonard to prepare a supplemental appropriations request in the amount of $5 million to submit to White House officials for consideration. At the same time, Freeman directed Leonard to devise a public relations strategy for the department to get the request approved. That done, the secretary took under advisement Leonard's other request—a further rise in the food stamp program's authorization level for fiscal year 1969 and $20 million more in appropriations to run it after July.

In his communications with Leonard and White House officials on budgetary matters in 1968, Freeman was performing some of the most important duties associated with the role of the cabinet officer in the American system of government. After sifting through policy recommendations from his aides, Freeman presented options to White House advisers for the president's approval and briefed Johnson and his aides about the political implications of various combinations of action and inaction. Meanwhile new complications in presidential policy making had appeared. Lyndon Johnson's decision taking himself out of the presidential race after the New Hampshire primary in March 1968 immediately split Democrats in Congress and the executive branch into factions.[6]

While this maneuvering was going on, Freeman continued to try to use the renewed public interest in food policy brought on by the activities of antihunger groups to increase the department's appropriations. About 300,000 additional people, he told White House officials, had joined the food stamp program by the end of 1967, and more growth was expected as counties in the South started up program operations during the spring of 1968. During March alone, department officials estimated, approximately 177,000 people would be added followed by 160,000 in April and 300,000 in May and June. Freeman's preferred political strategy to cope with these dramatic jumps in program participation was to put the burden for a budget increase on Congress.

In other words, Freeman told the president in a March 11, 1968, letter, the USDA was publicly committed to go ahead, but had run out of money (National Archives, Food Stamp Program). Pressure directed at important aspects of the program had offset the usually important conservative influence on program operations of three key sets of political actors: leaders of the agricultural policy community in Congress; state and local government officials who wanted to maximize their autonomy in program administration; and officials within CMS who worked with local government officials on a daily basis.

BATTLING FOR THE PRESIDENT'S "HEART AND MIND"

Freeman's budget problems were made more complicated by the fact that after renouncing another term in office Johnson had further surprised his advisers by cutting back on his legislative efforts. The only exception was his determination to win votes from conservatives in Congress to enact a tax increase. The Secretary of Agriculture's legislative situation was also made more difficult by the complexity of the budgetary process in the spring of 1968. Administration officials had to make decisions simultaneously on several food policy issues: (1) the USDA's supplemental budget requests for fiscal year 1968, which was almost over; (2) a new food stamp authorization bill that Leonore Sullivan had introduced in 1968 to increase the size of the program for calendar year 1968 and future years in light of the growth that was occurring in the number of its new recipients; (3) Agriculture's need to respond publicly to the demands made by the Citizens' Crusade Against Poverty and the Poor People's Campaign; and (4) calculations about the level of food assistance outlays in the agricultural appropriations bills for the next fiscal year.

The need to respond to specific governmental deadlines, especially those set by the legislative process, contrasts with the ad hoc nature of the pressures from program critics the year before. Freeman was involved in the development of each of the plans presented to the president by Califano, but responsibility for the details rested with White House aides, not officials at the USDA. For the first time since Myer Feldman had overseen development of food aid policy at the beginning of the Kennedy administration, presidential aides were getting a close look at the philosophy and the details of the food aid programs. They also were aware of what had happened whenever Congress had considered food stamp program legislation before: the food stamp program had always been linked with votes on price support. At Freeman's urging, the administration had joined other food stamp supporters when Congress had renewed the program's basic authorization in 1967. The outcome, after Freeman had brokered trades between food aid and agricultural issues, had been a compromise extending the program for two years.

Now Sullivan and other Congressional supporters wanted to take advantage of the increased public attention to hunger and malnutrition to improve on the bill that had been written the year before. When Califano first brought it to the president's attention in the spring of

1968, the new Sullivan bill was still in the early stages of congressional consideration. Johnson would have a chance to embrace it at any of several key points in the legislative process. A memo to the president dated April 25, 1968, shows that Califano wanted to get the president to go on record in support as soon as possible (Johnson Presidential Library, Files of DeVier Pierson). However, Johnson refused to take any action and the first deadline slid past. After the Poor People's Campaign had set up shop in Washington later in the spring, Califano tried again. For over a month, he met several times a week with a White House working group, which included DeVier Pierson and James Gaither of his own staff, Charles Zwick of the Bureau of the Budget, Charles Murphy, and representatives from Agriculture (usually Rod Leonard and Undersecretary John Schnittker) in order to draft an administration response to the Sullivan bill.

The issue was whether or to what degree to supplement what the administration had recommended for Agriculture's budget for the year beginning July 1, 1968. Raising the food stamp authorization, as Sullivan's bill would do, was the first step. Larger appropriations would also be needed if this were done. Califano kept proposing versions of four policy options for Johnson to consider.[7] The first would have had the three main program categories—food stamps, commodity distribution, and child nutrition—remain at the 1968 levels outlined in the president's budget, a position that no one in the working group favored or thought was tenable given the aroused public mood. It was sometimes referred to as the "no new starts" position and was considered politically unviable by White House aides, because it did not allow for the opening of any new food stamp sites after April of 1968. By taking no action, Johnson was in effect subscribing to that position.

Under this first option, the three major programs would stand at the following amounts: (1) food stamps—$225 million; (2) commodity distribution—$168 million; and (3) child nutrition—$503 million, according to figures cited in a memo from Califano aide DeVier Pierson to Charles Murphy on May 9, 1968 (Johnson Library, Files of DeVier Pierson). After eight years in office, an administration that approved of expanded food aid to poor families had not yet secured an authorization for these low-income programs any larger than that for the mostly middle-class child nutrition programs. The problem was that these programs were not priority considerations for the one official whose support really counted, Lyndon Johnson. White House officials and the USDA representatives who had been meeting with them favored versions of the other three alternatives.

A second possibility was for the administration to ask for a budget increase of about $100 million for fiscal year 1969, which would apply about equally to each of the three program areas. Most of the members of the working group felt that would not be enough money to meet program demand and soon developed a consensus around a third option, increases of about $300 to $400 million as soon as possible. This choice, they argued, would allow for several of the options that, in the winter of 1968, Freeman and Leonard had explored. If this third option were adopted, the food stamp program would be expanded modestly to $275 million, but two new features with important long-term implications could be phased in: (1) free stamps for those whose family income was at or below $20 per month; and (2) an enrichment of the bonus for others. Thus, "poorer families (would) spend no more than 30% of their income on food" (Johnson Presidential Library, Files of DeVier Pierson).

The fourth option was a dramatic, long-range statement of national objectives. It would commit the country to helping the complete universe of people thought to need food aid, a figure that the Califano group estimated at 10 million. Support for this option came from the president's counselor (and former Undersecretary of Agriculture), Charles Murphy, in a May 1, 1968, memo to the president (Johnson Library, White House Central Files EX CM). Although the others did not find it politically practical under the budgetary strictures of the moment, they privately agreed with Murphy that it would eventually become the basis for food aid policy. Thus, within a few weeks the Califano group had privately agreed on both short- and long-term measures, which, if implemented, would have meant major changes in food assistance policy.

BEHIND THE SCENES: THE BATTLE CONTINUES

During the rest of Johnson's term in office, the president's advisers used events outside the White House (e.g., congressional deadlines for consideration of authorizing and appropriations legislation and the quickening pace of political protest in the streets) to lobby the president to accept their plan. After each presidential rebuff, they came back with new combinations of budget totals and new versions of their preferred third option.[8] For example, Califano used the occasions of the CBS television documentary "Hunger in America," and the arrival of the Poor People's Campaign to show Johnson new versions of his group's budget totals, but to no avail. Johnson did not want to be criticized by members of Congress (whose help he needed on other legislative matters) for giving in to the demands of street demonstrators. Nor would he take a public position on pending legislative initiatives, like the Sullivan bill. As Johnson continued to put off his aides' recommendations, it became increasingly obvious that the food aid issue—at least in the president's mind—had become caught up in larger political concerns involving the costs and purposes of federal domestic spending generally.

Meanwhile, Freeman continued to take the public blame for the administration's refusal to respond to the new round of criticism. Each time before, in 1964 and 1967, the secretary had arranged a vote trade in connection with Representative Sullivan's food stamp program bills. Freeman wanted the president to do so again in 1968 so that the Agriculture chief could urge liberal and urban members of the House to support agricultural legislation that otherwise would face an uncertain future on the House floor. The secretary had routinely testified on behalf of the administration's original food stamp program request for $245 million earlier in the spring. By early June 1968, he was summoned back to Capitol Hill under pressure of the new food stamp controversy, but had no guidance from Johnson about how to proceed. On June 12, Freeman testified in favor of Leonore Sullivan's new amendment and seems to have been genuinely surprised at Johnson's angry reaction afterward.[9]

After the Poor People's Campaign disbanded and the image of disarray among government spokespeople on food aid policy had somewhat receded, Califano's group tried once more to get Johnson to endorse expanded food aid spending. This time their efforts coalesced around a three-year program to combat hunger and malnutrition that was a new version of their middle-range proposal, redesigned to have a low startup cost. Califano wanted it to take the form of a message to Congress, timed to coincide with the final vote on the Sullivan food stamp extension bill debate on the House floor. However, Johnson repeatedly refused to sign on to his aides' new plan and even forbade the administration's congressional liaison staff from admitting after the fact to reporters from *Congressional Quarterly* that White House officials supported the intent of the Sullivan bill. This can be seen in an August 1, 1968, memo from White House aide Barefoot Sanders to the president (Johnson Presidential Library, White House Central Files, EX BE 5–5/AG7).

Yet Johnson never absolutely and unequivocally forbade Califano from continuing to work on food aid policy issues, and his rebukes of Freeman are similar to the way that the president treated other loyal administration officials on occasion; he was encouraging Freeman and humiliating him at the same time. Since he was not running for reelection, Johnson did not need farm state support in the upcoming election, but Freeman and his friend Hubert Humphrey did. The secretary felt increasingly adrift, left on his own by the White House to round up votes for Agriculture's legislative program. In the end, Sullivan got another food stamp program increase, but did not succeed in winning approval for an open-ended authorization. This result ensured that food assistance policy would remain on Congress' agenda for the foreseeable future.

FOOD POLICY GAINS IN 1968: A FINAL ASSESSMENT

When the amended Sullivan bill was ready to be signed by the president, Johnson's advisers tried again to get him to take additional action in response to the hunger issue. They wanted the president to send a supplemental appropriations request to Congress to deal with the growth in the food programs that would be occurring throughout fiscal year 1969. This would mean spending at the revised authorization level of $315 million decided on in the Sullivan bill. This time Johnson agreed and Congress approved part of this amount before adjourning.[10] If the president's intention all along had been to let Congress pull him into higher spending after a convincing show of reluctance on his part, then his strategy had worked. By the end of 1968, Congress had enacted a supplemental appropriation for the current fiscal year, increased the food stamp authorization level, and passed a supplemental authorization for the next fiscal year. Never had the program been in such flux.

In 1968 the hunger lobby, as food aid advocates were often described in the media, continued to concentrate attention on Orville Freeman and the USDA. This pressure helped the secretary win some legislative, administrative, and budgetary concessions from Congress that he had not succeeded in getting before. No one—not the food aid advocates who saw him as a burned-out veteran of too many bureaucratic battles, nor his liberal allies in Congress and the White House, nor subsystem insiders at the USDA who felt the familiar terrain of bureaucratic politics shake beneath them—gave him much credit for what happened. Nor was Freeman himself able to appreciate, while the battle raged around him, the degree to which food aid advocates shared his own goals and values. At the time, most Washington observers thought that the main battles over food policy during 1968 were the ones involving the USDA and the Congress. Few suspected that Califano and other White House aides had tried so hard to make food aid policy a key item on the president's domestic policy agenda during Johnson's last year in office.

This attempt illustrates several points about the food aid policy process. First, while media attention to the hunger coalition's activities kept pressure on the USDA and spurred White House officials to come up with new initiatives, it was the workings of the legislative calendar that forced the president to make the few tentative decisions that he did. Second, this extended internal debate marked the first time that food assistance policy was debated on its own merits within the executive branch; it had always been linked to farm policy before. After 1968, there was no going back. Ties to the USDA's mainstream farm income programs were never again such determining factors in decision making on food policy. Thereafter, the food programs were judged on their usefulness as welfare programs and tools of antipoverty policy. Finally, this episode attests to the problematic role of the president in the policy process.

The food assistance programs had gotten their start in the Kennedy years because of action by officials of the executive branch of government. Now they stand as one of the most important legacies of the Great Society years, even though Lyndon Johnson never linked hunger and malnutrition with his administration's concerns about the effects of poverty and refused to mount a full-scale food aid initiative during his term of office. This disinclination to act on the part of the chief decisionmaker within the executive branch of government created a vacuum that congressional liberals began to fill in 1968. Food stamp authorization limits and budget totals rose by a larger amount in 1968 than in any previous year, although by not nearly so much as program supporters in and outside of government had hoped.[11]

The last and least expected victory that antihunger forces achieved in 1968 turned out to have been the most successful of all. Late in the session, a bipartisan coalition of Senate liberals led by George McGovern (D-S.Dak.) administered a stinging rebuke to that body's agricultural establishment. It got the Senate to create a Select Committee on Nutrition and Human Needs with membership drawn from two other bodies, the rural-oriented Agriculture and Forestry Committee and the more urban Labor and Public Welfare Committee, the latter the parent of the Senate Poverty Subcommittee. As a select committee, it was intended to be a congressional watchdog over the USDA and the food and agriculture-related committees in the U.S. Senate. Its creation represented an important institutionalization within government of the nation's continued preoccupation with hunger and malnutrition. The Select Committee had been McGovern's idea, but it represented a logical extension of what antihunger activists had also been seeking, a governmental forum from which to push Congress and the executive branch to take further action.

8

Best Laid Plans Oft Go Awry

Just after Richard Nixon won the presidency, Washington journalist Elizabeth Drew reviewed for readers of the *Atlantic* how government officials had reacted to the politics of hunger and malnutrition. The current lack of progress toward feeding the poor, even the administration's friends conceded, had been its "most serious domestic failure" (Drew 1968:7). Two objectives for food aid policy were at the top of the public agenda in 1969. First, antihunger groups would press Nixon administration officials to make a major political commitment to expand the food aid budget. That is what Johnson's White House aides had been engaged in, vainly, for the past nine months and had already proved difficult to achieve. The second objective—decreasing local control of food program operations in order to introduce equity into the distribution of food aid around the country—might prove equally difficult to achieve given the strong pressures toward decentralization that pervaded the American federal system.

Drew's predictions proved correct. Her reporting also reinforces another point that had become increasingly clear that year, that USDA and White House officials no longer had a monopoly on the development of new food aid policy initiatives. Congress was taking a much more important role. This chapter examines the conflicting pressures felt by officials in the office of Secretary of Agriculture and in the USDA agency that administered the food aid programs during the Nixon and Ford years. The president's men and women at Agriculture had a very frustrating time during this period. Right from the beginning, executive branch officials had to work hard to keep up with developments already underway on Capitol Hill and to meet deadlines imposed by the legislative calendar.

TO END HUNGER IN AMERICA?

The 1968 election had divided control of government between the two political parties; the Republicans triumphantly took charge of the executive branch, but Democrats retained control of both houses of Congress. In the process many Democratic committee chairmen and a whole generation of middle-level Democratic liberals in Congress were freed from the need to subordinate their policy agendas to White House coordination and supervision. So, much of Richard Nixon's first term in office was dominated by competition between Democrats and Republicans to see which party could propose more politically attractive solutions to the nation's social problems. The new Senate Select Committee on Nutrition and Human Needs got started before Secretary of Agriculture Clifford Hardin had drafted an antihunger program for the president to consider.

In the winter of 1969 McGovern held hearings on the findings of new nutritional studies about the effects of hunger and malnutrition, and, accompanied by members of the committee from both political parties, he also made several fact-finding trips designed to increase public pressure on the hunger issue. These activities attracted the attention of the media when Senator Ernest F. Hollings (D-S.C.), a relatively junior member of the southern establishment in Congress, dramatically described the toll of suffering by poor and minority people in South Carolina in testimony before the Senate Select Committee on February 19. Soon thereafter Hollings and McGovern paid a joint call on Hardin to test the department's willingness to break with past administrative practice. What did the secretary propose to do about the plight of poor people in Beaufort, South Carolina, who could not afford to participate in the food stamp program? Hardin's response may have surprised his guests. He offered to take a step that Freeman had resisted to the end of his term in office, making food stamps free of cost to the poorest applicants in South Carolina.

This decision was in line with a package of proposals that USDA officials planned to send to the new president's cabinet-level Urban Affairs Council. Another issue that White House officials had to decide was whether to fold food aid into the administration's deliberations over welfare reform. Secretary Hardin wanted to go ahead with food aid reforms separately because of the high degree of public concern that existed on the hunger issue. However, he did not get the administration's go ahead in time for food aid to be included within the revised budget that Nixon sent to Congress in the spring of 1969. Instead, during April and the early part of May while the McGovern committee was publicizing problems associated with the status quo, Hardin's proposals remained bottled up in the White House.

At that point, congressional pressure forced the administration to adopt a position on food aid policy and defend it publicly. Senator McGovern helped this process along by introducing his own food stamp reform bill and inviting Hardin and Secretary of Health Education and Welfare Robert Finch to react to it at hearings held by the Select Committee on May 7. Congressional food aid supporters also obtained a copy of the proposal that Agriculture was trying to sell to White House officials and leaked it to the press. Several observers have suggested that these two events sprung a trap that had been carefully set by McGovern and committee staffers. If no decision had been reached by White House officials on the antihunger issue when the hearings began, Hardin would have had to publicly explain why the administration did not believe the problem was as severe as Agriculture's report had said it was. The administration was caught and, on the eve of the hearing, President Nixon sent a message on hunger and malnutrition to Congress that basically endorsed the Agriculture plan. In it the president called for an end to hunger in America (Berry 1984:62; Burke and Burke 1974:118–9; and Kotz 1969:223).

Subsequently, Hardin outlined the details, which called for a major expansion of food stamp benefits; the key feature of this plan was a promise to pay for food stamps for the poorest of the poor, an extension of the experiment that Hardin had agreed to try in South Carolina. Second, the USDA proposed to develop and apply uniform national eligibility standards for the program. Benefits also would be increased so that they constituted a diet that could be considered nutritionally adequate. The effect of all of these changes would mean substantially higher costs for the program. Although he heard some advice that he ought to take money away from mainstream agriculture programs, the president was reported to have told his Budget director to find the money somewhere else, thus avoiding the necessity for his new Agriculture secretary to commit political suicide so soon after coming to office. A year before such an announcement would have been astounding. Now the question was whether Congress would go even further.[1]

That some kind of legislative action on food aid would be taken by the 90th Congress seemed a foregone conclusion whatever actions Secretary Hardin took on his own. After eight months in office, President Nixon had come out in favor of two food aid and social welfare programs that delivered benefits to a wide range of families including those of the working poor; plans for the Family Assistance Program and the revamped food stamp program constituted a major break with past practice that had limited welfare benefits to families outside of the workforce. It was also much more than any Democratic president had agreed to support, and because of continued pressure from food aid advocates, there were no major philosophical conflicts between the administration's proposals and those supported by Senator McGovern and other congressional food aid advocates. Even so, it took the rest of the congressional term for the food stamp reform legislation to be enacted.

The chief reason for this slow pace was that agricultural policy insiders needed time to link changes in the food stamp program with agricultural price support legislation. With the election of a Republican president, responsibility for developing vote trades linking farm and food policy had passed to agricultural policy insiders in Congress. Republican presidents could be expected to favor lower farm program subsidies. Consequently, congressional supporters of commercial agriculture needed to attract urban and liberal Democratic support for farm programs. The legislation finally approved in 1971 extended the food stamp program for three more years and timed its expiration to coincide with the deadline for reenactment of major farm support programs. It also put Congress' stamp of approval on free food stamps for families with monthly incomes under $30, down from the $50 figure that administration officials had originally recommended.

Several other provisions liberalized or clarified interpretations that USDA officials had made of existing legislative authority. For example, the new legislation required that no household would have to spend more than 30 percent of its monthly income on stamps, another provision that the administration had supported in its legislative proposals. To describe the value of the coupon allotment the legislation used the term *nutritionally adequate diet*, but left the concept to be operationalized by the Secretary of Agriculture. Congress also went on record allowing both family food programs—food stamps and distribution of surplus agricultural commodities—to operate simultaneously in a given area, a goal that had been advocated by food aid supporters for many years. In return, the administration won agreement that the food stamp program was the preferred food delivery system for the future.

The bill made three other changes that had far-reaching consequences. First it allowed those sixty years and older to use stamps to purchase meals from government or nonprofit organizations. This was the first of several food aid initiatives tailored to the requirements of a special population. It attested to Congress' fondness for categorical programs and made food program administration more complicated. Second, conservatives failed in their attempt to require state financial participation in food stamp program costs. Consequently, the program remained different in design from traditional welfare programs such as AFDC. Program supporters did accept conservative language in the House bill requiring able-bodied adults to register for and accept available employment as a condition of participating in the program.

This workfare provision attests to the increasing integration of the food stamp program into the nation's arsenal of social welfare programs. Finally, in the process of the legislative give-and-take over the workfare issue, liberals won another victory. Besides substantially increasing the food stamp authorization for fiscal year 1971, legislators agreed to allow open-ended food stamp program authorizations for fiscal years 1972 and 1973. As a result of these changes, the value of food stamp benefits going to each household increased dramatically during the period from 1970 to 1972. Some people got more food for the same purchase price they had paid before and many others got free food for the first time. These changes inevitably increased pressure on Congress and the White House to come up with needed program funds.

The other major legislative change that antihunger activists achieved in the food stamp program during the Nixon administration was amendments passed in 1973 mandating that all counties offer the program by July 1974. That meant greater geographic coverage and a larger potential pool of recipients. Taken together, liberalization of food stamp program costs and benefits and its extension to nationwide coverage were the main reasons why the program was rapidly becoming an important supplement to the federal government's existing cash income maintenance programs. Ironically, while food aid increased, several political factors—including conservative opposition in the Senate, disagreement among supporters of increased social welfare spending about which population groups should benefit most, and declining interest in the program by the president himself—prevented enactment of Nixon's main domestic policy priority, the Family Assistance Program, during the president's first term in office.

HOPSCOTCH: TRYING TO ACHIEVE THE ANTIHUNGER AGENDA

The workings of the legislative calendar allowed food assistance program supporters to divide their work between food stamp and child nutrition legislation. Food stamp program changes were enacted in 1969, 1970, 1973, and 1977 while Congress passed major child nutrition legislation in 1970, 1972, 1974, and 1975. During this period, Congress was continually engaged in liberalizing one or another of the food assistance programs. As was the case with food stamps, the Republican administration started out supporting legislation advanced by the antihunger forces designed to liberalize existing child nutrition programs and, again, food aid advocates successfully pushed for more program spending. Another key objective of the antihunger lobby was to extend free lunches to all of the nation's low-income school children. Local school officials, like their counterparts who ran the family food programs, were accustomed to administering child nutrition programs as they saw fit.

Food advocates focused on the school lunch program first because it was the main delivery system for child nutrition assistance and the most popular child feeding program in Congress. In 1969 Congress approved an emergency transfer of Section 32 funds to the school lunch program in order to finance more free lunches for low-income children. Then, PL 91–248, which went to the president for his signature on May 4, 1970, significantly strengthened provisions in existing legislation that applied to children from poor families. This act provided for an open-ended authorization of Section 11 of the Child Nutrition Act and declared meals for the neediest to be the top congressional priority for the child nutrition programs. Congress also directed that beginning in January 1971 all poor children had to be provided reduced price lunches.

Finally, in the same legislation, Congress expanded the school breakfast program (*Congressional Quarterly Almanac* 1970:179–82). The Nixon administration acquiesced in these reforms, but thereafter executive branch support for further changes dropped. Food aid advocates' successes in 1970 came as the result of several behind-the-scenes maneuvers. First, they took advantage of a lack of organization in the new administration by playing different presidential spokespeople off against one another. USDA school food policy decisions were strongly influenced by comments made in the administration's name by Jean Mayer, a nationally known nutritionist and part-time consultant for the president, who organized and presided over a White House conference on hunger and nutrition issues held late in the fall of 1969.

To the chagrin of other administration officials, Mayer made very broad promises of support for food aid spending in his public comments during the conference. Food aid supporters declared them to be the equivalent of the president's own comments earlier in the year endorsing expansion of the food stamp program's legislative and budgetary authority. Thereafter, the hunger lobby tried to force administration officials to live up to the costs that these promises required. Public interest lawyers used Mayer's language in court cases to support their position that existing law and public policy demanded broader coverage and greater spending. So even before the passage of HR 515 in May 1970, which expanded school food programs for low-income children by mandating uniform national eligibility standards for the school food programs, Department of Agriculture officials had felt the effects of the White House school food promises.

Mayer's comments gave antihunger advocates an opportunity to claim that the Nixon administration would back up increased program authorization with sweeping increases in program budgets. As Deputy

Assistant Secretary for Marketing and Consumer Services Elvin Adamson put it in a memo to Secretary Hardin on May 12, 1970, school officials "expect the Federal government to finance federally mandated programs" (National Archives, Food Program 7-School Lunch Program). Almost immediately after the new legislation passed Congress on May 4, 1970, antihunger lobbyists launched a campaign to influence the regulations that would implement it. Throughout the rest of the year members and staffers of the Senate Select Committee kept the issue alive through a combination of public hearings and private pressure. Chairman McGovern's initial objective, which administration officials understood and successfully frustrated, was to have draft regulations ready early in the summer when a group of food advocates planned to meet for a conference and workshop on the subject.

By scheduling a meeting of interested groups early in June in Washington, D.C., food advocates hoped to force the department to develop regulations well in advance of the start of the school year in September. After they finally appeared on August 3, food groups adopted a double-barreled approach. First, they criticized the USDA for delaying the regulations and taking too narrow an interpretation of legislative intent. Then, they switched their attention to monitoring implementation at the local level. Women's organizations, like the ones that had authored the national school lunch participation study in 1968, and Washington-based public interest advocacy groups like the Children's Foundation took the lead on this issue. Other antihunger groups joined in later in an effort to increase pressure on USDA officials timed to coincide with the first anniversary of the White House hunger conference.[2]

Thereafter, conflict over school food spending simmered for several years. Each time administration officials tried to cut back on growth, food advocacy groups rallied Congress to the program's defense. USDA officials felt caught in between. Congress won the budget battles that took place in the spring of 1971. But administration officials decided to accomplish the objectives Congress had rejected via tightened eligibility for the child nutrition programs. Once again the McGovern committee provided a forum for food aid advocates to fight the administration's proposals. On June 25, 1971, members of the Senate Select Committee heard testimony that needy children would be especially hurt by cutbacks the administration planned in the summer lunch program. Among those testifying that day were the mayors of Detroit and Newark; each described great need in his city for increased funds.

Then, on July 22 the committee turned its attention to another problem, proposed cutbacks in commodities in the food distribution programs for needy families and the special supplemental commodity program for women, infants, and children (Senate Select Committee

1971a). After the hearings ended, USDA officials issued regulations cutting the federal school lunch contributions, leaving the states with less money than they had the year before. In response, food aid supporters got both houses of Congress to pass a joint resolution endorsing increased spending in the summer programs. Faced with certain defeat, the administration backed away from its plans. Congress had responded predictably to a crisis that had been provoked by administration strategists.

USDA officials privately grumbled that they had been caught in the crossfire between the White House and food program supporters. First, they had had to follow the Office of Management and Budget (OMB) directives. Then, they had to shift gears and administer the programs at a higher funding level than they had planned. White House officials responded to the string of congressional victories that food advocates had won by making the changes they wanted through revised regulations for the summer food programs. That action also drew a quick, and hostile, response. Almost immediately, in October 1971, fifty-nine senators cosigned a protest letter to the president. Soon thereafter, the House reported out its own resolution to make sure that administration officials got the message.

Legislative intent was crystal clear: members of Congress did not want to fund programs for low-income children at the expense of the middle class and did not want any further tampering with the school food programs. Both the secretary and Assistant Secretary Richard Lyng, Hardin's deputy for food policy, were very frustrated by this point. Congressional food aid supporters were still blaming USDA officials for the administration's repudiation of Mayer's commitment to feed all eligible low-income children. Portraying a cabinet secretary as the villain and allowing White House officials to have the leeway of a later disavowal or change in policy is an old political ploy. Lyng showed in a September 9, 1971, memo to Hardin that he was well aware of the position in which department officials found themselves (National Archives, Food Program 7-School Lunch Program).

He and Hardin had little room to maneuver between OMB's determination to put a lid on rapidly escalating costs and pressures from "the highly organized 'Hunger Lobby,'" whose leaders kept reminding the press and the attentive public of White House commitments to feed all of the nation's low-income children attending school.[3] During the fall of 1971, department officials watched helplessly as Republicans on Capitol Hill deserted the administration and joined their Democratic colleagues in publicly criticizing the department's actions. This protracted struggle over the administration's interpretation of congressional intent for school food assistance is a classic illustration of how antihunger groups and their congressional allies were able to bring pressure to bear on the department during this period. Even after the administration gave in, congressional determination to expand food aid policy continued.[4]

In 1972 legislators created several new food assistance programs, each aimed at a different audience. Congress sent legislation to the president extending the nonschool food program through fiscal year 1975, authorized $25 million for each of the first two years for a new program of supplemental food for women, infants, and children (what came to be known as the WIC program), and made special nutrition grants to the states for serving the elderly. Administration officials argued that many of these legislative initiatives were unnecessary, but they chose not to openly oppose aid to such politically attractive populations as poor children and older Americans. Instead, White House planners developed a new strategy. They increasingly sought to evade Congress altogether and make major policy changes on their own through the budgetary process, administrative rule making, presidential vetoes, and impoundment of federal funds.

Food aid supporters were also monitoring the effects of implementation of food aid policy at the grass roots level. Many of these local efforts followed up on issues that had been raised in *Their Daily Bread*, the report of the Committee on School Lunch Participation, which had so impressed Orville Freeman in 1968. Beginning in 1969, local antipoverty lawyers and Washington-based public interest groups like the newly formed Food Research and Action Center (FRAC) began filing court cases challenging the USDA's management of the school lunch program. These cases had important policy implications whether they were later settled out of court or led to court decisions. First, they pushed state and local education agencies to expand their participation in the USDA child nutrition programs. Food aid activists hoped that increased participation (e.g., starting up a school breakfast program or serving reduced-price lunches to needy children) would strain local school budgets and prompt local school bureaucrats and policymakers—teachers, school board officials, school food service workers, and local administrators—to urge Congress to expand the USDA's budgetary authority and appropriations further.

Food advocacy groups also regularly participated in the notice and comment process by which the Department of Agriculture promulgated child nutrition program regulations. Through this technique they brought information about local program operations to the attention of Food and Nutrition Service officials in Washington and pushed the department to monitor program administration by state agencies more strictly. Their aim was to affect all parts of program management by local, state, and federal officials and they were becoming increasingly sophisticated at the many ways of doing so. Antihunger activists still felt there was much to do. They favored increasing the number of free meals in school, eliminating any stigma attached to school lunch participation by low-income children, and increasing the possibilities of getting food to poor children in settings outside of traditional school hours—at breakfast, in the summer, in preschool and Head Start programs, and in a variety of child care settings.

WHITE HOUSE OPPOSITION TO FOOD PROGRAM EXPANSION MOUNTS

By 1973, Congress and the Nixon administration were clearly moving on opposing tracks on food policy. Over the past four years, a strong legislative authorization and appropriations base had been constructed for getting food to low-income people via the food stamp and school lunch programs. Several other food programs had also found increased congressional support, including school breakfast, the child care and summer food programs, and commodity assistance for poor women and their children. So far, however, the administration had not registered its growing disapproval of any food aid initiatives through the use of the president's veto power.

The first intimations of a change in that direction came in 1973 when administration officials prepared legislation to consolidate several existing categorical programs into a child nutrition block grant. They hoped that this reorganization effort would hold down further escalation in program costs, bring together the disparate child nutrition programs, and shift part of the burden of program costs and administration to the states. White House officials made no objection to the food stamp program's reauthorization, the main food aid initiative before Congress that year, but they did object when legislators again increased the size of the child nutrition budget by adjusting school lunch payments upward to account for food price inflation.

In 1974 Congress rejected the administration's block grant proposal, and conflict shifted to the issue of reauthorization of the programs in their current form. First, the congressional child nutrition bill had to be recommitted to a conference committee because it exceeded the targets set by the new congressional budgetary process. Congressional supporters felt that they could defend the final product against charges of fiscal irresponsibility by White House spokespeople. Even with lower figures, however, it attracted a veto from President Ford. Coming in a year of conflict with Congress over a wide range of issues, Ford's veto was easily overridden in both the House and the Senate. But this open conflict signaled the start of a new phase of executive–legislative conflict over food aid policy.[5]

Part of the reason why people on Capitol Hill and elsewhere in the

Washington community believed that the Nixon–Ford administration was now in the process of hardening its position on food assistance policy was a change in style that had occurred when Secretary Hardin stepped down. His position went to another economist, Earl Butz, who had been involved in food policy issues in the department during the Eisenhower administration. Secretary Butz employed a more combative style than Hardin in defending the department's mainline agricultural programs and expressed little sympathy for its new social welfare responsibilities. By then, too, the open and experimental Nixon administration decision-making style that had seemed so refreshing compared with the Johnson administration was gone.

No matter how much money the administration might have been able to save if this child nutrition block grant legislation had been enacted, the attention of executive branch budget cutters would eventually have been drawn to the food stamp program. So far, a de facto ceasefire had prevailed publicly over food stamp expansion, but that disintegrated in 1974. Fighting between the administration and Congress broke out that year over the issues of food stamp eligibility and program costs. The triggering incident was an attempt by administration policymakers to write into food stamp regulations a requirement that recipients pay 30 percent of their net income for the stamps they received. The only exception to this rule would be the poorest of the poor, who were exempt from paying for their stamps at all.

Congress had approved the 30 percent figure in the 1970 food stamp bill as a ceiling on income payments, but USDA officials had charged much less in actual practice. If the new regulations went into effect, prices for the stamps could rise considerably without members of Congress having had a chance to react. At the same time that the administration was launching its initiative to cut back on future food stamp program costs, food aid advocates were trying to expand them further. Program supporters were concerned that benefits to the poor had not kept pace with inflation since the reforms of the early 1970s. Because low-income people spent a higher proportion of their income on food and other necessities, they had been especially hard hit by food price increases caused by the administration's shift to more market-based prices for agricultural products. Food aid advocates reacted to the new regulations on two fronts: (1) congressional program supporters immediately started looking for ways to get the administration to rescind the new regulations; and (2) public interest groups like FRAC promised to fight them in the courts.

Food aid advocates also wanted a mechanism to ensure that people got program benefits automatically. They believed that government agencies should do more program outreach. As it was, poor people had to hear about the program in some way, inquire about their eligibility, and then be certified by local welfare officials. Eligibility had increased after Congress eliminated the purchase requirement for the poorest of the poor. Now the 30 percent requirement was a serious threat for the working poor. Having to pay more money for the benefits they received might drive many people out of the program who still had to pay for their stamps and discourage others from signing up at all. At a hearing called to consider the effects of the proposed regulations in June of 1974, FRAC's Ronald Pollack told members of the McGovern Committee that the food stamp allotments contained in the program's rules did not meet the law's requirement that food stamps provide a nutritionally adequate diet (Senate Select Committee 1974b).

USDA planners had advanced the 30 percent proposal after officials at OMB had directed them to come up with increased food aid savings for inclusion in the budget, which the president planned to submit to Congress in January 1975. But following an outpouring of congressional protest mail to the White House and the USDA, Congress blocked the administration's actions by passing a bill freezing the old system in place for another year.[6] This action did not completely deal with the issue, however, because FRAC continued to press the courts to decide if existing program benefits met the test of a nutritionally adequate diet. The administration's postmortems after the hostile congressional action concentrated on how to reintroduce the 30 percent issue. However, no one in the administration remarked on the emergence of a new issue, the relationship of food stamp program increases to the worsening state of the nation's economy.

After recovering from the jumps in program participation that had resulted from liberalization and nationalization of program coverage since 1969, departmental and OMB officials, by the middle of 1974, were hoping that program growth would begin to level off. But that seemed increasingly unlikely in late 1974. After all, eligibility for government benefits can change in several ways: (1) administrative officials can interpret or enforce legislative mandates differently; (2) elected officials can change existing laws or add new provisions; and (3) more people can qualify under existing statutory language because of deteriorating economic conditions. Congress had just blocked an attempt by the administration to employ the first option. In the early 1970s, the second option, legislative changes aimed at benefit enhancement and broader eligibility, had made the food stamp program available and attractive to more people.

Now the third alternative was taking over. Many more Americans were becoming eligible for food stamps and reduced-price school food benefits automatically as the recession caused their income levels to drop. Combined with the program's open-ended budget authority gained in the 1973 law, this meant that the food stamp rolls would continue to expand and accept all those who met the income requirements until the economy improved. Because the program was doing its job—paying out benefits to needy Americans—food stamp costs in 1974 and early 1975 outdistanced all of the administration's budget forecasts. Consequently, late in the spring of 1975 President Ford set up a cabinet-level food stamp review group to draft new legislative proposals designed to hold down food program costs and put the administration's mark on the food stamp program;[7] but in the middle of a recession, prospects for completing these tasks did not appear auspicious.

Once the group got organized, White House Domestic Council staffers advised that participation would likely rise to 21 million people or more by early in fiscal year 1976. The group's task was also made difficult by a decision handed down on June 12, 1975, in one of FRAC's court cases. Despite administration arguments to the contrary, the judge's opinion struck at the heart of the regulations that USDA had issued to implement the 1971 Food Stamp Act amendments. Agriculture officials had not made sure, the court held, that the food stamp coupon allotment schedule would ensure recipients a nutritionally adequate diet. The legislation had "marked a major shift in the policy of the Act, a shift from supplementing the diets of low-income households to guaranteeing those households the opportunity for an adequate diet. Congress plainly intended the 1971 amendments to assure that no eligible family go malnourished" (*Rodway* v. *USDA*, No. 74–1303, U.S. Court of Appeals, 668).

If benefits to each household rose as a result of the decision, that meant that food stamp program costs would soon go even higher. No end seemed in sight for food stamp budget increases. But as the program grew in size, it was attracting a different kind of media attention than food aid supporters and USDA officials were accustomed to hearing. Conservatives were charging massive fraud and abuse in food stamp program administration. A March 9, 1975, editorial in the *San Diego Union*, "Food Stamp Waste Escalates," illustrates the newly critical tone. "It is clear that the food stamp program is duplicative, unfair and rife with inequities. It represents all that is bad about over-generous, open-ended welfare programs." Other articles, however, stressed the human cost of the recession and the real needs of two key populations: those who had recently become unemployed and the working poor. The latter, it was believed, were especially vulnerable to the effects of rising food prices and other forms of inflation.

WHAT IS TO BE DONE? FOOD STAMP REFORM BECOMES A REPUBLICAN PARTY ISSUE

Now it was not the farmer in his expensive car going to pick up his check from the government that was drawing critical attention in the media, but the welfare mother or the unemployed middle-class steelworker seeking governmental benefits. The administration's search for a package of legislative changes that would control skyrocketing program costs was fueled by growing divisiveness within Republican party ranks. Before President Ford could act on his staff's recommendations, a group of Capitol Hill Republicans stole a march on the administration. Two conservatives, Representative Bob Michel (R-Ill.) and Senator James Buckley (R-N.Y.), introduced food stamp legislation of their own, which embodied work done by staffers on the House Republican Study Committee, an organization sponsored by conservative legislators in Congress.

Many of the ideas in the bill were believed to have come from David Swoap, a former official in the gubernatorial administration of Ford's chief intraparty rival Ronald Reagan of California.[8] Since Reagan was likely to be Gerald Ford's main challenger for the Republican nomination in 1976, the president's political and policy advisers wanted to develop legislative proposals of their own as soon as possible as an answer to the growing food stamp reform issue. But the administration took too long resolving its internal differences to get serious congressional consideration for its legislative proposals in 1975.

After laboring mightily, the president sent Congress a message urging food stamp reform, but did not break his proposal into individual bills for Congress to work on.[9] In consequence, it was largely ignored by members of the House and Senate agriculture committees, who had jurisdiction over the food stamp program. Ford finally sent a comprehensive food stamp reform bill to Congress on October 25, 1975, but by then the president's rivals within the party had benefited from almost a year of publicity about their proposals. The president's supporters argued that the administration's bill targeted food stamp funds where the need was greatest. It would help low-income people at the expense of their counterparts at the high end of the scale of those currently eligible, clean up fraud and abuse, and save more than $1 billion. The president's food stamp proposals called for net income eligibility to be set at the Buckley-Michel figure, $5,050, a considerable reduction over the subcommittee's plans, and proposed a $100 standard deduction. The 30 percent concept was reintroduced as the purchase requirement for all but the very poorest and eligibility was tightened or eliminated for several groups previously covered by the program.

Although Ford's legislative proposals were finally available in a form that Congress could act on, legislative prospects for them did not look good despite continued attention in the media to food aid's rising costs. Accordingly, OMB Director James Lynn suggested that the administration try to demonstrate the president's commitment to food stamp reform by implementing the 30 percent proposal administratively after the one-year ban that Congress had enacted expired. Presidential advisers also urged Ford to try for joint action with Buckley, Michel, and the Republican congressional leadership as evidence of a good faith effort to come up with a common party position during the election year; but Republicans on Capitol Hill, who had raised the issue first, reacted coolly to this idea.

So, in the end, no grand Republican compromise emerged in 1976 on the issue of food stamp reform. Instead, as the political primary season got under way, positions in the two main camps hardened further. A judgment which domestic Council Chief Jim Cannon made of the conservative position in a report on October 16, 1975, appears to apply to both sides' motives with equal force: "Our bottom line assessment on our current situation is that we want reform of the food stamp program while our friends on the Hill would prefer to have the issue" (Ford Presidential Library, *Meeting on Food Stamps*, White House Central Files, WE 10–4). Rather, in 1975 and 1976 all of the major Republican groups preferred to score political points, rather than reach a compromise with one another or with other food aid program critics in Congress. Since neither the Buckley–Michel nor the Ford administration bills came to a vote, it is hard to tell how strong the sentiment for food stamp reform actually was on Capitol Hill that year, or which direction it would have taken.

Meanwhile, attempts by a bipartisan coalition of legislators led by Senators McGovern and Robert Dole (R-Kans.), who wanted to expand the program, were also put on the back burner as members of Congress turned their attention to the fall election campaign. Administration officials decided to go ahead with Lynn's plan to implement the 30 percent proposal administratively. Two days after they were published, however, a federal judge issued a temporary restraining order staying implementation of the 30 percent rule until the court could consider a case brought by FRAC and other antihunger advocates. Throughout the summer of 1976 the number of plaintiffs in the suit grew. By fall, twenty-six states, several cities, seventy-three households receiving food stamps, and about one hundred organizations including the U.S. Conference of Mayors had joined FRAC's new court suit. So, in the end, no changes were made in the food stamp program during Ford's last year in office.

9

Budget Realities and the Results of Reagan's War on the Poor

Food assistance policy in the 1980s owes a great deal to the four years that the Carter administration spent in office. During this period, executive and legislative branch officials began to grapple with several issues that remained unanswered when Ronald Reagan left office a decade later. The most important question was how much of a claim food aid supporters could make on the federal government treasury during a period of inflation and economic stagnation. After the Reagan administration took office in January of 1981, White House strategists succeeded in tightening eligibility and cutting back on benefits in all the food aid programs. After that, food aid supporters tried to undo those changes, arguing that hunger and malnutrition are still very real issues in the United States, and that the food assistance programs represent the most effective means that currently exist for dealing with these problems.

THE CARTER ADMINISTRATION'S CONTRIBUTION TO FOOD AID POLICY

Food advocacy, consumer, and antipoverty groups provided a knowledgeable personnel pool for appointive positions at the USDA after the 1976 election. The new team at Agriculture was led by Bob Bergland, formerly a Democratic member of Congress. As a Minnesotan, he shared the same approach to food aid policy as other congressional Democrats from the upper midwest, and had built up a solid record of support for food and agriculture policy during his service on the House Agriculture Committee. On food-related issues, Secretary Bergland relied on Robert Greenstein, who had worked for one of the leading Washington-based food advocacy groups of the 1970s, the Community

Nutrition Institute (CNI), which itself was headed by Rodney Leonard, who had administered the food aid programs for Orville Freeman during the Johnson administration. The other major USDA official involved in food assistance policy on a daily basis in the Carter Agriculture Department was Carol Tucker Foreman, Assistant Secretary for Food and Consumer Services, who came to government from the Consumer Federation of America.

Along with the president, these new officials at Agriculture quickly signaled a break with past practice by endorsing elimination of the purchase requirement. This brought the administration into agreement with bills introduced by food aid supporters like Senators George McGovern (D-S.Dak.) and Robert Dole (R-Kans.) (Demkovich 1977). In 1977, the core of the antihunger lobby included groups like FRAC, CNI, the Childrens' Defense Fund, and the Children's Foundation, all of whom assigned staffers to monitor USDA policy making and administration regularly. These organizations specialized in different areas of food aid policy, but worked together on issues of common concern. Strategy sessions on major legislative issues often included representatives from all these groups, along with key congressional staffers—especially people associated with the House Education and Labor Committee, the House Subcommittee on Domestic Marketing, Consumer Relations, and Nutrition, and the Senate Select Committee on Nutrition—and Washington-based representatives for church, civil rights, and union organizations.

As had happened at the beginning of the Nixon period, Carter's domestic policy advisers decided to separate the food assistance programs from the administration's preliminary discussions about welfare reform (i.e., the income transfer programs housed in the Department of Health, Education, and Welfare). They would, they decided, reform the food stamp program first.[1] They took this action partly because of the exigencies of the congressional calendar and partly because of pressure from food aid lobbyists. Instead of being on the defensive about food stamp program operations that year, supporters were able to defuse the continuing conservative critique by redefining it. They claimed that elimination of the purchase requirement would cut back on fraud and abuse and streamline program administration by eliminating the necessity for massive amounts of money to change hands each month. The antihunger lobby emphasized fraud committed by vendors, whereas program critics usually focused on fraud perpetrated by recipients.

Food stamp reform that year recognized that food aid had played a part in alleviating the effects of the recession. By 1977, many commentators had discovered the role of food aid as an instrument of social policy (U.S. Congressional Budget Office 1977; Nathan 1976; Schlossberg 1975; Steiner 1971). In return for making the program free to all who were eligible, a move that Food and Nutrition Service officials estimated might bring in 3 million more people, congressional food aid advocates agreed to two new program limitations in 1977. They accepted a proposal to tighten eligibility at the upper end of the income scale. According to administration estimates, this provision would remove about 1.3 million people from the program.

The net increase in participation resulting from these changes might be a population of 1.7 million. That could mean a total of 18.5 million recipients after transition to the new program had been completed, but no one was really sure just how big the program might be (*Congress and the Nation* 5:681–85). Senate conferees also agreed to a provision in the House version that placed specific authorization ceilings on the program during the four-year life of the legislation. This "cap" on expenditures, which the administration opposed, was an attempt to keep the program from getting as large as it had been in the mid–1970s, and represented a break with the practice of open-ended authorizations.

The changes that Congress made in 1977 were the most important and far-reaching for program operations since the food stamp program was first enacted in 1964. Several aspects of the final legislation—new assets tests, the work requirements, and the new standard deduction—were complicated issues (Food Research and Action Center 1978). The new program regulations would surely add more complexity to program management. The most complicated element turned out to be the food stamp spending cap, because the estimates about participation on which it relied were unrealistically low. In 1979, even before transition to the program's new rules had been completed, more than 19 million people were participating. Congress had to do something quickly before the depleted food stamp budget brought program operations to a halt.

Legislators were faced with at least two unpleasant options. More money could be authorized and appropriated. Alternatively, benefit levels and/or program eligibility could be changed. In 1979 and again in 1980, Congress chose the first alternative, raising food stamp authorizations to meet program demand. While the food stamp program was clearly not an entitlement program as written, Congress was treating it that way in practice. Through the medium of capping food stamp expenditures and then raising the cap whenever a financial crisis loomed over the program, Congress had begun to acknowledge financial constraints in its consideration of the food program long before Ronald Reagan came to office. Food aid supporters had won a major victory in 1977 in eliminating the purchase requirement, but they had not solved the money issue, which was a natural consequence of program expansion. After all, that was what had provoked the conservative attack on the program in 1974.

Food stamp supporters and critics remained sharply divided on the merits of the program throughout the remainder of the 1970s, but, because the administration and a majority in both houses of Congress remained supportive, no further changes were made while Jimmy Carter remained as president. Some members of the congressional agricultural policy community welcomed doing yearly reauthorizations because it increased their influence over program operations. They again had something—their acquiescence in raising the food stamp cap—that they could trade for approval of legislative issues they cared more about.

Another reason why Congress settled into this habit of capping and uncapping the food stamp program, instead of cutting back on eligibility, lay in the profile of the new participants in the program. Food aid supporters had been correct: there was a lot of new interest once people knew they were eligible and did not have to make a sizeable cash contribution each month. Many of the newcomers were rural and/or elderly people who came from population groups that commanded strong political support on Capitol Hill, and did not fit the conservative stereotype of shiftless people or the undeserving poor (House Subcommittee on Domestic Marketing, Consumer Relations, and Nutrition 1979). So, during the remainder of the Carter years, food assistance policy was caught up in a growing debate over the costs of redistributive policy designed to benefit people at the lower end of the income scale.

With a stalemate in place between critics and supporters of the food stamp program, concern about the growing cost of the food aid budget spilled over onto the child nutrition programs. Administration officials first signaled their concern about child nutrition program spending when Congress was considering legislation extending the WIC and child care food programs for five more years in 1978.[2] At that time, the administration backed a stronger school breakfast program than Congress had been willing to accept, favored elimination of the special milk program, and proposed a cutback in eligibility for WIC for children aged three to five years. The objective was to shift resources within the food assistance program budget rather than increase it. That meant taking money from school feeding programs for middle-class children and giving more funds to programs for children from low-income families.

As earlier administrations had also discovered, it proved extremely difficult to reorient popular middle class programs toward the poor. Because Congress was reluctant to go along, no major child nutrition bill was passed in 1978 or 1979, even though budget concerns became more pronounced as time went on. In 1980 the administration's proposed child nutrition changes received support in the Senate. In a final House vote, which many members admitted they took reluctantly, House conferees were instructed to meet the $500 million cut that the Senate had voted.[3] No bill emerged from the House–Senate conference, however. Instead, House, Education, and Labor Committee Chief Carl Perkins (D-Ky.) engineered an unusual last minute compromise. After holding out against cuts in the child nutrition programs for weeks, Perkins, who had been the chief legislative sponsor for most of the child feeding programs enacted by Congress since the mid–1960s, gave in and agreed to cuts in the programs he had championed for so long.

The chairman gave the reconciliation bill conferees the child nutrition savings they wanted. The price they agreed to pay in return was early reauthorization of several child nutrition programs in the reconciliation measure, rather than through the regular legislative process. Perkins thought he could get a better deal by having Congress reenact child nutrition legislation through the budgetary process than by having reauthorization bills come up in 1981 during the political honeymoon of a popular new Republican administration (*Congressional Quarterly Almanac* 1980:707–10). Republicans complained about Perkins' tactics, but used a similar process themselves to enact more far-reaching changes in eligibility and benefit levels under the auspices of the Omnibus Budget and Reconciliation Act (OBRA) of 1981.

Something new had happened. For the first time in over a decade, congressional supporters had had to accept a cutback in the rate of growth of major food aid programs. Ever since 1968, their chief aim can be summed up in Oliver Twist's attitude about food. They wanted "more," more food aid and more money to pay for the USDA's programs, although they seldom phrased their requests so meekly as Dickens' character did. Now they suddenly had to settle for "less." In the last years of the Carter administration, their first priority was to raise the food stamp cap, so that people who qualified for the program could get enough to constitute a nutritionally adequate diet. Food stamps had become a major income transfer program for the working poor. Moreover, food stamps and the various child nutrition programs bore the full burden of assistance for many low-income families because AFDC payments were still inadequate or nonexistent in many parts of the nation.[4]

In 1979, food advocates tried to make their case in a new set of congressional hearings designed to summarize the development of food aid policy since the discovery of hunger in America in the late 1960s (Senate Select Committee on Nutrition 1979). Media accounts focused on the good news; some of the same doctors who had testified a decade before reported that hunger and malnutrition had been greatly alle-viated in the interim. But food advocates worried that the media had missed the more subtle message that they had been trying to convey. Yes, the programs were working, but just barely. Millions of needy people still were not being served and benefits were constantly being eroded by inflation. In the absence of welfare reform, they would con-tinually need upgrading. The problem that they were fighting was a product of their many victories during the 1970s.

The real test would come if and when a new administration claimed that food program successes meant that the war on hunger had been won and, so, scarce resources could safely be diverted to more pressing concerns. By the time that the Reagan administration took office in 1981, food stamps went to almost one-tenth of all Americans, a much broader universe than that of any other means-tested welfare program. The total cost of benefits had reached almost $9 billion. Several million people received aid from WIC and the child nutrition programs too. Distribution of surplus agricultural commodities, which had once been the larger of the two family food programs by far, now took less than 1 percent of total food aid funds. That cost-cutting was taking place during the administration of a sympathetic Democratic president meant that pressures would likely continue whoever won the White House in 1980.

COST-CUTTING: HOW THE NEW ADMINISTRATION ACHIEVED ITS BUDGET VICTORIES

As the leader of his wing of the Republican party, Ronald Reagan had the benefit of years spent by conservative activists developing a welfare policy agenda (Anderson 1978; Stockman 1975; Swoap 1982). Because White House officials did not have enough political support in Congress to reshape social programs outright through the legislative process, they pushed for benefit and eligibility cutbacks like the ones that had nearly been approved by Congress during the last year of the Carter administration (Barrett 1983; Bawden 1984; Grieder 1981; Stockman 1986). It is not surprising that the budgetary process became the instrument for presenting the Reagan administration's first year legislative program to Congress. As has already been shown, the House and Senate had begun to engage in "continuous budgeting" (Schick 1984) in connection with the food stamp program even before Reagan was elected president.

In 1981, the new administration succeeded in winning congres-sional approval for budget cuts in most of the major food aid pro-grams. Only WIC remained largely unaffected by this increased official skepticism about the intent and achievements of food aid policy. People at or slightly above the poverty line, the so-called working poor who had been receiving food stamps and child nutrition program benefits, were hardest hit as Congress slowed the rate of budget growth by tightening eligibility and lowering benefits. Three separate pieces of legislation were needed to make the food stamp program changes in 1981. First, the cap on food stamp program funds had to be raised to cover the realities of unemployment and inflation (Wehr 1981). Before Congress could complete this action, however, a new surge in program activity forced the administration to increase its supplemental appropriations request by about $300 million. Then, before this emergency funding legislation was signed into law late in June, congressional committees began to work on legislation to extend program authorization.

The Senate cleared a bipartisan compromise bill on June 10, coauthored by Chairman Dole (R-Kans.) of the Senate Nutrition Subcommittee and his Democratic counterpart, Patrick Leahy (D-Vt.). This called for deeper budget cuts than President Reagan asked for in the program; supporters were trying to protect the program against more serious changes offered by Senator Jesse Helms (R-N.C.), the new chairman of the full committee and long a leader among food stamp program critics. The budget reconciliation bill made changes in the way that the USDA indexed food stamp program benefits by delaying participation for newcomers to the program. It also cut program eligibility by lowering the maximum adjusted allowable income level. OBRA, the reconciliation bill, projected further savings by exempting certain shelter-related costs from being used as deductions from gross income.

In the process, senators voted by an overwhelming margin to keep the food stamp program free for those who met the stiffer eligibility guidelines, defeating moves by Helms in committee and Senator Steven Symms (R-Idaho) on the floor to reinstate the purchase requirement. This proposed reform, which the administration did not support, would have signaled a major change in congressional sentiment about food assistance policy.[5] Because of the defeat of Senator George McGovern and several other Democratic liberals in the 1980 election, control of the Senate and its committees had shifted to the Republicans. That meant that food aid supporters had to search for a new set of congressional allies. Starting in 1981, Senator Robert Dole, McGovern's long-time partner on food aid issues, played a central role.

In the end, Congress authorized $11.3 billion for fiscal year 1982. This figure compared with the authorization level of over $9 billion that had originally been set for fiscal year 1981. That meant a slower rate of program growth than the $11.5 billion that had finally been agreed to in the 1981 supplemental bill. The reconciliation conferees had aimed at about $1.4 billion in savings during fiscal year 1982 and ended up with savings estimated over $1.6 billion. All of this was contingent, however, on participation levels falling as expected once the tighter eligibility rules took effect (*Congressional Quarterly Almanac* 1981:466–71). In other words, the success of the administration's cost-cutting depended on the health of the economy.

The avowed purpose of the cuts urged by the Reagan administration for the school food programs, as with food stamps, was to target increasingly scarce program benefits on the truly needy. In 1981, Congress came close to eliminating the special milk program altogether, a favorite target of budget officials in presidential administrations going back to Lyndon Johnson's term in office. Instead, OBRA restricted its operations to schools that had no other federal food program. Second, the summer food program, which served children in nonschool settings, was narrowed substantially, but not totally eliminated, as the administration had originally requested.

The biggest savings were expected to come where most of the child nutrition budget was concentrated, in the school lunch and breakfast programs. The basic legislation, the Child Nutrition Act of 1966 as amended, called for differing subsidies for three target populations of school children: (1) those from families with poverty level incomes; (2) the working poor; and (3) all others. OBRA reduced the upper limit of eligibility for free breakfasts and lunches to children whose families had incomes no higher than 130 percent of the official poverty level, 185 percent for reduced price meals. If these had been the only changes made in program operations that year, a strong argument could be made that the child nutrition changes were doing just what administration officials professed to be most interested in, that is, targeting scarce benefits on the most needy.

The problem that proponents of this position faced was that the changes went further than that. In order to meet the lower budget figures asked of the reconciliation conferees that year, OBRA also reduced the cash value of the subsidy for free and reduced-price meals and cut the basic subsidy (set partly in cash and partly in commodities), which went to all children. Similar changes—subsidy cutbacks, tightened eligibility, and reduced benefits—were made in the child care food program (*Congressional Quarterly Almanac* 1981:497–99). Still, as with the food stamp program, the basic outline of program operations was not altered in 1981, although Congress did authorize the Food and Nutrition Service (FNS) to examine whether existing regulations could be revised to effect further cost reductions without sacrificing nutritional content.

THE REAGAN ADMINISTRATION'S FOOD AID REFORM AGENDA STALLS

This conservative insurgency led food advocacy groups to forge coalitions with the defenders of other social programs that had also been cut back. The concentration on budget issues also prompted the formation of a new public interest organization, the Center for Budget and Policy Priorities, headed by Robert Greenstein, who had been Secretary Bergland's chief food policy adviser.[6] Despite this activity, food aid advocates were not successful in convincing members of Congress to reconsider their decisions. However, food aid supporters scored one victory late in the year when they successfully mobilized opinion in Congress against changes the administration proposed in school lunch program regulations. Under authority granted in OBRA to effect further cost-cutting, FNS had redesigned the Type A lunch, the meal that was the cornerstone of all the school food programs. Led by the FRAC officials, food aid supporters immediately publicized the new rules, arguing that they would make fundamental changes in program operations that Congress had not intended.

They charged that parents would no longer be assured that their children were receiving at least one-third of their daily dietary needs when they ate lunch at school. Food program supporters eagerly demonstrated how a school might satisfy the loosened nutritional requirements by serving a lunch consisting of french fries, ketchup (as the vegetable), a combination meat and soy patty, one slice of white bread, and a reduced portion of milk. In a well-orchestrated media event on Capitol Hill, previously beleaguered congressional food aid supporters gleefully posed for television cameras eating this Spartan fare.[7] The resulting flurry of negative news reports was quickly followed by a storm of hostile editorials, scathing commentaries by news columnists and cartoonists, indignant calls for congressional investigations, and equivocations from White House and USDA spokespersons.

In light of all this unfavorable publicity, administration officials quickly backed down and withdrew the proposed regulations. This was soon followed by one of the first top-level resignations from the Reagan administration, that of G. William Hoagland, head of the Food and Nutrition Service. The administration's embarrassment over the abortive school lunch regulations helped congressional food aid supporters face down proposals for additional cuts when White House officials presented the president's legislative program in 1982. After scaling back spending for food assistance programs during its first year in office, the administration's officials tried to move on a broader front with respect to food aid policy in 1982. They proposed folding the child nutrition programs into a block grant to be operated by the states; and the president announced in his State of the Union message that he wanted the states to assume funding for the food stamp program within the context of a swap of state and federal social welfare responsibilities.

Neither plan attracted much support on Capitol Hill. The block grant idea met with immediate opposition from school food supporters in the congressional committees that had jurisdiction over the child nutrition programs but with little enthusiasm elsewhere, even among the administration's usual allies on Capitol Hill. Members of both houses introduced resolutions declaring it to be the sense of Congress that the school food programs should not be cut any more. The House went even further, passing a bill to restore some of the cuts made the year before, but it died when the Senate did not take similar action. The result was continued stalemate; Congress did not want to make further changes or to restore the cuts already made.

Food program supporters alleged that the administration's stated intention of targeting child nutrition program benefits on the truly needy had backfired. Some schools dropped the programs altogether after the 1981 cuts in subsidies to middle class children had begun to be felt. What good did federal government nutrition aid do for poor kids if local school officials were not willing to operate the child nutrition programs at the lower reimbursement levels, supporters asked.[8] The administration's 1982 food stamp proposals were even more far-reaching than what White House officials were pushing for in the child nutrition area. They represented a new version of an idea that the National Governors Association had proposed before Ronald Reagan had come to office.

The governors' group, along with the U.S. Advisory Commission on Intergovernmental Relations, had been interested in some kind of sorting out of federal–state responsibilities, especially in the social welfare area. However, instead of the "swap" originally suggested by the governors and their allies, which would have resulted in increased federal government responsibility for most social welfare programs (including food stamps), the Reagan administration proposed a different kind of exchange in 1982. As the centerpiece of his New Federalism initiatives, the president proposed shifting food stamp program spending and administration to the states. In return, the federal government would assume the states' portion of Medicaid costs (Beam 1984; Williamson 1983).

After an initially cautious welcome while the governors read the fine print of Reagan's proposal, state officials grew increasingly wary about the long-term financial implications of this idea. As a result, negotiations with White House officials fell apart almost as soon as they began. Throughout President Reagan's first term, official spokespersons insisted publicly that the swap remained a top administration priority, but the White House never followed up the president's references to it in his speeches in 1982 by sending any legislation to Congress. Apparently, it was soon considered a dead issue. Even with this defeat, the president and his allies had succeeded in redirecting the public debate about food assistance policy. They had been careful to assure Congress and the public about their commitment to a *social safety net*, including food assistance programs designed to protect those most in need in American society.

Part of the success of the president and his allies came because they had tapped into popular attitudes about fraud, waste, and abuse that seem to be permanently attached to means-tested social programs in the United States. Until they proposed the food stamp swap and the child nutrition block grant, they had been careful to steer clear of more extreme schemes, like restoration of the food stamp purchase requirement or proposals to count as income the meals that low-income children received in school in determining their families' food stamp eligibility. Food advocacy groups worked hard to rally public opinion against these proposals, but it was events outside of their control—in particular the administration's management of the economy and the effects of the worsening recession—that ultimately protected the food aid programs from further changes.

Late in 1981 media accounts began publicizing the effects of a new economic slowdown. Simultaneously, USDA officials administering the food aid programs felt the effects of a surge in food program participation. Spending levels were rising dramatically because of growing unemployment. As in the Ford administration, food stamp participation was proving sensitive to deteriorating economic conditions. Even with the stricter eligibility levels enacted in 1981, more people were qualifying for participation, and food stamps, unlike AFDC, still helped the working poor, drawing in people who had jobs as long as they met the stricter income guidelines. Families did not need to be "on welfare" to get food aid.[9]

As the recession worsened, the number of people who needed help bumped up against the appropriations levels in all the food programs. But tightened administrative requirements meant a longer time before new applicants qualified for food subsidies. These conditions created a new set of tensions and gave rise to media stories about the problems of the "new poor." This publicity, in turn, increased political pressure on Congress and the administration, forcing acquiescence to spending above administration budget requests and above the spending caps enacted by Congress (House Subcommittee on Domestic Marketing, Consumer Relations, and Nutrition 1983b). Each side accepted this outcome (i.e., raising food aid authorization ceilings and appropriating more money during the recession) grudgingly because it was marginally preferable to all of the other available alternatives.

Administration officials acquiesced to a temporary expansion of the food assistance budget because they did not want to reverse the program changes made in 1981. Food aid advocates, however, accepted small budget increases because they believed that they could not yet muster majority support in Congress for full restitution of the cuts made in 1981. The Senate's composition was crucial to both sides' calculations. The reduced number of food aid supporters in that body after the 1980 election, combined with the popularity of the president, ensured continued stalemate, but did not prevent several small initiatives from being considered.

LET THEM EAT CHEESE: THE RISE OF SOUP KITCHENS AND FOOD PANTRIES

One set of marginal changes involved an expansion of surplus disposal efforts. Alarmed by the deepening recession, Reagan administration officials announced late in 1981 that they would use new farm program authority to increase the kinds and quantities of surplus food that could be distributed to needy individuals and households. Ever since the food stamp program reached all parts of the nation in 1974, use of agricultural commodities had declined and what remained had gone principally toward supplementing the child nutrition programs. Now, rather than risk losing hard-won legislative gains incorporated into OBRA from the year before, administration strategists were proposing to act administratively to beef up surplus distribution efforts.

This idea had several advantages. Rather than wait for congressional acquiescence, USDA officials could get started right away; and they had more administrative flexibility. Like other postwar administrations, Reagan's officials liked the idea of having the Secretary of Agriculture dispose of surplus agricultural stocks by distributing them to needy families.

As a result, when the next national debate about the extent of hunger and malnutrition developed, farm and food assistance policy once again became linked in media accounts about USDA programs and policies.

In 1981, USDA and White House officials viewed the distribution of surplus cheese as a one-time only action. The arrangements worked out by USDA officials for what they called the Surplus Dairy Distribution Program (SDDP) closely paralleled surplus food distribution efforts during the 1960s. State officials made distribution arrangements for the commodities after the USDA delivered them to a central location in each state (Lipsky and Thibodeau 1985). From the perspective of state agriculture officials used to other USDA programs, the new commodity distribution effort went through a predictable cycle. According to an Iowa official, the "initial message that went to the states was to be very liberal and broad in their eligibility guidelines, as there is a great deal of surplus food that needs to be distributed across the U.S." (Senate Subcommittee on Nutrition 1983a:16–17).

Soon, however, complaints about the new program sounded very similar to what USDA officials had been used to hearing before the introduction of the food stamp program. Industry trade groups complained that surplus cheese giveaways were causing disruptions in regular retail sales of their products. That prompted the administration to suspend the cheese distribution pending action by the states setting eligibility guidelines, which would ensure that surplus food only went to the truly needy. But that step did not solve the competition issue. Inexorably, this emergency effort began to take on the trappings of a permanent program, just what neither food program supporters nor administration officials, for different reasons, wanted.[10]

While state officials grumbled that their federal colleagues were making the operation of the new program excessively complex, staffers and volunteers working for local government and community agencies blamed both sides for the makeshift delivery system they had to use to get surplus food to needy people. At congressional hearings in 1983, Salvation Army directors, church groups, local welfare officials, and heads of community food banks and soup kitchens, who presided over the actual distribution of surplus cheese and other dairy products, severely criticized the surplus food delivery system. They cited poor planning by government agencies, the inappropriate size in which the products typically came, and the costs of processing and distributing the commodities that the states and the USDA passed along to them. Many also noted disapprovingly the embarrassment and shame that needy people felt when obliged to stand in the cheese lines (House Subcommittee on Domestic Marketing, Consumer Relations, and Nutrition 1983b; Senate Subcommittee on Nutrition 1983a; and Senate Subcommittee on Rural Development, Oversight, and Investigations 1983).

The attraction for White House and other administration officials was the same as it had been from the New Deal to the New Frontier period—financially and politically inexpensive. The federal government had already paid for the food that the USDA was making available to local groups. Here was a way that more could be distributed without breaking the budget or acquiescing to calls for undoing the 1981 budget cuts. The administration did not want to be committed to specific statutory requirements for what officials still hoped would be a temporary measure. Food program supporters preferred to have money restored to the food stamp and child nutrition programs, rather than diverted into what they considered a makeshift and demeaning delivery system. However, when Congress began to react to media accounts about increased hunger and malnutrition early in 1983, the final result was a compromise: legislative enactment of a new food program which was not the preferred choice of either side in the controversy.

This authority for a Temporary Emergency Food Assistance Program (TEFAP) was included in PL 98–8, an emergency jobs bill enacted later in 1983. Administration officials were able to hold the line on the changes made in the food stamp and child nutrition programs in 1981, but food supporters got an increase in program funds and a tacit admission that the existing safety net was not working satisfactorily. TEFAP authorized $100 million, half of which would be distributed by a national board of voluntary associations to meet emergency food and shelter needs. Another $50 million would go to the states to cover some of their expenses carrying out these programs. All of this new money had to be spent in just a few months, before the end of September 1983 (Wehr 1983a).

Almost immediately after the jobs bill was signed by the president, food aid supporters in Congress introduced legislation to expand and continue TEFAP past its September cutoff date. Both the jobs bill and the new legislation drew on testimony in congressional hearings during the spring of 1983. These hearings, by three different subcommittees of Congress, dramatized the extent of the new hunger problems of the 1980s. First, legislators were told that not just the recently unemployed or new poor (i.e., those who did not qualify for a mainstream food aid program) were showing up at soup kitchens and food pantries to get food for their families, but food stamp recipients came too after their monthly benefits ran out. That showed, program supporters argued, that the mainstream food aid efforts were grossly underfunded. Nor was it only the most blighted areas of the nation's cities that were affected. Representative Leon Panetta's Subcommittee on Domestic Marketing, Consumer Relations, and Nutrition heard evidence that hunger and unemployment had spread to suburbs. Finally, the hearings Panetta held in Cleveland, Ohio, and Birmingham, Alabama, showed the recession's effects on the theretofore stable working class (House Subcommittee on Domestic Marketing, Consumer Relations, and Nutrition 1983b).

Panetta followed up these findings with testimony from officials who specialized in food aid policy and programs—food advocates, state agriculture officials, school food service administrators, the grocery trade, and some agricultural producer groups. All supported increased food assistance efforts. Senator Robert Dole, Panetta's counterpart on the

Senate Nutrition Subcommittee, who represented the bipartisan support that the food aid programs had in rural areas of the country, confirmed the Panetta committee's findings in hearings that he held in Washington that spring. Dole also used his subcommittee's hearings to publicly caution the administration to implement the spirit as well as the letter of the jobs bill (Senate Subcommittee on Nutrition 1983b).

In testimony before the Dole Subcommittee, Robert Greenstein, of the Center for Budget and Policy Priorities, summarized the overall indictment that food program supporters were making. Administration assurances to the contrary, the poor had not been held harmless against the food program changes that Congress had enacted in 1981.[11] Let's give the poor a break, Greenstein argued. TEFAP was being used by those who had fallen through the cracks of the administration's social safety net. Dole was not that blunt, but noted that most Americans were embarrassed by the return of Depression-era images in the 1980s (Senate Subcommittee on Nutrition 1983b). In short, these hearings and the accompanying media attention to cheese lines and soup kitchens were putting hunger and malnutrition back on both the public's and Congress' policy agenda.

HUNGER IN AMERICA REVISITED: URBAN AND RURAL POVERTY IN THE 1980s

In August 1983, White House officials finally acknowledged the seriousness of the hunger situation. This change of heart was caused by a combination of events. First, media accounts about hunger and malnutrition had built up, especially coverage on the major television networks' evening news programs. The administration also was embarrassed by the appearance of several government reports critical of the 1981 budget cuts and the extent of poverty in America in the 1980s. By the end of July 1983, it became clear that Congress would present the president with legislation extending the new food donation program. By cooperating with Congress to renew TEFAP's authority, administration officials hoped to regain the political offensive on the hunger issue and have some influence in the legislative bargaining already under way.

Acknowledging public concern about hunger in America, the president reported that he had asked White House adviser Edwin Meese 3d to study the hunger problem. Meese himself became the target of a spate of Christmas-time editorials later in 1983 when in the course of his study he expressed skepticism about the existence of hunger and malnutrition, views that were at considerable variance from President Reagan's public expression of concern about hunger and its effects (Wehr 1983b). Food aid supporters used Meese's comments to try to discredit the report's generally conservative conclusions when it was made public soon thereafter. They charged that the results had been foreordained, that the establishment of the commission had been only a public relations gesture, and that the Reagan administration had never taken seriously the reports of growing human service needs across the country.

The fact that the report had little new to offer also strengthened their case. Its chief recommendation—creation of a food assistance block grant that would allow states to drop out of the food stamp and other federal food programs—also met with a united front of opposition from groups representing state and local officials who dealt with the problems of hunger and poverty on a daily basis, such as the National Governors Association, the U.S. Conference of Mayors, and the National Association of Counties. A hearing, sponsored by the three major congressional subcommittees with responsibilities for writing food aid policy, reviewed the task force report in January 1984 and provided critics with a public forum in which to air their views (House Subcommittee on Domestic Marketing, Consumer Relations, and Nutrition 1984). It demonstrated yet again the wide degree of bipartisan consensus that existed in Congress for continued federal government responsibility of the food aid programs.[12]

None of the program proposals suggested by the Meese task force was taken seriously by Congress. As the recession waned, discussion about hunger and malnutrition gradually receded from media attention. Since then, food aid policy has remained out of public view except for periodic discussions about complex social problems like lingering unemployment and homelessness.[13] Each year since then, executive branch officials have reluctantly acquiesced to small increases in the food aid program budget. By the time that Ronald Reagan left office, food supporters in Congress still had not been fully able to turn around the eligibility and benefit changes effected in 1981. Instead, they settled for trying to rub the sharp edges off the changes that the Reagan forces won when they first came to office. As the issue of federal budget deficits has crowded many domestic policy concerns off Congress' agenda during Reagan's second term, supporters have continued to modify their objectives to fit the straightened circumstances in which the Department of Agriculture's food aid efforts still find themselves.

10

Conclusion: Still Hungry After All These Years

This chapter returns to several themes that have run through this book. First, it outlines food aid's current relationship to social welfare policy. Second, it reexamines the connections that the food programs have to the political economy of agriculture in America. The rest of the chapter is given over to conclusions about the politics of the food aid policy process and, in particular, to an assessment of the tactics and accomplishments of the groups and individual activists who have been food aid policy's most important and effective supporters for the past two decades.

THE IMPORTANCE OF FOOD AID PROGRAMS TO SOCIAL WELFARE POLICY

Before the 1970s, food aid policy's welfare benefits could be easily ignored. After all, most social policy experts knew that food aid had been designed to help agricultural producers rather than low-income consumers. Also, the total federal food aid budget was still quite low. During that decade, civil rights, poor people's lobbies, and other food aid advocates won unprecedented increases in program funding, and liberals who had been harsh program critics switched and became staunch program defenders. At the same time, conservatives, who had successfully defused these policies' redistributive rhetoric through their control over how they were implemented, became highly critical of program operations, costs, and philosophy.

Because of this new support (and despite inconsistent presidential commitments to it), food aid policy expanded dramatically in the 1970s. Still, both Presidents Nixon and Carter were more interested in comprehensive welfare reform. Their welfare plans addressed what might be called the reform ideal, a set of goals held by many social policy analysts and social work professionals. In this view, successful social welfare reform had to do four things. First, it should correct problems caused by the existing multiplicity of federal income maintenance programs and the current methods of intergovernmental service delivery. At the same time, it had to provide low-income people with a decent standard of living, and, realists among them would argue, a welfare reform plan had to provide incentives for low-income people to work themselves out of poverty and toward self-sufficiency in order to attract majority support in both houses of Congress (Maney 1987b).

For reasons of political exigency, both administrations decided to separate food aid policy from the issue of welfare reform. Twice the importance of food aid—tucked away in the unlikely venue of the USDA—was underestimated by those pushing for welfare reform within the Department of Health, Education and Welfare (now Health and Human Services) and on the president's domestic policy staff. Administrative changes in the USDA's food programs played a much more central role, however, in the welfare reform plans that conservatives designed in the 1970s and again during the Reagan years. Then, in the mid–1980s, the pendulum began to swing back. In the final version of the Gramm-Rudman-Hollings plan enacted in 1985, Congress explicitly included food aid, along with AFDC, SSI, and a handful of other programs as the main exceptions to the deficit reduction timetables designed to cut defense and domestic program spending. Poor people, Congress averred, had already taken their fair share of cuts.

For the fact that food aid grew to supplement the ramshackle set of income support programs for the nation's poor, while the nation remained stalemated on welfare reform, credit goes not to social policy analysts eager to try out alternatives to mainstream income maintenance programs, but to the antipoverty activists working in the South and in Washington in the 1960s and 1970s. Food aid was a vital part of this campaign. These activists were successful in getting influential publics to examine contradictions implicit in the contrasting images that America presented—of agricultural abundance on one hand and dire poverty on the other. They made the country confront the issue of whether the poor should benefit from America's agricultural abundance and on what terms. Poverty declined substantially in the period from 1960 through the recession of the mid–1970s, because of the combined effects of transfer payments and strong economic growth, but the decline of the poverty rate slowed considerably in the late 1970s and the number of people mired in poverty began to grow again after 1979. Poverty also became more difficult to uproot or treat. Female-headed and minority families have not fared well in the private employment markets of the 1980s, even when economic conditions have improved (Schwarz 1983).

Food assistance spending got to be so high in the period from 1969 to 1980 because further growth of in-kind benefit programs seemed preferable to key veto groups to the prospect of achieving welfare reform through a guaranteed annual income, negative income tax, or similar comprehensive approach (Nathan 1976; MacDonald 1977; Moynihan 1973). And food aid spending stabilized and began to grow again, although at a slower rate, during the Reagan years because members of Congress have preferred these programs to each of the alternatives yet put forward for consideration. Food aid policy is interesting on its own and for what it shows about the policy process generally. As an old but not yet settled policy area subject to strong ideological claims, it highlights several continuing concerns researchers have about how groups can and do try to influence policy making and implementation.

By the end of Ronald Reagan's second term as president, stalemate still prevailed between the administration and Congress over how much money the federal government should spend on food aid policy. As a new administration came to office in 1989, the programs discussed in this book remained politically controversial, despite the growth and institutionalization that had occurred since the early 1970s. Because of the political conflicts that always have swirled around food aid policy, it probably is unwise to forecast anything except continuing ferment for the near future. Hard times in the 1980s spurred new debate about the adequacy of the nation's social welfare system of which the food assistance programs had become so crucial a part (Furniss 1985; Page 1983; U.S. Congressional Research Service 1986b; U.S. General Accounting Office 1983) The Reagan administration started this debate during the 1980 election campaign by arguing that actions taken under previous presidential administrations had made the social welfare system too elaborate and costly. Fraud, waste, and abuse could be rooted out without dismantling the basic protections of what administration spokespersons termed the "social safety net."

A less intrusive government role in the economy would, they argued, spur private investment and economic activity. That, in turn, would create new employment opportunities for low-income workers and ease the welfare rolls. The administration's legislative successes in its budget and tax cut proposals during 1981 attest to the persuasiveness and political attractiveness of these ideas. But the economy did not respond as Reagan administration officials expected. Between 1981 and 1986, food aid's ties to agriculture were reinforced, sometimes in surprising ways. The administration found itself operating first one and then a second food distribution program for those hurt by the recession and for a politically sensitive category of the "new poor" who did not qualify for traditional types of food aid. Food aid will remain an important tool of economic and social policy and a subject of continued political dispute for the foreseeable future until politicians come up with new themes and coalitions for governing.

LINKAGES BETWEEN FARM AND FOOD AID POLICY

Agricultural support for subsidizing consumer food spending was an acquired taste. The initiation of food aid policy reflected public officials' views about wise public policy, rather than a direct response to agricultural pressure groups. Food aid policy's major supporters were not general purpose farm groups like the American Farm Bureau Federation, the National Farmers Organization, or the National Farmers Union, nor was it the preferred course of action of the agribusiness or commodity groups that have grown so much in power and influence during the postwar period. Instead, it was designed by bureaucratic technicians, the agricultural economists charged with stabilizing farm income and making the farm support system work more effectively. Until the 1960s, the debate over the means and ends of surplus disposal policy remained largely confined to specialists in agricultural policy at the USDA and in the agricultural committees in Congress. Most farm organizations always spent more time and effort on price support than surplus management policy.

Nor has the debate attracted much attention from the general public. When they pay attention to farm policy, Americans usually look at the price of food in the supermarket and at the overall amount of government aid going into the farm economy, not at the details of surplus management programs. Since the New Deal, support for expanded food assistance programs within the agricultural policy community has come from pragmatists worried about how the farm economy will fare in the increasingly urban and consumer-oriented society they see around them. In their ranks were four key sets of activists: (1) a handful of mavericks at the USDA like Frederick Waugh; (2) a few influential members of Congress from both political parties such as Senators George Aiken, Robert Dole, and George McGovern; (3) appointees to senior USDA policy-making positions under successive Democratic administrations like Orville Freeman and Bob Bergland; and (4) only occasionally spokespeople for farm groups (e.g., National Farmers Union, National Grange) and producer interests.

During the 1980s, half a century after the New Deal drastically changed American agriculture, farm policy again faced problems of massive proportions, some of which still came because of its unprecedented successes. By applying the fruits of science and technology (and with the aid of government), American commercial agriculture has achieved unparalleled abundance and immeasurably improved the lives of those who continue to work on the land. Like their counterparts in the agricultural areas of other advanced industrial societies, most rural Americans today do not live isolated lives or labor in a subsistence economy. American farm families shop for bargains in the same supermarkets that their city cousins enjoy and send their children to high school and college. In short, most live middle-class lives in the mainstream culture of the nation. But these gains, unimaginable just a generation ago, have come at a high price.

While millions of farm families have succeeded beyond their expectations, many more have left farming altogether. The spectacular gains in productivity, which consumers take for granted, have meant that fewer and larger farms remain. Government programs have eased the migration of middle-class farm operators out of agriculture in this decade, but did not help low-income (both white and black) farmers make the transition from rural to metropolitan areas in earlier years (Baldwin 1968; Fligstein 1981; [The] People Left Behind 1967; Poverty on the Land 1964). The plight of sharecroppers, tenants, and migrant farm laborers briefly attracted the concern of the larger political system in the 1960s after it was too late to help those who had already left and many who were still clinging to their traditional livelihoods. The situation in which many poor farm families found themselves was made worse by the legacy of racial discrimination and the effects of the caste system, which dominated the southeast and parts of the southwest through the 1960s.

That the effects of the federal farm programs begun in the New Deal helped force many rural tenants out of agriculture seems clear in retrospect. Ironically, though, the food aid programs that were in place by the end of the Johnson administration assisted the last group of migrants from rural America once they got to the cities. Equally ironically, after encountering charges of insensitivity to the plight of agricultural laborers and the rural poor, USDA officials are now being accused of pursuing policies that are hurting the very middle-class farm families who were supposed to be the main beneficiaries of government farm programs. In the mid–1980s, states in the midwestern farm belt experienced rates of farm failures and bankruptcies that have been unparalleled since the 1930s. Banks failed all over the country, and the farm credit system courted collapse because of mounting debt loads. More recently in 1988, farmers battled drought conditions that reminded people of the Depression years.

Besides initiating the food aid efforts that have been our principal concern in this book, Franklin Roosevelt's New Deal laid the foundation for nearly all the forms of governmental intervention in the agricultural economy that producers depend on today. But beneath this surface pattern of stability, much change has taken place in farm and food policy. Changes in the nation's demographics have contributed to changing sentiment in Congress about farm and food policy over the past fifty years. Throughout the postwar period, rural House districts have lost representation on Capitol Hill, and those rural areas that remain send different kinds of people to represent them in Congress now. By the early 1970s, most of the formal and informal Democratic party leaders of the agricultural policy community in Congress represented different kinds of farming areas than had traditionally been the case.[1]

Depopulation of rural areas during this period, including those with large numbers of poor people, has meant that low-income people who wanted help from the federal government have become increasingly concentrated in America's cities. That has given urban members a wider stake in the USDA's programs. In the process, food aid policy, and the dollars that these programs have brought to the USDA's budget, have become a means for the Department of Agriculture to broaden its missions (as Secretaries Wallace and Freeman had hoped) during an era of uncertainty about whether the older ones, which stressed help to families in the farm economy, remain politically viable.

INFLUENCING THE POLICY PROCESS

The material presented in this book also adds to what is known about how pressure can be generated on government decisionmakers by (and on behalf of) low-income people in the contemporary American political system. Most political science studies of interest group lobbying have a snapshot quality. The best outline and analyze the tactics that activists or groups use during work on one bill, or concentrate on legislative maneuvering involving a set of policy issues during one or more sessions of Congress. This study has been organized differently. It has examined a broad policy area made up of several sets of programs, looking for similarities and differences in tactics and activities over time as groups form and old ones reorganize, refocus their activities, and/or move on to other issues.

In the late 1960s, a small group of antipoverty and civil rights activists created a new public issue, the continued existence of hunger and malnutrition, and put forth a solution, expansion and liberalization of the Department of Agriculture's food aid programs. In order to evaluate their activities, it is necessary to start with conventional interest group analysis and add insights from the literature on public interest groups and political protest (Berry 1977; Maney 1987a; McCann 1986; Piven 1976; Piven and Cloward 1977). Until the mid–1960s, the main supporters of food assistance policy outside of the agricultural policy community came from important sections of the New Deal political coalition. Churches, liberal groups, and organized labor were involved along with a few urban representatives in Congress like Representative Leonore Sullivan and Senator John F. Kennedy.

On the strength of the ties that New Deal officials had forged between farm and union groups, organized labor's political leaders also remained sympathetic to the problems of small and medium-sized agricultural producers and the rural poor. They supported increased surplus disposal efforts by the USDA and were instrumental in interesting urban legislators in food aid policy as a political issue during the Eisenhower administration. Later, when antipoverty and antihunger groups began to focus attention on hunger and malnutrition, a younger generation of liberal activists took over, but their numbers also included many people who had previously been affiliated with labor and civil rights organizations. The United Auto Workers, for example, played a key role in organizing and supporting the first Washington-based food advocacy group, the Citizens Crusade Against Poverty.

Civil rights and antipoverty activists were able to put their knowledge of the conditions of urban and rural poverty and their connections with liberal farm activists to use in the 1960s and 1970s to lobby Congress and the executive branch to expand food aid spending. They wanted to use food assistance policy to implement an uncompleted agenda of social reform after the momentum of the civil rights movement had begun to run down. By 1966, the first stage of federal action designed to secure the citizenship rights of blacks and other minorities—dismantling segregation, eliminating discrimination in public accommodations, and securing voting rights—had been enacted. Liberal activists saw the USDA's programs as a means to deal with a second stage of economic, social, and psychological impoverishment that still remained.

Some characteristics of food aid policy making are surprising given earlier studies showing the prominent role of executive branch policymakers in the Great Society period. Presidents and their domestic policy advisers have not been the chief movers on food aid issues within government or with the attentive public since the Kennedy administration. Congress has. Conventional peak associations—the Chamber of Commerce, the National Association of Manufacturers—have not been arrayed on either side until quite recently. Indeed, there was no formal opposition at all to increased food aid until conservatives developed arguments about what should be acceptable and unacceptable upper limits on food program costs in the mid–1970s. Instead, during most of the period for which evidence has been presented here, food advocacy groups with few conventional political resources have been the main organized interests pushing Congress on these issues.[2]

Unlike programs and policies that started out more avowedly redistributive and became less so over time, food aid policy appears to have gone in the opposite direction. The conclusions that can be drawn about the activities of the public interest groups under study here add to the growing research agenda that exists on that subject. This information falls into two general categories: about the characteristics of the groups themselves and about their tactics and activities. During most of its existence, the antihunger lobby has been made up of four main elements, with the importance of each varying over time.

The first category includes activity at the *community level*. Local civil rights activists were the first to see food aid as part of the nation's uncompleted antipoverty agenda. They never gained the formal authority to run food stamp or school food programs that they sought during the Freeman years, but they continue to play key roles monitoring the decisions of the school boards and county social service departments that remain the official local implementors. Nonprofit community organizations do run many of the newer food aid programs, however.

Organized groups of actual or potential food aid recipients (e.g., civil rights and poor people's groups active in the South, public assistance recipients organized by the National Welfare Rights Organization in the cities of the North in the early 1970s, etc.) also fall into this category of community-level organization. Besides expanding existing programs and monitoring implementation once programs are in place, individual activists and community groups have been a continuing source of information for Washington-based food advocacy groups. They know how the programs actually operate and what problems need further attention from federal government decisionmakers.

The second part of the antihunger lobby has been the *food advocacy groups* and individual activists working in Washington, D.C. They established contacts with sympathetic members of Congress, pressured executive branch officials, and recruited specialists and allies from a wide circle of organizations for specific campaigns. Although only a small number of organizations were involved, including the CCAP, the Committee on School Lunch Participation, FRAC, the Children's Defense Fund, the Children's Foundation, the Community Nutrition Institute, and the Center on Budget and Policy Priorities, they have had an effect on food aid policy out of all proportion to their size and available political resources. These organizations have been able to influence food aid policy formulation and implementation because of detailed knowledge about how these complex programs operate.

And they have worked together as part of a network or community that shares information and tries to develop complementary specialties. Marion Wright Edelman, Ronald Pollack, Rodney Leonard, and Robert Greenstein are good examples of the people involved. Together with past and present officials at Agriculture, a few people in the media like Nick Kotz, some state and local officials who oversee or implement the USDA food programs, and a handful of congressional staffers who have worked for the Senate Select Committee on Nutrition and Human Needs and other congressional committees, they constitute a variant of an "issue network" (Heclo 1978). One of the main functions that these Washington-based public interest activists have performed has been to build coalitions or alliances with sympathetic organizations that have broader policy interests.

These *allies* constitute a third set of organizations involved in the food aid policy process and take on important tasks in connection with lobbying campaigns. Church, labor, civil rights, and specialized liberal organizations such as the National Sharecroppers Fund are examples of the types of organizations involved. Associations of local officials, like the National Association of School Food Service Workers, have also played prominent roles, and organizations of elected officials (e.g., the National League of Cities and the U.S. Conference of Mayors) have become food policy allies recently. The mayors' support was activated during this decade in response to the problems of the homeless, the "new poor," and others who use the expanded network of soup kitchens and food pantries that now exists. Antihunger activists have employed several techniques to mobilize these allies. In the 1960s, for example, CCAP officials used personal contacts to persuade doctors and other medical professionals to testify in Congress about the human cost of hunger and malnutrition. Later, CNI's newsletter provided a forum to publicize food policy issues generally and to alert members of each advocacy group about what other organizations were working on at any given time.

The final element in the antihunger forces has been made up of *congressional food program supporters*. Senators Robert Kennedy and Joseph Clark and the staffers on the Senate Poverty Subcommittee comprised the first generation of supporters in Congress when food aid was becoming an antipoverty and civil rights issue. Senator McGovern and his colleagues dominated the scene during the early 1970s, even though the Select Committee on Nutrition and Human Needs could not author or report out legislation on its own; bills its members favored still had to work their way through the House and Senate agriculture committees. Important work also has been done by Chairman Carl Perkins (D-Ky.) and others on the House Education and Labor Committee, which has jurisdiction over the school food programs. The role of members and staffers on the House Subcommittee on Domestic Marketing, Consumer Relations, and Nutrition, the Senate Nutrition Subcommittee, and the new House Select Committee on Hunger has also been crucial.

STRATEGIES, TACTICS, AND ACCOMPLISHMENTS OF FOOD ADVOCATES

Political scientists have done a better job describing the behavior of governmental and private sector political actors than they have outlining the context or setting in which they operate. Much of what has happened in the period covered in this study has been influenced by a set of political practices inherited from the New Deal. The "shadow" cast by Franklin Roosevelt on the present has been variously interpreted, but recent studies agree on its importance (e.g., Leuchtenburg 1983; Mollenkopf 1983; Skocpol 1980). Roosevelt and his appointees at the USDA acted in a manner consistent with the independent role that theorists see public officials pursuing in a liberal democratic state (Elkin 1987). The regime that Roosevelt and his advisers put into place lasted into the 1960s; both Democratic presidents Kennedy and Johnson attempted to complete the New Deal agenda. It is in this context that the accomplishments of the protest and public interest groups discussed earlier in this chapter need to be viewed.[3]

Besides assuming leadership from an earlier generation of liberal activists, members of the antihunger coalition changed the regime of food aid policy in important ways. This happened in three phases: (1) a period of protest activity during which popular discontent reached national decisionmakers; (2) a decade of Washington-based public interest advocacy that helped to secure enactment of numerous legislative initiative; and, finally, (3) a period of concentration on defending redistributive policy outcomes from conservative attack. Food aid supporters first gained national attention through their association with the protest activities of civil rights and antipoverty organizations in the rural South in the late 1960s. Because of the difficulty of sustaining the kind and degree of organization needed to influence governmental decisionmakers, the most likely outcome of *protest* as a political resource is bursts of highly charged activity interspersed with periods of apathy, inaction, and anger at the meager results achieved (Button 1978; Lipsky 1970; Piven 1976; Piven and Cloward 1977).

When protest occurs, friends and foes compete to offer explanations for what the protestors want. That is the situation that antihunger groups and activists worked hard to exploit during the late 1960s. Most of the time no one in Washington pays close attention to the political demands that are voiced by poor people and their organizations; but for a short time during the late 1960s, poor people's demands posed problems for the Washington community that officials could not easily ignore. By the winter of 1967, long-established social, political, and economic relationships had come under severe strain in the rural South. People who had previously been kept from participating in the political system in conventional ways were suddenly engaged in a wide variety of unconventional political activity that threatened the implementation network through which food aid had been organized locally. By early 1967, Washington-based antihunger groups and activists were at work trying to convey some of the ferment and urgency expressed by southern community organizations.

Protest as a political tactic came to Washington with the Poor People's Campaign and then largely subsided from view. Besides its prominence in the short term, the use of protest had several important longer range effects. These included the institutionalization of the Senate Select Committee on Nutrition and Human Needs as a powerful congressional ally, and the mobilization of a congressional coalition to push for changes in existing food policy authority and operations. Thereafter, middle-class sympathizers and a small group of antipoverty lawyers continued to monitor implementation of food aid policy. In the period from 1969 to 1977, it proved hard to sustain the grass roots mobilization of poor people, although some political organizers worked hard to do so. Part of the reason for this falloff in local activity was a product of the antihunger forces' previous successes. Because many of the demands for action had been answered, more people were receiving food assistance benefits.

The characteristic activity of antihunger activists during the second period was *public interest advocacy* by small Washington-based public interest groups such as FRAC and the Children's Defense Fund. That has changed somewhat during the 1980s. Faced for the first time with a serious outside threat to the redistributive policy gains won in the 1970s, food aid supporters engaged in a wide variety of defensive activities. They looked for telling evidence about the effects of inflation and budget cutbacks on the benefits that low-income and needy people received from the food aid programs. Grass roots activity revived in the form of food banks and soup kitchens. A new generation of local organizations concerned about hunger, malnutrition, poverty, and homelessness formed and Washington-based public interest organizations linked up again with community organizations.

Poor people may not have joined antihunger organizations during the 1980s recession, but they have kept pressure on the political system during most of the Reagan presidency as they had several times before (e.g., in the South in the late 1960s, during the recession in the mid–1970s, and after the food stamp reforms in 1977) by trying to get back onto the rolls of the food programs and by creating embarrassingly long lines at soup kitchens and food pantries. The most important characteristic of this period is the heightened meaning that the USDA programs have acquired as examples of *redistributive* policy. The collective results of millions of individuals seeking government benefits and of group (e.g., protest and movement activities) behavior by poor people should be evaluated as political participation. Such collective behavior matters for the political system, but not in the ways that political scientists have most often written about.

American government remains inhospitable to poor peoples' demands most of the time. Any account of the growth of food assistance spending in the last two decades, however, must take account of the impact of low-income and minority people on program operations. Recipients have regularly shaken the foundation of this ramshackle network of programs, pushed decisionmakers to vote for larger appropriations, and sent supporters and opponents back to the drawing board again and again to design program changes. Given the political stalemate that currently exists in Washington, it is likely that battles over redistributive policy will continue to be played out under the guise of deficit reduction during the administration that follows Ronald Reagan to office. Because of the inability of elected officials and government managers to keep the economy growing in which low-income people live, it is also likely that sharp spurts in food aid spending will again occur in the future.

Notes

CHAPTER 1

1. Congressional policy making provides the most authoritative base for new public initiatives, but policy directives can also be issued by the president and other executive branch officials in the form of executive orders, guidelines, etc. In the case of food aid—the distribution of surplus food, a food stamp program, the child nutrition programs, etc.—Congress waited until after executive branch initiatives had been in existence for several years before codifying them legislatively and funding them as regular governmental programs.

2. The literature on implementation, already extensive, is still growing. Useful treatments include Ingram (1977), Lipsky (1978), Pressman and Wildavsky (1984), and Van Horn (1979, 1985). A very complete bibliography can be found in Montjoy and O'Toole (1979) and O'Toole and Montjoy (1984).

3. Ripley and Franklin argue that since the president's attention must be spread over so many tasks, this official's influence is greatly diminished and Congress and the bureaucracy dominate policy implementation. They form "the core of the American national governmental policy process" (Ripley and Franklin 1980:5), a conclusion confirmed by the findings of this study. Others have been even more specific. Implementation decisions will usually be in the charge of a *dominant coalition* in the agency in question (Montjoy and O'Toole 1979).

4. Interest groups and the media serve as important conduits of information to congressional and executive branch officials. The term *subgovernment* has often been used to describe the symbiotic relationships that can grow up among three sets of political actors who have strong stakes in a given area of public policy—nongovernmental groups that benefit from bureaucratic activity, agency officials who want to protect their bureaucratic turf, and members of Congress seeking influence over a particular area of public policy.

5. Even when a "new" problem is discovered, as was the case with environmental protection in the late 1960s, Congress often grafts legislation onto older foundations of public policy. The same thing happened to domestic food

aid policy after concern was raised about hunger in the United States in 1967. The model of the policy process outlined earlier also needs adjusting to account for distinctions between old and new areas of public policy.

6. Henry Wallace and his aides had also made most of the important decisions about FSRC operations, as can be seen from one of the corporation's earliest actions, buying up and distributing surplus pork until the well-publicized USDA pig and sow slaughter campaign of 1934 (Leuchtenburg 1963:73; Rasmussen and Baker 1972:26). Wallace recalled later that the FSRC had been set up as a byproduct of the pig slaughter episode (Columbia University, Wallace Oral History, 2:399).

7. The best overview of the New Deal's philosophy of diverting surplus agricultural commodities to use by the needy can be found in a report that one of its designers, USDA economist F. V. Waugh, later wrote for the National Planning Association in which he describes the USDA's New Deal activities as unplanned responses reached as a result of trial and error (Waugh 1962).

8. The basic outline for the food stamp program can be seen in articles and reports written by Waugh and his colleagues (Gold, Hoffman, and Waugh 1940; Waugh 1961, 1962). The importance of agricultural economists and other social scientists employed by the USDA during the Roosevelt administration can be seen in several accounts of the department's growth and bureaucratic development (Baker 1963; Baldwin 1968; Christenson 1959; Cochrane 1979; Fite 1980; Hadwiger 1982; Hadwiger and Talbot 1965; Kirkendall 1982; Matusow 1967; Peterson 1977; and Rasmussen and Baker 1972).

9. The "no-cash" problem came about "mostly in the south," where relief payments were so low that people were just given blue stamps (Gold, Hoffman, and Waugh 1940:12).

10. Later, the USDA's Waugh summed up the results of food purchases made under the Depression-era food stamp program. It helped most, he noted, to stimulate demand for perishable foods that were not getting government support. "[T]hey are foods with a real future in the domestic market. In the long run, we clearly need to shift from some of the so-called 'basic crops' to animal products and related foods that will be needed in the diets of domestic consumers. A good national food stamp program would help this shift" (Waugh 1961:11).

11. Benedict (1955:290) has estimated the total cost of the New Deal food stamp program at $285.8 million for the years it operated, 1939–1943. Secretary Wallace later said that he would have liked to see a worldwide food stamp program set up in the postwar period under the auspices of the U.N.'s Food and Agriculture Organization (FAO) (Columbia University, Wallace Oral History, 6:4902).

CHAPTER 2

1. At odds with the White House and most fellow Republicans on this issue, Aiken had to defend his proposal against attack from the right. His defense was to liken it to other politically popular subsidies, including those to agricultural producers. Aiken and other farm spokespeople had to be concerned about how long the majority nonrural sector would pay for agriculture's idled

productive capacity. At the same time, Aiken's was not just a humanitarian argument; he appealed to the combination of shrewd self-interest and altruism that coexisted in rural America. Vermont farmers were dissatisfied with the high cost of government payments to agricultural producers that showed up in the prices they were charged when they bought feed for their dairy herds.

2. Sullivan recalled that she first became interested in reviving the Depression-era food stamp program after observing the effects of the recession on low-income people in her St. Louis district in 1954. She had become indignant at the existence of hunger in a time of agricultural surplus. Food assistance would benefit farmers and consumers both. Why not combine food stamps with public assistance payments, she reasoned (House Agriculture Committee 1958:40).

3. For the first few years after he took his seat in the Senate, Kennedy had paid little attention to agricultural issues. When he had to vote on farm issues, he relied on Clinton Anderson (D-N.Mex.), former Secretary of Agriculture, for his orientation to these issues (Kennedy Presidential Library, Willard Cochrane Oral History, 1).

4. In a speech, "The Dairy Farmer—the Challenge Ahead," prepared for delivery November 15–19, 1959, Kennedy poked fun at the suddenness of his conversion to farm issues. He acknowledged a similarity between himself and former Civil War general Winfield Scott. The first presidential hopeful to tour the United States hoping to influence his party's nominating convention, Scott would invariably say that he was traveling around the country looking for sites for military hospitals. "I have not come to seek votes," Kennedy quoted Scott as saying, "I have come on a mission of great public charity" (Kennedy Presidential Library, Pre-Presidential Papers).

5. The other major candidate for Secretary of Agriculture was a second midwestern liberal, Representative George S. McGovern. Kennedy and his advisers ended up dividing responsibility for agriculture-related matters in the new administration into two parts. McGovern assumed leadership of a reorganized and expanded position heading up the distribution of surplus agricultural products abroad under the auspices of the Food-for-Peace program (Kennedy Presidential Library, Feldman Oral History, 324–27).

6. In an attachment to the Cochrane memo, "Background Statement on the Food Distribution Program," committee staffer Faith Clark described how they expected the subsidy to work:

The Task Force's Report states that the proposed food stamp plan is intended to provide participants the purchasing power to obtain a "nutritious economy diet." This is estimated to cost "about $5" a person a week. For those families with no income, the subsidy would be the full amount, i.e., about $5; others would receive less depending upon their incomes. The average subsidy is estimated to be $2 per person per week. (National Archives, Farm Program 6–1)

7. The Waugh committee had access to the scholarly studies of shopping patterns from which the $5 figure was derived. Its members also reviewed studies that home economists had done on what constitutes a nutritionally adequate food budget. That figure represented a geographic average for national shopping patterns with a built-in correction for low-income families. It

also assumed clever shopping, all meals prepared at home, a minimum of plate waste, and the purchase of only a few food accessories like coffee and tea.

8. Administration officials kept Leonore Sullivan informed in a general way about food stamp program planning, but did not consult her about how the program would operate. A letter she wrote to Freeman on February 16, 1961, shows that she believed that the department was proceeding under the authority contained in the legislation she had sponsored in 1959, not through a new interpretation of Section 32 authority (National Archives, Farm Program 6–1–1). Freeman's letter to Mississippi Governor Ross Barnett on February 14, 1961, is representative of the information the secretary was sending to all governors about the actions taken under Kennedy's first executive order (National Archives, Farm Program 6–1).

9. According to departmental records, the first food stamp projects opened on May 29, 1961, in West Virginia. By mid-June, Assistant Secretary John P. Duncan, Jr., reported in a memo to Tom Hughes in the secretary's office that six of the eight sites were in operation (National Archives, Farm Program 6–1).

10. With that money, Agriculture proposed to double its case load and add twenty-three counties and one city. Freeman's office carefully spread new sites over eighteen states for maximum political benefit in Congress. Administration planners estimated that that would bring program participation to almost 365,000 people nationwide. Memo, John P. Duncan, Jr., to the Secretary of Agriculture, "Proposed Initial Expansion of the Food Stamp Program" on April 20, 1962 (National Archives, Farm Program 6–1–1).

CHAPTER 3

1. USDA officials could also make use of food stamp program decisions to win support for the administration with influential representatives in Congress. A July 9, 1962, memo to Lawrence O'Brien, Kennedy's congressional liaison chief, from Ken Birkhead, O'Brien's counterpart at the Department of Agriculture, shows how political considerations influenced food stamp program site selection. USDA officials wanted to include St. Louis, Missouri, in the next round of food stamp program expansion because it was represented by Leonore Sullivan in the House even though it was not among the areas that most needed economic development funding (National Archives, Food Stamp Program).

2. The school lunch program operated as a grant-in-aid program to the states. For its part, the Department of Agriculture entered into contracts with a state agency agreeing to pay a portion of the food costs that that agency incurred, donated surplus foods, and purchased other food specifically for the program. The federal share came to about 22 percent of the total cost of the school lunch program in 1962 and rose to 25 percent in 1965 (U.S. Department of Agriculture 1963).

3. In a memo written on April 23, 1963, the AMS' S. R. Smith reminded Freeman aide Tom Hughes of topics that Whitten might bring up at an upcoming meeting with Freeman. AMS officials provided similar background information on food programs and commodity purchases in Louisiana in ad-

vance of Freeman's visit with Allen Ellender (D-La.), chairman of the Senate Committee on Agriculture and Forestry, so that the secretary could remind the chairman of help the department had given Ellender on commodity issues (National Archives, Farm Program 6).

4. Sometimes he portrayed a commodity decision that he was going to make anyway as a favor to an influential senator or representative, and in return asked for help for the department on another matter concerning agriculture. What he usually needed from them was help on a committee vote or a promise of nonobstructionism on some issue they did not care much about. He also used decisions about where to locate new food stamp project sites as bargaining chips to build support among urban representatives in Congress for the administration's position on other farm-related issues. Officials in AMS (or the Consumer and Marketing Service as the agency came to be called) helped out by keeping an elaborate box score of favors that department officials did for members of Congress and Democratic governors.

5. Here is how Cochrane described the dilemma in his June 7, 1963 memo:

There is a basic conflict between varying purchases from year to year to stabilize prices and incomes to producers, and the use of Section 32 funds to provide the relatively constant food needs of schools, institutions, and needy persons. Thus, we need to spell out our objectives more clearly in the use of Section 32 funds. (National Archives, Farm Program 6, p. 2)

6. Under pressure from White House officials to take remedial action, Freeman prodded AMS officials to set up a surplus distribution delivery system in these two counties jointly with state officials. Freeman skirted around the politics of the situation in a March 29, 1961, letter to Representative William F. Ryan (D-N.Y.). "While the decision (by county officials) not to expand the program (in Le Flore County) and the establishment of headquarters for voter registration activities in the county were made at the same time, we have no evidence that the action of local officials was predicated on anything other than the lack of tax funds" (National Archives, Farm Program 8–1).

7. Many of the food aid programs that used surplus agricultural commodities in the deep South operated on a seasonal basis. County officials withdrew from the program in the spring of each year, when tenants and sharecroppers returned to work in the fields, even though they could have used a government food subsidy year-round. Then when the crops had been harvested, counties signed up again in order to receive federal aid during the winter months. For many poor people, food aid was the only type of welfare or relief program available (Maney 1988).

8. Conrad (1965), Baldwin (1968), and others have written about the effects of New Deal programs on poverty in the rural South. Looking at the Farm Security Administration (FSA), Baldwin stressed the intergovernmental dimensions of its programs. "Paradoxically, the FSA was dismissed by its critics at the national policy level as economically irrelevant, while locally it was condemned as a threat to the economic status quo" (Baldwin, 1968: 263).

9. Lampman suggested that an accounting be made of the tendency for people in these groups to move in and out of poverty. In delineating groups that were likely to be particularly affected, Lampman noted that poverty was

more prevalent in the South and in smaller communities. Although his comments indicate that he was familiar with the notion of a self-perpetuating *culture of poverty*, his emphasis on movement between the worlds of the poor and the nonpoor shows that he considered that poverty was solvable as a public issue. In keeping with the Kennedy administration's rhetorical emphasis on the importance of governmental officials taking action on important public issues, he argued that an antipoverty effort was a matter of the society, through its political institutions, committing itself to tackle a difficult but not impossible task. See his memo to Heller on June 10, 1963 (Johnson Presidential Library, OEO Legislative Background, 3).

10. Gilbert Fite has noted that liberals had been lukewarm about the original proposal for different reasons. By and large, they did not believe that many small farmers could continue to survive in the modern agricultural economy (1980:222).

11. Freeman addressed the golf course issue in his June 30, 1964, *Weekly Report* to White House officials. See also a *Des Moines Register* article attached to the memo (Freeman Papers).

CHAPTER 4

1. Part of the congressional and interest group support for the school lunch program had come because of information that USDA officials publicized during World War II about childhood nutrition and health. Congressional supporters—liberals and conservatives alike—have often cited studies attributing health and educational problems among young men called up to be drafted into the armed services to childhood dietary deficiencies experienced during the Depression years. For example, testimony by local government officials before a hearing of the House Committee on Education and Labor held on March 18, 1966, hailed the program's "national security" component (p. 45).

2. The administration's bill that year was an amalgam of legislation introduced by John Brademas (D-Ind.), a member of the House Education Subcommittee, and Chairman Bailey. O'Hara also had drafted a new version of the bill he had authored in 1960 (House General Subcommittee on Education 1961). In addition, similar bills had been introduced in the Senate as well (Senate Subcommittee on Agricultural Research and General Legislation 1962).

3. After a similar discussion about funding food programs a few years later, a weary White House official summed up the problem this way in a background paper used by the administration during the 1968 controversy over hunger and malnutrition. "In the Congress, obtaining the authority for a program is only half the battle. The other half is getting the money appropriated. The Child Nutrition program is a classic case" ("Child Feeding Programs," Johnson Presidential Library, Files of DeVier Pierson).

4. Freeman's basic pitch to farm state interests can be seen in this quote:

Increases in markets for these foods will help to relieve the general problem of overcapacity in agriculture. Particularly, increased markets for animal products would use more feed grains and, thus, a food stamp program could make an important contribution to the total effort to bring our feed grain supplies into balance with demand. (House Agriculture Committee 1964)

5. To enforce this provision, USDA officials would have been obliged to strike any retailers from program participation who discriminated against minority customers. Administration officials should have been ready for the attempt to rouse southern Democrats on civil rights issues, because this tactic also was being tried on other domestic policy initiatives before Congress in 1963 and 1964. Since major civil rights legislation also was under consideration in Congress at the same time, these issues were extremely touchy subjects, which Secretary Freeman preferred not to address directly or deal with unilaterally (Senate Committee on Agriculture and Forestry 1964).

6. Freeman had been particularly concerned about removing the amendment authored by Representative Al Quie (R-Minn.) that had called for a 20 percent financial contribution by the states. In an April 21, 1984, memo to Larry O'Brien, Freeman warned White House officials that he opposed it because it could "effectively kill the program in the areas where it is needed the most—e.g., Mississippi, West Virginia, etc." (Johnson Presidential Library, White House Central Files (WHCF), EX/LE/BE 5–5/AG7).

7. The substance of these issues of program design masked a more important concern—which political actors got to define the terms of the program. Ostensibly, the sequence ought to have been an original determination by Congress; then, any subsequent clarifications should have been the responsibility of the Secretary of Agriculture. Instead, many interpretations were made by operating officials at AMS. They only came to the attention of Freeman and others in his office when problems attracted a broader audience than just the state and local government officials, producer groups, and commercial interests who usually paid attention to food stamp program administration. For an idea about how large a role AMS administrators had, see Berry (1984).

8. After a trial run in 1964, White House officials used task forces to put together the administration's legislative program. Freeman usually was included in the deliberations whenever farm and food issues were involved, unlike some other cabinet members who were intentionally excluded from policy development via the task force process. Besides Joseph Califano, the president's chief policy adviser, and his aides, presidential counsel Harry McPherson and senior staffers such as Bill Moyers participated in decision making on child nutrition issues during 1965.

9. Here is an excerpt from that task force report:

In other words, the National School Lunch Act, as now constituted does not lend itself to the future approach under which the schools will become real educational centers, open many hours of the day year-round. An important attraction for low-income children particularly—as demonstrated in Head Start this summer—is a nutritionally adequate meal. (Johnson Presidential Library, WHCF, EX FG 600/Task Forces, 1)

10. Since the school programs were under his department's jurisdiction, Secretary Freeman had to explain and defend the administration's decision on Capitol Hill. He stayed away from the first scheduled hearing held by the House Subcommittee on Dairy and Poultry in early May 1966 while the administration regrouped. He sent a fairly low-level USDA administrator from the

Consumer and Marketing Service instead, who tried in vain to deflect congressional wrath.

11. This language also can be construed as an oblique attack on the Office of Economic Opportunity's Head Start program (Senate Committee on Agriculture and Forestry 1966a). Conservatives on the congressional agriculture committees wanted to safeguard the authority of the USDA over these programs from raids by other federal agencies such as HEW or OEO. The matter was put quite succinctly by the Agriculture Committee leadership in its report to the full House. "The administration of these food assistance programs is an important part of the Department of Agriculture's total responsibility to farmers and consumers" (Senate Committee on Agriculture and Forestry 1966a:8).

12. After one of his first talks with Johnson about the USDA's legislative program, Freeman noted in a memo for his files on January 13, 1964, that Johnson seemed "uncertain" about agricultural legislation and about agriculture in general (Freeman Papers). The secretary was uneasy about how much the new president would rely on old congressional allies and fellow southerners like Senator Richard Russell (D-Ga.) and Representative W. R. Poage (D-Tex.) for advice about agricultural issues.

13. That may have accounted for his willingness to let Mrs. Sullivan take public credit for the administration's food stamp successes in Congress. Several years later during another food stamp legislative controversy, he reminded President Johnson about what he called his "cold turkey" deal with Sullivan in 1964, that is, urban votes on the cotton/wheat bill in exchange for rural votes for food stamps. He would try to make the same deal with her in 1968, he told the president, in order to get the next farm bill approved in Congress. For years, farm bills had passed the House under a process of intercommodity log-rolling. Supporters of different food producing groups represented on the House Agriculture Committee got favorable provisions written into farm legislation in committee and then agreed to support each other's bills on the House floor. See also House Agriculture Committee 1964.

14. A key problem was opposition to the administration's programs from two of the most powerful southern conservatives, Senator Holland and Representative Whitten. Both had shown themselves implacable in their opposition to the administration's modest efforts to reorient spending to help the poor. Not to put too fine a point on it, Freeman noted, in the same October 24 memo, Whitten opposed Section 11 funding because many of the poor children that it would help were black.

CHAPTER 5

1. In the early 1960s, local activists and northern volunteers, supported by churches and other private groups, began to develop new community institutions parallel to the schools and other segregated community institutions in the delta region. Among the most famous of these were the local "Freedom Schools" located in Mississippi cotton belt counties like Le Flore and Panola, where much of the state's black population was concentrated. Besides the usual school subjects, they stressed self-help, literacy training, political organizing, and social action. Children received meals, health exams, and a start on ed-

ucation. Parents and other adults in the communities served were encouraged to participate, advise, and hold paraprofessional jobs (Belfrage 1965; Greenberg 1969; Watters 1971; Watters and Cleghorn 1967).

2. Increasing use of mechanization was changing the face of cotton production in the rural South and making the complex equation of balancing employment needs and the costs of welfare programs more difficult for county officials to calculate. By the mid–1960s, changing workforce needs were prompting officials in some delta counties to question whether they should continue to bear the administrative costs associated with running the family distribution program. Two cost-cutting possibilities were tried out. Some local officials pressured USDA officials to take over the state and local share of the distribution program's administrative costs. Others sought to shift over to the new food stamp program because it operated through normal retail channels and offered local officials the benefits of expanding the food programs without paying for them. Fite quoted a black farmer from Alabama who noted that white landowners got especially interested in mechanization after the passage of the Civil Rights Act of 1964 (Fite 1984: 219–23).

3. NSA's first communication with USDA officials came in connection with a project mounted in the fall of 1964. College students throughout the nation were asked to donate food to minority communities in the South. Scheduled over the Thanksgiving holiday, this campaign was intended to be a dramatic reminder of the extent of poverty in the United States despite the nation's general affluence.

4. Zippert's letters demonstrate the extent to which regional and locally based USDA officials supported the racial and economic status quo in the deep South. Zippert charged that local officials regularly discriminated against blacks in elections to govern the county's ASCS program. Also, USDA offices in that part of Louisiana maintained segregated facilities, according to Zippert, until his complaints to department officials in Washington ended these illegal practices. Letter to Freeman aide William Seabron on November 1, 1965 (National Archives, Food Stamp Program). Like the correspondence between NSA officials and staffers in Freeman's office, Zippert's letters provided USDA administrators with an independent channel of information about what was going on in the field, which helped officials on the secretary's staff measure the accuracy of the reports they regularly received from CMS officials.

5. In an April 26, 1965, memo to Assistant Secretary George Mehren the CMS' Roy Lennartson revealed some of the political considerations that USDA officials routinely took into account. He was, he said, looking for food stamp sites that would give Freeman good publicity (National Archives, Food Stamp Program). An example of how designation of a food stamp site could help the administration's friends in Congress can be seen in Ken Birkhead's February 10, 1966, letter to Paul E. Goodling in which USDA officials promised to help arrange for Senator Claiborne Pell (D-R.I.) to receive public credit for a new food stamp site in Providence to help his reelection effort (National Archives, Food Stamp Program).

6. The NSA position paper noted that Tom Hughes had suggested a mutually beneficial arrangement: "If we can use you to use us to make those

counties join the Department's program, what could be better?" (National Archives, Farm Program 8–1 Domestic).

7. The experiences of the new OEO preschool programs operating in Mississippi could have shown USDA officials how grass roots groups use federal programs in community organizing and movement-building. During 1965 and 1966, some of the same civil rights and antipoverty groups that were active on food aid issues were also working hard to support a multiracial, grass roots organization, the Child Development Group of Mississippi (CDGM), which had won OEO backing to operate a network of local Head Start programs across Mississippi.

8. Almost as soon as the OEO's Head Start programs got under way in Mississippi, they drew strong criticism from the state's white political establishment led by Senator John Stennis (D-Miss.). This controversy was settled in OEO's favor, but only after civil rights groups got White House officials to intervene. CDGM officials and their allies professed not to be surprised that state and local politicians felt challenged by this experiment in political empowerment. For their part, OEO officials did not relish another protracted conflict with powerful southerners in Congress, but felt that if they could stand up to such attacks USDA officials should be more critical of the local political establishment (CDGM Files).

9. Much of the philosophy and operating style of the OEO-funded programs of the Child Development Group of Mississippi came from the earlier Freedom Schools and other self-help projects that had been associated with the southern civil rights movement. CDGM's organizers included several well-known black professional people with roots in Mississippi's civil rights movement, including Dr. A. D. Beittel, a former president of Tougaloo College, Marian Wright, an attorney with the NAACP Legal Defense Fund in Jackson, and Rev. James McCree, a minister and civil rights activist in Canton. Black universities, groups like the National Council of Churches, and individual religious denominations provided technical and administrative services and set up political liaison efforts with decisionmakers in Washington, D.C. (CDGM Files).

10. Freeman's comments were written in the margins of his copy of the November 27, 1966, article, "Negroes Leaving Farms in South," which was attached to a memo from Lee M. Day to the Undersecretary dated February 16, 1987 (National Archives, Food Stamp Program). Birkhead's and Cochran's responses are also included as attachments to Day's memo.

CHAPTER 6

1. The *New York Times* reported on the two-day meeting of the Mississippi Advisory Committee to the U.S. Civil Rights Commission in a story by Walter Rugaber, "Food Plan Hurts Mississippi Negro," on February 19, 1967. USDA officials saw this and a transcript of the group's proceedings (National Archives, Food Stamp Program).

2. CCAP had been founded soon after the Economic Opportunity Act of 1964 had been enacted and was intended as an umbrella organization for groups interested in supporting a comprehensive attack against poverty's causes. It was the idea of United Auto Workers President Walter P. Reuther,

and got the largest part of its funding from that union and its close ally, the Industrial Union Division of the AFL-CIO.

3. The rural affairs group also considered recommending the transfer of the USDA's food aid programs to the federal department of Health, Education and Welfare, but came to no formal position on that issue. Freeman and other farm state liberals who wanted the food programs to remain under agriculture's jurisdiction correctly perceived that this was a subtle threat that food aid advocates and their allies could keep in reserve indefinitely or activate on short notice.

4. While members of CCAP's rural affairs group were working out a common approach to the food aid crisis in Mississippi, many of its members continued to be involved on parallel fronts in the same policy area as individuals or through their affiliations with other organizations. For example, Henry McCanna corresponded with Secretary Freeman about conditions in Mississippi in 1967 wearing his United Church of Christ and Delta Ministry hats. He also sent along an advance copy of the testimony that he planned to deliver about the operation of USDA food programs before the House Agriculture Committee.

5. In his oral history for the Kennedy presidential library, Edelman emphasized the effect of Kennedy's experiences in Mississippi in 1967. According to Edelman, Robert Kennedy's developing concerns about food aid and anti-poverty programs in the rural South became a crucial way station in the senator's growing estrangement with his political past, symbolized by Johnson, Shriver, and Freeman. From this middle ground, he developed an increasingly outspoken affiliation with the grass roots groups that he later embraced during his 1968 presidential campaign (Kennedy Presidential Library, 5:108).

6. Edelman reserved principal credit for discovering the problem of hunger in America for the civil rights movement and the grass roots groups that it spawned, especially what he termed the "poverty infrastructure," which included groups like CDGM and experienced political strategists like Wright. These were people who "had political sophistication, who knew how to yell all the way to Washington, when they had a problem, and who also were the kind of people that liberal Democrats would want to show off as exemplary of the success of the poverty program when they were starting a road show, to try to develop national support for the poverty program" (Kennedy Prsidential Library, Edelman Oral History, 8:13–4).

7. White House officials assumed an extremely low public profile during this period on matters concerning food aid policy although Freeman briefed Johnson and his aides privately. All public comments came from the USDA, not the White House. The tone was set at the outset when White House aides went to almost comical lengths to avoid responsibility for acknowledging the Clark subcommittee's letter. Kennedy and Clark walked a fine line in public before the hearings resumed, withholding further criticism of the Secretary of Agriculture, but continuing to pressure their colleague, Orville Freeman, in private.

8. The first indication that Freeman had accepted Leonard's recommendations can be seen in a handwritten note dated March 28, 1967, from Leonard to Undersecretary John Schnittker (National Archives, Food Stamp Program).

9. He had already taken precautions aimed at defusing criticism from that quarter by verifying the subcommittee's charges about conditions in the delta. After the senators had returned, he dispatched two departmental investigators to Mississippi with instructions to retrace the senators' steps and reinterview people who had testified at the hearings. One of the travelers, Freeman's aide Bill Seabron, came back to Washington after this trip deeply affected by what he had seen there.

10. Besides the fifty cents issue, Leonard spent considerable time and effort during the spring of 1967 backtracking the department's position on the "emergency" issue. A memo from Leonard to Freeman on May 3, 1967, shows the ticklish political situation in which USDA officials found themselves (Agricultural History Branch, Freeman files).

11. Besides press reports of the doctors' findings, most of the participants at the July hearings had also read a strongly worded article in the *New York Times* Sunday magazine that followed up on the earlier findings of hunger and malnutrition in the Mississippi delta (Sherrill 1967).

12. This litany of medical problems attendant upon malnutrition in childhood was devastating, as this excerpt shows.

Let me now summarize what we have seen: Evidence of vitamin and mineral deficiencies; serious untreated skin infections and ulcerations; eye and ear diseases; unattended bone diseases; secondary to poor food intake; prevalence of bacteria and parasitic disease; the chronic anemias we have discussed; diseases of the heart and lungs requiring surgery which have gone untreated; epilary and neurotic disorders receiving no care; kidney ailments that in other children would warrant immediate hospitalization.

Finally, in boys and girls in every county we visited, evidence of severe malnutrition with injuries to the body tissues, muscles, bones, and skin. Diarrheas, sores, untreated ligament and arm injuries and deformities have again been brought to your attention. (Senate Subcommittee on Employment, Manpower, and Poverty 1967, 11)

13. Soon after the hearings ended, antihunger advocates won a small, but highly symbolic, victory. Stung by congressional and media criticism of how officials in his state had responded to reports of increased poverty in Mississippi, Senator Stennis introduced legislation to provide money for emergency medical aid. Congressional food program supporters welcomed this gesture as a response by the state's political establishment to the issues that they had raised. They also saw it as a partial vindication of their strategy of dramatizing the effects of poverty and malnutrition on health and well-being. The Stennis bill appropriated money for the Office of Economic Opportunity, not the USDA, to use. That meant that members of the agricultural policy community in Washington were not ready to concede that malnutrition and poverty were Agriculture's problems. Still, a significant amount of this new money would be spent on food aid.

CHAPTER 7

1. In a June 12, 1967, memo to Walter Reuther, CCAP's Richard Boone outlined the purpose, membership, and procedures of this new body. Funds

would be sought from church groups, foundations, and private organizations. Modeled after CCAP's earlier work in support of community-based preschool programs in Mississippi, the group's membership would come from sympathetic private citizens in the business, church, and academic communities, as well as several subject matter specialties, such as medicine and nutrition. After some minor changes, this plan was approved and Reuther publicly announced the formation of a Citizen's Board of Inquiry into Hunger and Malnutrition (CCAP Files).

2. A February 1, 1968, memo that Freeman wrote to Joseph Califano illustrates the secretary's increasingly peevish mood and summarizes what he expected to happen when the food aid issue was again at the center of public attention.

I expect we will be hit by the Kennedy-Clark subcommittee of the Senate Committee on Food [*Sic*] before long. Nick Kotz of the Cowles Press is making a major muck-raking enterprise out of picking at our programs in any way he can, mostly by painting very pathetic word pictures of the people we are not yet reaching. We are, of course, thoroughly aware of this and are doing everything we can do to reach them. I am sure he will persist. We have also been in touch with the subcommittee staff. They will persist too. (Johnson Presidential Library, WHCF, EX AG7)

3. Here is how Walter Reuther summed up what food aid advocates wanted from the Secretary of Agriculture in a letter to Freeman on June 20, 1968, timed to coincide with the arrival of the deadline—June 30, 1968—that Freeman had imposed the summer before for the completion of Project 331. Reuther seems to be responding to Freeman's testy tone in their earlier correspondence. "I am well aware," the labor leader concluded, carefully meting out portions of blame and exculpation, "of the limits which you have felt were imposed upon you by members of various congressional committees. Nevertheless, I am convinced that determined and dedicated leadership can and must produce action now to achieve the needed measures I have outlined" (CCAP Files).

4. Besides having been a guiding force on CCAP's Rural Affairs Committee, Marian Wright has been credited with originating the idea of the Poor People's Campaign and suggesting it to Dr. Martin Luther King, Jr., as a project for the Southern Christian Leadership Conference. After Dr. King was assassinated in Memphis in April of 1968, planning for the campaign faltered. Then, a decision was made to go ahead; campaign officials believed that it would be a fitting memorial to King's involvement in poverty, peace, and justice work. For one account of this planning, see Peter Edelman's comments in his oral history (Kennedy Presidential Library, 3:331–3).

5. Freeman had asked Rod Leonard to investigate the possibility of abolishing the fifty cents food stamp purchase requirement altogether for certain low-income groups. This initiative presents another example of how flexible and undogmatic the secretary could be in private, even while he was holding the line publicly against much less radical changes. The memo on October 25, 1967, from Freeman to Leonard, in which the secretary raised the subject also shows that he seriously questioned the commitment that lower level officials in the department had in solving problems of hunger and malnutrition. After

outlining the arguments on both sides of the purchase price issue, Leonard cautioned against such a change at that time (National Archives, Food Stamp Program).

6. Soon after Johnson's decision about his own political future was revealed, Vice President Hubert Humphrey of Minnesota, Senator Robert F. Kennedy of New York, and Senator Eugene McCarthy of Minnesota began to campaign actively for the Democratic party nomination. Orville Freeman served as a leader of the Humphrey campaign while serving out the remainder of his term as secretary. Others at Agriculture, like Schnittker, quickly became affiliated with other Democratic candidates.

7. The choices were constantly recombined and rearranged in the period from late April until the end of June. For example, DeVier Pierson's files show memos on this subject from Califano to the president on May 7, 22, 23, and 27 as well as June 12, 13, and 28 (Johnson Presidential Library).

8. They also wanted a public statement from the president committing the country to the goal of banishing hunger everywhere in the nation. The cost, they warned Johnson, was likely to be quite high. Even with what they considered to be a meager level of food assistance, the price tag for the current food aid budget was rapidly approaching the $1 billion mark. All the best evidence showed a need for more substantial food aid to reach about one half again as many people as the number that were being served under the existing programs. The White House working group also believed that the federal government should develop and phase in national eligibility standards for the family food programs, another change that promised to significantly increase program costs.

9. In a June 17, 1968, memo, White House aide DeVier Pierson sought unsuccessfully to convince the president not to repudiate Freeman's action or publicly rule out a food stamp authorization above the outdated $245 million figure.

I really believe you still want to take some additional action before the end of 1968—and would hate to see us appear to have been pulled kicking and screaming into a program. If we do get into this posture, it will be virtually the only program where Congress had seemed to be ahead of the Administration in social conscience. (Johnson Presidential Library, Files of DeVier Pierson)

10. On the occasion of the signing ceremony for the Sullivan bill's food stamp amendments, Califano tried but failed to persuade the president to voice a strong public commitment against hunger and malnutrition. As drafted by Califano's staff, the president's statement would have called for a "substantial increase in expenditures to meet the tragedy of hunger in America." This would have been done by explicitly linking America's agricultural abundance with food assistance. "The only question is whether [the nation] has the will to assure that no American is compelled to go hungry in this land of plenty." The proposed press release is attached to a memo from Jim Gaither to Joe Califano dated October 9, 1968 (Johnson Presidential Library, WHCF, EX BE 5–5 AG 7 # 35). Instead, the tone of Johnson's remarks was much more low key.

11. Congress also passed several small food aid initiatives that year. A nonschool program—lunches for preschool and day-care programs that had been deleted from the Child Nutrition Act when it passed in 1966—was finally enacted. Another bill, HR 17873, sponsored by Chairman Carl Perkins (D-Ky.) of the House Education and Labor Committee, authorized $100 million to be spent from Section 32 during the next three years in order to fund Section 11 of the school lunch program. This was considered by friends of this chronically underfunded program to be a major victory. And Congress authorized another new food assistance program, special commodity assistance for women, infants, and children, a forerunner of WIC.

CHAPTER 8

1. In the meantime, White House welfare reform planning was proceeding along another track. The result of these deliberations, the proposed Family Assistance Program, was unveiled in a presidential speech in August 1969. Immediately after that, food aid supporters caught administration spokespeople off guard and won assurances that the two programs would continue to operate separately.

2. Late in November of that year, telegrams addressed to the president and to USDA officials began arriving from all over the country. Among the senders were Jean Fairfax of the NAACP Legal Defense Fund; officials of the church and women's groups who had taken part in the national school lunch participation project; Marian Wright Edelman now with the Washington Research Project; Rod Leonard and others at the Children's Foundation; John Kramer, a lawyer and executive director of the National Council on Hunger and Malnutrition; Ron Pollack, one of the public interest lawyers litigating food policy issues for FRAC; and Richard Boone, formerly staff director of CCAP and now on the staff of the Robert F. Kennedy memorial organization (National Archives, Food Program 7—School Lunch Program).

3. In this communication, Lyng put the blame squarely on Mayer. The president's special nutrition consultant had, according to Lyng, gone beyond what Nixon intended the administration's commitment to hunger and poverty to be. Lyng reminded Secretary Hardin what Mayer had said about the price tag for the administration's antihunger effort, "it will cost what it will cost." Ironically for Lyng and Hardin, the department was spending two times what had been the case for the school lunch program when the Republican administration had come into office in 1969, but was getting scant public credit for doing so. Instead, the antihunger forces had created a "tremendous demand" for even more (National Archives Food Program—School Lunch Program). They also chafed at the attitude in Congress that if enough pressure was brought to bear the administration would back down as it had done before.

4. In the fall of 1971, even after the administration had secretly negotiated the terms of its surrender on this issue, letters continued to go out over Hardin's and Lyng's signatures in response to protests by state and local administrators, food service officials, members of Congress, and interested citizens. After Congress had settled the matter by passing House Joint Resolution 923, a USDA official, Philip Ollsson, summarized its effect in a November 30, 1971, letter

to Representative Page Belcher (R-Okla.) as "greatly expand[ing] the Federal contribution to the National School Lunch Program" (National Archives, Food Program 7—School Lunch Program). And at about the same time, food advocates signaled their next legislative objectives in this ongoing campaign over school lunch expansion efforts; the Senate Select Committee opened hearings to investigate the need for a universal school lunch program.

5. Another problem contributing to increases in program costs that year was Congress' mandate that the department continue commodity assistance to the child nutrition programs. As far back as the passage of the original School Lunch Act in 1946, the school food programs had received some financial help through the federal government's donation of surplus agricultural commodities to local education agencies. Now the surpluses were disappearing. Congress solved the problem temporarily by extending the Secretary of Agriculture's authority to purchase food for domestic food assistance programs at nonsurplus prices. The White House and the USDA's top leadership disapproved of that approach, however, and continued to press Congress to take what they felt was a more fiscally responsible approach (*Congressional Quarterly Almanac* 1973:550–52, 566–67; 1974:503–5).

6. According to testimony by Ronald Pollack of FRAC at hearings conducted by McGovern in June, 1974, food stamp recipients were worse off than most people thought. The first problem, in FRAC's view, was that many people who were eligible for food stamps had not joined the program, so it was still not reaching everyone in need. According to USDA figures, which Pollack claimed somewhat underestimated the extent of the problem, only about 35 percent of those who could qualify actually were being helped by the program (Senate Select Committee on Nutrition and Human Needs 1974b:821–7).

7. Originally, responsibility for the working group was assigned to the vice president, but in practice most of the staff work was done by Art Quern, an assistant to Domestic Council chief Jim Cannon.

8. In his public comments about the food stamp program, Governor Reagan had struck at the heart of the existing program by urging major changes in eligibility. "Are there," he asked rhetorically in a newspaper column written for publication in July 1975 and included in the files of the White House food stamp working group, "really that many poor and hungry people to feed? No, the problem lies with the liberal, loose eligibility standards for food stamps." See the memo from Jim Cavanaugh to Jack Veneman, July 7, 1975 (Ford Presidential Library, WHCF, WE 10–4). The Buckley–Michel bill incorporated much of that perspective. Its features included transfer of the food stamp program to HEW, strict limitations on the eligibility of students and strikers, a gross income test, and several changes in administrative procedures, such as photo identification cards and strong work requirements.

9. At one stage, Ford's Domestic Council staffers had taken a far more liberal position, balancing off tightened eligibility requirements by eliminating the purchase requirement and replacing the various itemized deductions currently in place with a standard deduction. Ford's advisers' long-term goal was to replace in-kind with cash benefits through a comprehensive welfare program. These recommendations represented a last attempt at welfare reform by officials like Jack Veneman, who had designed the Nixon administration's

original family assistance program proposal in 1969. The final version accepted by the president is outlined in a memo from Jim Cannon to Philip Buchen et al. on October 30, 1975 (Ford Presidential Library, Files of Art Quern).

CHAPTER 9

1. When Carter's welfare reform legislation, the Program for Better Jobs and Income (PBJI) finally appeared, it assumed (like the Nixon administration's Family Assistance Program also had done) that the food stamp program would eventually be cashed out. Carter administration officials had a welfare reform plan ready for Congress by late summer of 1977; but, like the Nixon plan before it, the Carter proposal never emerged from the Senate Finance Committee. Money, that is, the cost of the Carter PBJI proposal, was part of the problem. But even when the president submitted parts of his welfare plan separately to Congress, he still had little or no success to show for his efforts.

2. In the final compromise on the bill that became PL 95–627, Congress postponed making any major changes in funding and, in a show of strength by that program's supporters on Capitol Hill, awarded the WIC program entitlement status for two years. This came after the administration had objected to an earlier version that called for open-ended authorizations for WIC during the entire period that the bill was to be in effect (*Congress and the Nation* 5:691–92).

3. Under the administration's proposed changes, children from families just above the poverty line would be shifted from the free to the reduced-price category. That meant they would pay $1 a week for each child who had lunch in school. Those families between 175 and 195 percent of the poverty line would have to pay full price. The legislative maneuvering that greeted these proposals was extremely complicated.

4. The goal of food aid supporters was "more" in part because the alternative posed by program critics was always "less." In the process they had to defend programs that had developed separately as rational and necessary elements for an overall policy of improved nutrition. What supporters were really saying was that the special programmatic emphasis (e.g., WIC, child care food, etc.) that they had worked so hard to get Congress to approve might disappear if it were subsumed under block grant or more general legislation that left discretion about program activities to federal, state, or local officials.

5. In addition to the changes incorporated in OBRA, conservatives tightened requirements that food stamp recipients participate in "workfare" programs, made it more difficult for the families of strikers to qualify, won creation of a food assistance block grant for Puerto Rico in place of participation in the food stamp program, and placed more responsibility for reducing fraud and program costs on the shoulders of state administrators. Still, the main outlines of the food stamp program—uniform national eligibility standards with some variations for regional cost-of-living differences, no purchase requirement, and benefit levels determined by USDA estimates of the food needs of poor families—remained intact.

6. Groups that had supported food aid efforts in the past also became more active. Labor organizations, such as the Amalgamated Meat Cutters and

Butcher Workmen, and church groups, like Bread for the World and the group Interfaith Action for Economic Justice, are good examples.

7. These images proved even more telling when program supporters reminded members of Congress and the media that a steady diet of this kind of officially sanctioned junk food might have negative implications for national defense. After all, the school lunch program had originally been enacted in response to congressional concern about the health of young men examined for induction into the service during World War II (*Congressional Quarterly Almanac* 1981:498).

8. Dr. Jean Mayer, now president of Tufts University and a former food aid adviser to Richard Nixon, confirmed supporters' fears about how schools had reacted to the changes made in 1981. In congressional testimony delivered during March of 1983, he charged that school lunch program funds had been cut by 30 percent. That had translated into a reduction in participation by over 3 million children. Those who had been eligible for reduced-price meals and many who had been in the poorest category before had been hit the hardest.

I know there has been much talk of a safety net, but let me say that I do not see any evidence of it as regards many of the children's programs, and for that matter, we have a terminology whereby we speak about child nutrition programs, on the one hand, and food stamps, on the other. But I think it is important to remember that close to 50 percent of the food stamp recipients are children and that is the program that feeds the children day in and day out, and three meals a day (Senate Subcommittee on Rural Development, Oversight, and Investigations 1983:7).

9. But with each successive wave of food stamp reforms since the mid 1970s, the program had become increasingly complex. Many people who suffered economic reversals in the early 1980s could not qualify for food stamp benefits because Congress had changed to a system of calculating income based on past, not present, income levels. Others, especially middle-class families with assets higher than the program's limitations allowed, would be ineligible for program benefits even though the family breadwinners had lost their jobs.

10. Not surprisingly, state officials felt ill-used by the increasing requirements placed on them. First, they had been told to act as quickly as possible. Then, they were being blamed for taking quick action. In Wisconsin, for example, state agriculture department officials worked out an ad hoc distribution system for the new food donation program. In the process, they had to pull state workers away from their regular jobs and state government had to absorb all handling, storage, and transportation costs (Senate Subcommittee on Nutrition 1983a:37–40). They wanted a clear cut policy and a single set of rules to live by. Many preferred congressional action, which would give stability and predictability to program operations, to the ups and downs that they encountered when administrative discretion rested with White House and USDA officials.

11. Low-income Americans who qualified for safety net protections had suffered, Greenstein charged, because the OBRA cuts had included:

delaying and reducing annual cost-of-living food adjustments, cutting benefits for the working poor, reducing standard utility allowances, freezing deductions despite rising heating costs, reducing benefits through changes in rounding rules, etc. While some of these provisions did not, individually, have that large an impact on needy households, the cumulative effect of these numerous budget reduction changes has been significant and is clearly now being felt.(Senate Subcommittee on Nutrition 1983b:216–17)

See also Hoagland 1984; House Select Committee on Hunger 1984a, 1984b; Lelyveld 1985; U.S. Congressional Research Service 1986b; and U.S. General Accounting Office 1983.

12. Representative Panetta laid out the position taken by the administration's strongest critics. The report was not so bad as it might have been, he said, had White House officials not become embarrassed by the public furor that arose over Meese's remarks and made some last minute changes. Representative Carl Perkins (D-Ky.), chairman of the Subcommittee on Elementary, Secondary and Vocational Education, said that he read the task force report as a tacit admission that there would be no further changes or budget cuts in the food aid programs. Finally, Senator Dole expressed his reservations about administration policy. There were several useful suggestions in the report, Dole noted diplomatically; but he was not in favor of the food assistance block grant idea that was at the heart of its recommendations (House Subcommittee on Domestic Marketing, Consumer Relations, and Nutrition 1984:15–21).

13. Hunger and homelessness: House Select Committee on Hunger (1984a, 1984b, 1985, 1986); the Physicians' Task Force on Hunger in America (1985a, 1985b); U.S. Congressional Research Service (1986a, 1986b); and U.S. General Accounting Office (1985).

CHAPTER 10

1. The spokespersons for the Democrats today are more apt to be from Neal Smith's (Iowa) midwest and Tom Foley's (Wash.) northwest than the party's traditional area of rural strength in districts like those Representative Jamie Whitten represents in the old South. Even some urban and suburban Democratic legislators have acquired considerable clout on the food and agriculture committees of Congress.

2. Much of the recent literature on public interest organizations has focused on ones acting on behalf of middle-class populations (e.g., the Nader organizations, the environmental movement, and good government groups like Common Cause). Jeffrey Berry, however, included Washington-based organizations working for low-income people in his study of groups *Lobbying for the People* (1977).

3. In the case of food assistance policy, the delivery of benefits to low-income groups was mediated by local Democratic party organizations and supported by liberal and labor allies of the New Deal coalition. Some of this has striking parallels in rural America to what has been written about the New Deal's urban growth coalition (Mollenkopf 1983). This research also has implications for the growing debate about theories of the state (Benjamin and Duval 1985; Nordlinger 1981) in general and the relationship of low-income claimants to bureaucracies in particular (Skowronek 1982).

References

Agricultural History Branch Files. See U.S. Department of Agriculture.

Anderson, Martin. 1978. *Welfare: The political economy of welfare reform in the U.S.* Stanford: Stanford University Press.

Bachrach, Peter and Morton S. Baratz. 1962. Two faces of power. *American Political Science Review* 56:947–52.

Baker, Gladys et al. See U.S. Department of Agriculture. Agricultural History Branch.

Baldwin, Sidney. 1968. *Poverty and politics: The rise and decline of the Farm Security Administration.* Chapel Hill: University of North Carolina Press.

Barrett, Lawrence I. 1983. *Gambling with history: Reagan in the White House.* Garden City, N.Y.: Doubleday.

Barton, Weldon. 1976. Coalition-building in the United States House of Representatives: Agricultural legislation in 1973. In *Cases in public policy-making*, ed. James E. Anderson, 141–61. New York: Praeger.

Bawden, D. Lee, ed. 1984. *The social contract revisited: Aims and outcomes of President Reagan's social welfare policy.* Washington, D.C.: The Urban Institute Press.

Beam, David R. 1984. New federalism, old realities: The Reagan administration and intergovernmental reform. In *The Reagan presidency and the governing of America*, ed. Lester M. Salamon and Michael S. Lund, 415–42. Washington, D.C.: The Urban Institute Press.

Belfrage, Sally. 1965. *Freedom summer.* New York: Viking.

Benedict, Murray R. 1955. *Can we solve the farm program? An analysis of federal aid to agriculture.* New York: The Twentieth Century Fund.

———. 1966. *Farm policies of the U.S., 1790–1950.* New York: Octagon Books.

Benjamin, Roger and Raymond Duval. 1985. The capitalist state in context. In *The democratic state*, ed. Roger Benjamin and Stephen Elkin, 19–58. Lawrence: The University Press of Kansas.

Berman, Paul. 1978. The study of macro- and micro-implementation. *Public Policy* 26:157–84.

Berry, Jeffrey. 1984. *Feeding hungry people: Rulemaking in the food stamp program.* New Brunswick, N.J.: Rutgers University Press.

———. 1977. *Lobbying for the people.* Princeton: Princeton University Press.

Browning, Robert X. 1986. *Politics and social welfare policy in the U.S.* Knoxville: University of Tennessee Press.

Burke, Vincent J. and Vee Burke. 1974. *Nixon's good deed.* New York: Columbia University Press.

Button, James. 1978. *Black violence: The political impact of the 1960s riots.* Princeton: Princeton University Press.

Carson, Rachel. 1962. *Silent spring.* Boston: Houghton Mifflin.

Caudill, Harry. 1963. *Night comes to the Cumberland.* Boston: Little Brown.

Charles, Searle F. 1963. *Minister of relief: Harry Hopkins and the depression.* Syracuse: Syracuse University Press.

Christenson, Reo M. 1959. *The Brannan plan. Farm politics and policy.* Ann Arbor: University of Michigan Press.

Citizens Board of Inquiry into Poverty and Malnutrition in America. 1968. *Hunger U.S.A.* Boston: Beacon.

Citizens Crusade Against Poverty. Papers. Walter Reuther Archives. Archives of Urban and Labor History. Wayne State University. Detroit, Mich.

Cobb, Roger and Charles Elder. 1972. *Participation in American politics.* Boston: Allyn and Bacon.

Cochrane, Willard W. 1965. *The city man's guide to the farm program.* Minneapolis: University of Minnesota Press.

———. 1979. *The development of American agriculture: A historical analysis.* Minneapolis: University of Minnesota Press.

Columbia University Oral History Collection. New York.

Committee for Economic Development. 1962. *An adaptive program for agriculture.* New York.

Committee on School Lunch Participation. n.d. *Their daily bread.* New York.

Congress and the Nation. Washington, D.C.: Congressional Quarterly, Inc. Vol. 5.

Congressional Quarterly Almanac. Various years.

Congressional Record. 1962. 87th Cong. 2d Sess. Vol. 108, Pt. 7. 31 May.

Conrad, David E. 1965. *The forgotten farmers.* Urbana: University of Illinois Press.

Demkovich, Linda. 1977. The "odd couple" is whipping up a new dish on food stamps. *National Journal* 9:428–29. March 19.

Drew, Elizabeth. 1968. Going hungry in America. *The Atlantic* 222:53–61. December.

Edelman, Murray. 1964. *The symbolic uses of politics.* Urbana: University of Illinois Press.

Elkin, Stephen L. 1987. *City and regime in the American republic.* Chicago: Chicago University Press.

Fite, Gilbert C. 1980. Mechanization of cotton production since World War II. *Agricultural History* 54:1:190–207.

———. 1984. *Cotton fields no more.* Lexington University of Kentucky Press.

Fligstein, Neil. 1981. *Going north.* New York: Academic.

Food Research and Action Center. 1978. *Waiting for food stamps (or what to do until the new program gets here)*. Washington, D.C. July.

Ford, Gerald L. Presidential Library. Records of the Ford Administration. Ann Arbor, Mich.

Freeman, Orville. Papers. Minnesota State Archives. St. Paul, Minn.

Furniss, Norman. 1985. Political futures. In *The democratic state*, ed. Stephen L. Elkin and Roger Benjamin, 237–64. Lawrence, Kansas: University Press of Kansas.

Gold, Norman L., A.C. Hoffman, and F.V. Waugh. 1940. *Economic analysis of the food stamp program. A special report*. Washington, D.C.: U.S. Department of Agriculture.

Greenberg, Polly. 1969. *The devil has slippery shoes*. New York: Macmillan.

Grieder, William. 1981. *The education of David Stockman and other Americans*. New York: Dutton.

Hadwiger, Don F. 1982. *The politics of agricultural research*. Lincoln: Nebraska University Press.

Hadwiger, Don F. and Ross B. Talbot. 1965. *Pressures and protests: The Kennedy farm program and the wheat referendum of 1963*. San Francisco: Chandler.

Harrington, Michael. 1963. *The other America: Poverty in the United States*. Baltimore: Penguin.

Heclo, Hugh. 1977. *A government of strangers. Executive politics in Washington*. Washington, D.C.: The Brookings Institution.

———. 1978. Issue networks and the executive establishment. In *The new American political system*, ed. Anthony King, 87–124. Washington, D.C.: American Enterprise Institute.

Hoagland, G. William. 1984. *Perception and reality in nutrition programs*. Washington, D.C.: American Enterprise Institute.

Holt, Len. 1965. *The summer that didn't end*. New York: Morrow.

House of Representatives. See U.S. Congress, House.

Hunger U.S.A. See Citizens Board of Inquiry into Poverty and Malnutrition in America.

Ingram, Helen. 1977. Policy implementation through bargaining: The case of grants-in-aid. *Public Policy* 25:499–526.

James, David R. 1988. The transformation of the southern racist state. *American Sociological Review* 53:2:198–208.

Johnson, Lyndon B. Presidential Library. Records of the Johnson Administration. Austin, Tex.

Kennedy, John F. Presidential Library. Records of the Kennedy Administration. Boston, Mass.

Kirkendall, Richard S. 1982. *Social scientists and farm politics in the age of Roosevelt*. Columbia: University of Missouri Press.

Kotz, Nick. 1969. *Let them eat promises*. Englewood Cliffs, N.J.: Prentice-Hall.

Lasswell, Harold. 1936. *Who gets what, when and how*. New York: McGraw-Hill.

Lelyveld, Joseph. 1985. Hunger in America. The safety net has shrunk but it's still in place. *The New York Times Magazine* 16 Jun.

Leuchtenburg, William. 1963. *Franklin D. Roosevelt and the New Deal.* New York: Harper and Row.

―――. 1983. *In the shadow of FDR. From Harry Truman to Ronald Reagan.* Ithaca, N.Y.: Cornell University Press.

Lipsky, Michael. 1970. *Protest in city politics.* Chicago: Rand McNally.

―――. 1978. Standing the study of public policy implementation on its head. In *American politics and public policy,* ed. Walter Dean Burnham and Martha Wagner Weinberg, 391–402. Cambridge: MIT Press.

Lipsky, Michael and Marc A. Thibodeau. 1985. *Food in the warehouses, hunger in the streets.* Boston: Massachusetts Institute of Technology, July.

Lowi, Theodore J. 1964. American business, public policy, case studies and political theory. *World Politics* 16:677–715.

―――. 1972. *The end of liberalism.* New York: Norton. 2nd ed.

MacDonald, Maurice. 1977. *Food, stamps, and income maintenance.* New York: Academic.

Maney, Ardith L. 1985. Great society food programs then and now. A paper presented at the annual meeting of the American Political Science Association. New Orleans. August 29–September 1.

―――. 1987a. The antihunger lobby: Continuity and change. A paper presented at the annual meeting of the Southwestern Political Science Association. Dallas. March 18–21.

―――. 1987b. Innovation in the development of federal food and nutrition policy. A paper presented at the annual meeting of the American Political Science Association. September 3–6.

―――. 1988. The impact of civil rights issues on government benefits for the poor. In *John F. Kennedy: Person, policy, presidency,* ed. J. Richard Snyder. Wilmington, Del.: SR Books.

Matusow, Allen J. 1967. *Farm policies and politics in the Truman years.* Cambridge: Harvard University Press.

May, Judith V. and Aaron Wildavsky. 1978. *The policy cycle.* Beverly Hills: Sage Publications.

McCann, Michael W. 1986. *Taking reform seriously: Perspectives on public interest liberalism.* Ithaca, N.Y.: Cornell University Press.

Mollenkopf, John. 1983. *The contested city.* Princeton: Princeton University Press.

Montjoy, Robert S. and Lawrence J. O'Toole, Jr. 1979. Toward a theory of implementation: An organizational perspective. *Public Administration Review* 39:465–76.

Moynihan, Daniel P. 1973. *The politics of a guaranteed income.* New York: Harper and Row.

Nathan, Richard. 1976. Food stamps and welfare reform. *Policy Analysis* 2:1:61–70.

National Advisory Commission on Farm Labor. 1964. *Poverty on the land.* Washington, D.C. 18–19 May.

National Archives and Records Service. Records of the Secretary of Agriculture. Record Group #16.

Newland, Chester. 1984. Executive office policy apparatus: Enforcing the Reagan agenda. In *The Reagan presidency and the governing of America,* ed. Lester M. Salamon and Michael S. Lund, 135–68. Washington, D.C.: The Urban Institute Press.

Nordlinger, Eric. 1981. *On the autonomy of the democratic state.* Cambridge: Harvard University Press.

O'Toole, Lawrence J., Jr. and Robert S. Montjoy. 1984. Interorganizational policy implementation: A theoretical perspective. *Public Administration Review* 44:491–503.

Page, Benjamin I. 1983. *Who gets what from government?* Berkeley: University of California Press.

(The) People Left Behind. See President's National Advisory Commission on Rural Poverty.

Peterson, Trudy. 1977. *Agricultural exports, farm income, and the Eisenhower administration.* Lincoln: University of Nebraska Press.

Physicians' Task Force on Hunger in America. 1985a. *Hunger in America, the growing epidemic.* Middletown, CT: Wesleyan University Press.

———. 1985b. *Hunger counties 1986: The distribution of America's high-risk areas.* Boston: Harvard University School of Public Health. January.

Piven, Frances Fox. 1976. The social structuring of political protest. *Politics and Society* 6:297–326.

Piven, Frances Fox and Richard A. Cloward. 1971. *Regulating the poor: The functions of public welfare.* New York: Vintage.

———. 1977. *Poor people's movements.* New York: Pantheon.

Poverty on the land. See National Advisory Commission on Farm Labor.

President's National Advisory Commission on Rural Poverty. 1967. *The people left behind.* Washington, D.C.

Pressman, Jeffrey and Aaron Wildavsky. 1984. *Implementation.* Berkeley: Univ. of California Press. 3d ed.

Rabinowitz, Francine, Jeffrey Pressman, and Martin Rein. 1976. Guidelines: A plethora of forms, authors, and functions. *Policy Sciences* 7:4:399–416.

Rasmussen, Wayne D. and Gladys L. Baker. 1972. *The Department of Agriculture.* New York: Praeger.

Reuther, Walter. Papers. Walter Reuther Archives. Archives of Urban and Labor History. Wayne State Univ., Detroit, Mich.

Ripley, Randall. 1964. Legislative bargaining and the food stamp act of 1964. In *Congress and urban problems,* ed. Frederic N. Cleaveland et al., 279–310. Washington, D.C.: The Brookings Institution.

Ripley, Randall and Grace Franklin. 1980. *Congress, the bureaucracy, and public policy.* Homewood, Ill.: Dorsey.

———. 1986. *Policy implementation and bureaucracy.* 1986. Chicago: Dorsey. 2d ed.

Schattschneider, E.E. 1960. *The semi-sovereign people.* New York: Holt, Rinehart and Winston.

Schick, Allen S. 1984. The budget as an instrument of presidential policy. In *The Reagan presidency and the governing of America,* ed. Lester M. Salamon and Michael S. Lund, 91–125. Washington, D.C.: The Urban Institute Press.

Schlichter, Gertrude Almy. 1959. FDR's farm policy as governor of New York state, 1928–32. *Agricultural History* 33:4:167–76.

Schlossberg, Kenneth. 1975. Funny money is serious. *The New York Times Magazine*, 28 September.

Schwarz, John. 1983. *America's hidden success*. New York: Norton.

Senate. See U.S. Congress, Senate.

Sherrill, Robert. 1967. It isn't true that nobody starves in America. *The New York Times Magazine*, 4 Jun.

Skocpol, Theda. 1980. Political response to capitalist crisis: Neo-marxist theories of the state and the case of the new deal. *Politics and Society* 10:2:155–201.

Skowronek, Stephen. 1982. *Building a new American state*. New York: Cambridge Univ. Press.

Steiner, Gilbert Y. 1971. *The state of welfare*. Washington, D.C.: The Brookings Institution.

Stockman, David A. 1975. The social pork barrel. *The Public Interest* 39:3–30. Spring.

———. 1986. *The triumph of politics*. New York: Harper and Row.

Swoap, David B. 1982. Federalism: New directions at the Department of Health and Human Services. In *American federalism: A new partnership for the republic*, ed. Robert B. Hawkins, Jr., 121–130. San Francisco: Institute for Contemporary Studies.

Their Daily Bread. See Committee on School Lunch Participation.

Tugwell, Rexford. 1959. The resettlement idea. *Agricultural History* 33:4:159–64.

U.S. Congress, House Agricultural Appropriations Subcommittee. 1967. *Department of Agriculture and related agencies appropriations bill*. 89th Cong., 2d Sess. House Report 1446.

U.S. Congress, House Agriculture Committee. 1958. *Food-stamp program*. 85th Cong., 2d Sess. 16, 17 Apr. and 14 May.

———. 1964. *Food stamp plan*. 88th Cong., 1st Sess. 10–12 Jun.

———. 1985. *Food security act*. 99th Cong., 1st Sess. Part I. 13 Sep.

U.S. Congress, House Committee on Education and Labor. 1966a. *Amending the school lunch act*. 89th Cong., 2d Sess. House Report 1802. 3 Aug.

———. 1966b. *Establish a special school lunch program*. 89th Cong., 2d Sess. 18 Mar.

———. 1973. *Oversight hearings on the child nutrition programs*. 96th Cong., 1st Sess. 13 Mar.

U.S. Congress, House General Subcommittee on Education. 1961. *School lunch program*. 87th Cong., 1st Sess. 31 Aug.

U.S. Congress, House Select Committee on Hunger. 1984a. *Accessibility and effectiveness of anti-hunger programs*. 98th Cong., 2d Sess. Serial No. 98–1. 25 Jun. and 23 Jul.

———. 1984b. *Effective uses of agricultural abundance for hunger relief*. 98th Cong., 2d Sess. Serial No. 98–5. 20 Sep.

———. 1985. *Coordination and simplification of domestic federal assistance programs*. 99th Cong., 1st Sess. Serial No. 99–5. 9 Jul.

————. 1986. *Alleviating hunger: Progress and prospects.* 98th Cong., 2d Sess. Serial No. 98–2. 26 Jun.

U.S. Congress, House Subcommittee on Domestic Marketing, Consumer Relations, and Nutrition. 1979. *Food stamp program.* 96th Cong., 1st Sess. 9 May, 12–14 and 18–20 Jun.

————. 1983a. *Emergency food assistance and commodity distribution act of 1983.* 98th Cong., 1st Sess. Serial No. 98–4. 22 Mar.

————. 1983b. *Problems of hunger and malnutrition.* 98th Cong., 1st Sess. Serial No. 98–3. 28 Feb., 25 Mar., and 30 Apr.

————. 1983c. *Review of the fiscal year 1984 budget for the Food and Nutrition Service, United States Department of Agriculture.* 98th Cong., 1st Sess. 20 Apr.

————. 1984. Review of the President's task force on food assistance. 98th Cong., 2d Sess. 26 Jan.

U.S. Congress, House Subcommittee on Education. 1966. *National school lunch act.* 89th Cong., 2d Sess. 21 Jul.

U.S. Congress, Senate Committee on Agriculture and Forestry. 1959. *Food distribution programs.* 86th Cong., 1st Sess. 4, 5, and 8 Jun.

————. 1964. *Hearings on HR 10222.* 88th Cong., 2d Sess. 18 and 19 Jun.

————. 1966a. *Child nutrition.* 89th Cong., 2d Sess. Senate Report 1360. 7 Jul.

————. 1966b. *School milk and breakfast programs.* 89th Cong., 2d Sess. 21 Jun.

————. 1966c. *Special school milk program.* 89th Cong., 2d Sess. 12 May.

U.S. Congress, Senate Committee on Agriculture, Nutrition, and Forestry. 1985. *The food stamp program.* 99th Cong., 1st Sess. Committee Print. Apr.

U.S. Congress, Senate Select Committee on Nutrition and Human Needs. 1971a. *Nutrition and human needs, 1971—Part 6, Summer feeding program and USDA decision to withhold funds for section 32.* 92d Cong., 1st Sess. 25 Jun and 22 Jul.

————. 1971b. *Nutrition and human needs, 1971—Part 7, Crisis in the national school lunch program.* 92d Cong., 1st Sess. 7 Sep.

————. 1974a. *Family food programs, 1974—Part 7, Oversight: National school lunch program.* 93d Cong., 2d Sess. 5 Mar.

————. 1974b. *Nutrition and special groups.* 93d Cong., 2d Sess. 19 Jun.

————. 1979. *Hunger in America: Ten years later.* 99th Cong., 1st Sess. 30 Apr.

U.S. Congress, Senate Subcommittee on Agricultural Research and General Legislation. 1962. *National school lunch funds.* 87th Cong., 2d Sess. 9 Jun.

U.S. Congress, Senate Subcommittee on Employment, Manpower, and Poverty. 1967. *Hunger and malnutrition in America.* 90th Cong., 1st Sess. 11 and 12 Jul.

U.S. Congress, Senate Subcommittee on Nutrition. 1983a. *Oversight of commodity distribution programs.* 98th Cong., 1st Sess. 12 Jul.

————. 1983b. *Oversight of nutritional status of low-income Americans in the 1980s.* 98th Cong., 1st Sess. Serial No. 98–274. 6 Apr.

U.S. Congress, Senate Subcommittee on Rural Development Oversight, and

Investigations. 1983. *Effectiveness of federal food, nutrition and surplus commodity distribution programs.* 98th Cong., 1st Sess. 13 Jun.

U.S. Congressional Budget Office. 1977. *The food stamp program: Income or food supplementation?* Budget Issue Paper. January.

———. 1980. *Feeding hungry children: Federal child nutrition issues in the 1980's.* Budget Issue Paper for Fiscal Year 1981. May.

U.S. Congressional Research Service. 1986a. *Child nutrition issues in the 99th congress.* Issue Brief IB85055. By Jean Yavis Jones. 20 May.

———. 1986b. *Summary of reports concerning hunger in America, 1983–1986.* By Donna V. Porter and Marjorie H. Washington. 16 May.

U.S. Department of Agriculture. 1963. *Nonparticipation of urban schools in the national school lunch program.* Washington, D.C.

U.S. Department of Agriculture, Agricultural History Branch. 1963. *Century of service.* Washington, D.C.: GPO. By Gladys Baker et al.

———. Files. Washington, D.C.

U.S. General Accounting Office. 1978. *Federal domestic food assistance programs—A time for assessment and change.* CED–78–113. 13 Jun.

———. 1983. *Public and private efforts to feed America's poor.* GAO/RCED–83–164. 23 Jun.

———. 1985. *Overview and perspectives on the food stamp program.* RCED–85–109. 17 Apr.

Van Horn, Carl. 1979. *Policy implementation in the federal system.* Lexington, Mass.: Lexington Books.

———. 1985. *The politics of unemployment.* Washington, D.C.: CQ Press.

Watters, Pat. 1971. *Down to now: Reflections on the southern civil rights movement.* New York: Pantheon.

Watters, Pat and Reese Cleghorn. 1967. *Climbing Jacob's ladder.* New York: Harcourt, Brace and World.

Waugh, F.V. 1961. Food stamp program. *Agricultural Marketing* 6:11:10–16.

———. 1962. *Managing farm surpluses, A report by the National Agriculture Commission.* Washington, D.C.: National Planning Association. Apr.

Weaver, R. Kent. 1985. Controlling entitlements. In *The new direction in American politics,* ed. John E. Chubb and Paul E. Peterson, 307–41. Washington, D.C.: The Brookings Institution.

Wehr, Elizabeth. 1981. House approves $34 billion for farm and food programs. *Congressional Quarterly Weekly Report* 41:23:1151–2. Jun. 11.

———. 1983a. Food need weighed against tales of abuse. *Congressional Quarterly Weekly Report* 41:29:1513. Jul. 23.

———. 1983b. Hill, White House settle one food dispute. *Congressional Quarterly Weekly Report* 41:51:2742. Dec. 24.

Williamson, Richard S. 1983. The 1982 new federalism negotiations. *Publius* 13:2:11–32.

Young, James Sterling. 1966. *The Washington community, 1800–-1828.* New York: Harcourt, Brace and World.

Index

About the Author

ARDITH L. MANEY is Associate Professor of Political Science at Iowa State University. Among her earlier publications are *Representing the Consumer Interest* and *Government and Employer Roles in Child Care Policy*.